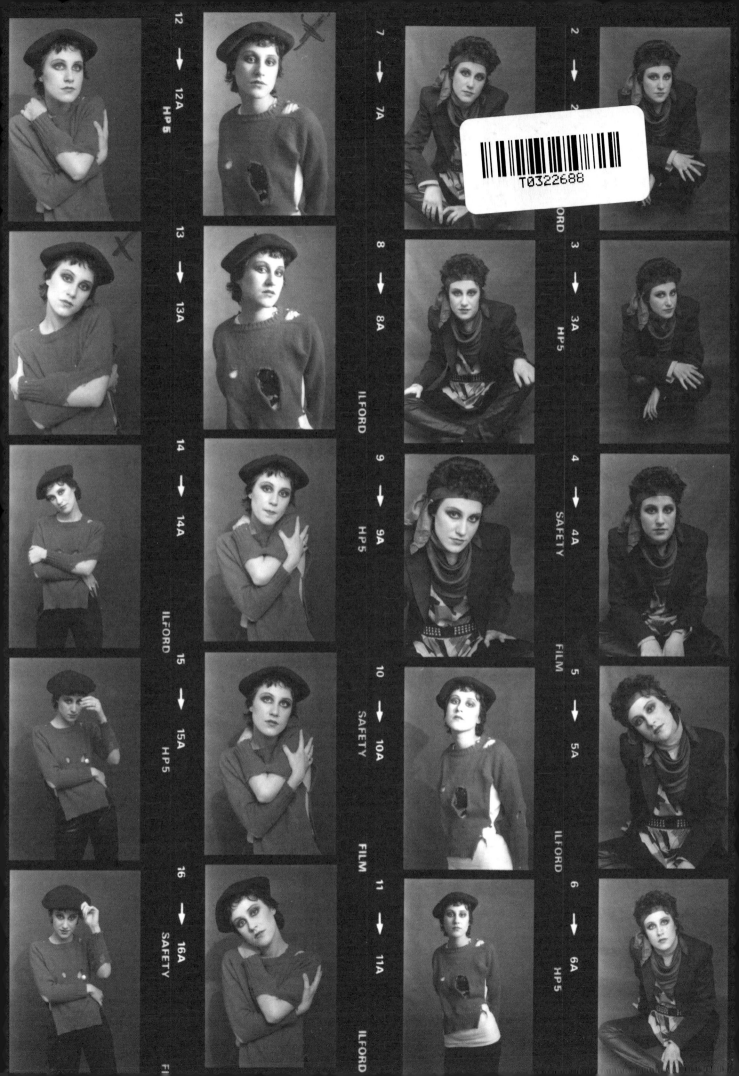

# LIFE'S A GAMBLE

*For Jean and Al, Alex and Grace*

# LIFE'S A GAMBLE

## PENETRATION, THE INVISIBLE GIRLS AND OTHER STORIES

### PAULINE MURRAY

**OMNIBUS PRESS**

London / New York / Paris / Sydney / Copenhagen / Berlin / Madrid / Tokyo

Copyright © 2023 Omnibus Press
(A division of the Wise Music Group, 14–15 Berners Street, London, W1T 3LJ)

Design and Art Direction: Russ Bestley
Creative Advisor: Paul Harvey
Picture research by the author

ISBN 978-1-9131-7270-1
Special Edition ISBN 978-1-9158-4106-3

Every effort has been made to trace the copyright holders of the photographs in this book but one or two
were unreachable. We would be grateful if the photographers concerned would contact us.

Front cover and endpaper images © Ray Stevenson
Back cover image © Kev Anderson

'Thundertunes', songwriter: Pauline Murray © Eaton Music Ltd and Pauline Murray
'Movement', songwriter: Pauline Murray © Eaton Music Ltd and Pauline Murray
'Danger Signs', songwriter: Pauline Murray © Eaton Music Ltd and Pauline Murray
'Judgement Day', songwriter: Pauline Murray © Eaton Music Ltd and Pauline Murray
'Challenge', songwriter: Pauline Murray © Eaton Music Ltd and Pauline Murray
'Shout Above the Noise', songwriter: Pauline Murray © Eaton Music Ltd and Pauline Murray
'The Visitor', songwriter: Pauline Murray © Eaton Music Ltd and Pauline Murray
'Silent Community', songwriter: Pauline Murray © BMG Rights Management UK Ltd and Pauline Murray
'Soul Power', songwriter: Pauline Murray © BMG Rights Management UK Ltd and Pauline Murray
'Beat Goes On', songwriter: Pauline Murray © Pauline Murray

A catalogue record for this book is available from the British Library.

Printed in the Czech Republic.

www.omnibuspress.com

# CONTENTS

# INTRODUCTION

**I began to write my life story a few years ago, mainly for my children.** Once you're no longer here, many details of your life are lost forever. I know that, now my own parents are gone, there are many things I wished I'd asked them; not that it makes any difference but everyone has a story to tell.

The original draft of the book you're reading now was written purely from memory and ended before Penetration reformed. Friends Russ Bestley (designer/academic) and Paul Harvey (guitarist/artist) informed me that they had approached Omnibus Press with a view to me writing an autobiography. I gave it no more thought until news came through at the end of 2021 that Omnibus were keen to go ahead with the project. I was delighted, excited then filled with trepidation at the reality of the prospect. The last time I had even written an essay would probably have been as a sixteen year old at school: the brief of 60,000+ words was mind boggling when I looked at the bigger picture. How do you even set about such a task? I read many examples of musicians' autobiographies but soon realised that I wasn't Bruce Springsteen, Sting, Debbie Harry or Patti Smith. I was me, Pauline Murray, and would have to tell my own story and pick my life apart in fine detail. The realisation that this would be paraded in front of the public and total strangers filled me with anxiety and I almost gave up on several occasions.

With no guidance or knowledge, I decided that the best way to approach this mammoth task was to apply the method of working in bite size chunks that would hopefully all come good in the end. This solitary endeavour would require patience, perseverance, stamina, faith and a fair bit of research to bring sketchy memories back to life. Childhood memories can seem vivid and bright but once I got into my teens, everything seemed to revolve around which bands I'd seen, and I had to delve into the details of when these events had taken place chronologically as my memory was misleading. For the years 1977-1981, I relied on scrapbooks of press cuttings that outlined my activities with Penetration and The Invisible Girls. For the whole of 1978, I'd filled in a Boots diary every day, so I have an authentic account of what my 19/20 year old self was doing, thinking and feeling at the time and some of the comments are taken directly from this resource. I filled in a diary for 1979, but lapsed with my entries and had to return to my memory, the scrapbooks and the internet to keep things in order.

As I got deeper into the story, I began to enjoy the process though the end never seemed to be in sight. When I finally reached my destination, the long and arduous journey has been transformed into a great sense of personal achievement which I'm now happy to share. Hope you enjoy!

Opposite page: Photograph by Jen Shutt.

# UNBROKEN LINE

I am the sun of many hearts
My sister is the same as me
The bearers of forgotten lives
Beneath the branches of the tree

Another link in the unbroken line
Of generations that go back in time

You are the vision of our love
A combination of the two
The evidence in flesh and blood
The X and Y that we live through

Another link in the unbroken line
Of generations that go back in time

A part of me, a part of you
I see it written in your face
A part of me I never knew
Another time, another place

Another link in the unbroken line
Of generations that go back in time...

# CHAPTER ONE
# THE VILLAGE THAT DISAPPEARED

**There is something eerie about Waterhouses Wood, even in the daytime.** The trees, planted in a grid of tubes over forty years ago, grow close together, their tall, thin trunks reaching high into the sky, their mantle blocking out the light. The wind, whispering through the branches, sounds like the voices of spirits trapped within a secret, meticulously concealed. The remnant of a brick wall, covered in moss and creeping weeds is the only evidence that a settlement once existed here. A man was killed in recent times, hit by a falling tree as he was walking his dog through the wood.

In my memory, a village stood on this ghostly site. Situated about five miles west of Durham in the Deerness Valley, it was built in the mid-1850s by Quakers Joseph Pease and Partners, the Darlington industrialists who'd been granted a license to establish a coal mine and railway line for the transportation of coal. This purpose-built village included seven streets of houses, a school, the Miners' Institute and a Methodist chapel, all of which were replete with running water, electricity, outside toilets and large gardens for the enjoyment of the mine workers and their families. The coal mine was at the heart of the community.

While it's hard to imagine it now, with nature having taken over so completely, I was born in this village, at number 1 Arthur Street, a one-bedroom, end-of-terrace house, on the evening of Saturday, 8 March 1958. I arrived so quickly that my mother Jean and father Al (Alwyn) almost had to deliver me themselves. They were hoping for a boy – they'd even named him (Colin) – but they received another girl instead. My five-year-old sister Lorna slept through the commotion and upon waking, discovered a new baby asleep in her twin dolls' pram.

My father was a coal miner at Waterhouses Colliery, which was within walking distance of the house. He was the sole wage earner (the miners' wages included free rent and coal) and would take on extra shifts to make sure his family had a decent standard of living. In his spare time, he, along with a friend, would scrap cars

Chopping sticks with my father, Al, at 1 Arthur Street.

on a nearby field for pocket money. At 33 years of age, he was a strong, gentle, handsome, hardworking man, who didn't say much but was highly principled.

My father's family can be traced back to Ramshaw, an isolated and inhospitable location in the North Pennines. They were associated with farming and then lead mining as the Industrial Revolution took hold. My great grandparents moved into the next valley and operated a successful blacksmith's business where their youngest son, my grandfather Ernest, served his apprenticeship. The business collapsed after fifty years when his father died and horse-drawn vehicles became

My grandfather, Ernest, with the colliery exhibition circa 1933.

obsolete with the advent of motor cars. Ernest now had to find his own way in life.

My grandfather Ernest had a vision – a calling – to build a model coal mine. Although he had never set foot in a mine, the model, which apparently took fifteen years to complete, was highly detailed, fully mechanised and painstakingly constructed, with moving parts and carved wooden figures. It was powered by steam and was the size of a fairground sideshow. He built a trailer to house the exhibition and became part of a travelling fair that would transport the attraction to many towns and villages in the region, who hosted the fairground for a week at a time. Every year between 1933 and 1939, the 'Model Colliery Exhibition' would pitch up on Newcastle's Town Moor next to the boxing booth and 'Wall of Death' at the Hoppings: the largest fun fair in Europe. My father was born in a caravan and grew up with his older brother, John, in this nomadic travelling community. Dad

worked on the Waltzer as a young teenager but he could barely read or write at the time as he'd only attended school when the fairground was 'overwintering' in different locations. He received a different kind of education in the school of life, outside of the confines of conventional society.

A parting of ways came when the fair was due to travel to Europe: because the family were not 'showmen born and bred' and not part of the Showmen's Guild, they weren't permitted to travel abroad. They were left stranded in Langley Park, County Durham, and had to find new options fast. Ernest found employment at Langley Park Colliery as a blacksmith shoeing the pit ponies and my father Alwyn became his apprentice. They lived at 1 Thomas Street and the model coal mine – or 'exhibition', as they called it – was stored at the side of the house, shuttered up as World War Two approached. At the end of the war, there was no demand for the skills of a blacksmith, so Alwyn ended up 'down the pit' (coal

My grandmother, Doris, in the box office.

mine), a dangerous job which was the only option for many young men in the area at the time.

My mother was a stylish, vivacious woman with twinkling blue eyes and a creative spirit, but by the age of 29, she, like so many working-class women of this era, had resigned herself to being a full-time housewife, immersing herself in household chores. The house in Arthur Street had a cast iron, coal-fired range used for heating and cooking. I remember linoleum on the floor with home-made rugs and basic items of furniture. It was spartan, yet clean and cosy. She listened to the wireless (radio), to programmes such as *Housewives' Choice* and *Mrs Dale's Diary*, which reinforced and supported her current role in life. Lorna was at school and I was left outside in my pram for long periods of time (which was standard practice for mothers in the 1950s), apparently crying frequently, possibly from lack of attention and stimulation. My recently widowed Nana Murray would come to the rescue from Langley Park and take me out for long walks, giving my mother a break and me some much needed social interaction.

Nana Murray, Doris (or 'Dot', as my father called her) was born in Halifax, Yorkshire, in 1901. She was well-spoken, artistic, open-minded, smelled of Tosca 4711 perfume and had lived an interesting life. My mother said that Doris was a 'romancer', meaning that she made things up. The perceived story of her upbringing was that her father had been chief of police in the Yorkshire Constabulary and that her parents had died in a car crash when she was very young. Upon researching her family history in recent years, I discovered that her father was a stone miner who died at 28 from typhoid fever, when she was 1 and her brother 4. Her mother died five years later from thyroid problems, so Doris was an orphan at 6. Doris and her older brother relocated to Bishop Auckland, County Durham, where she lived with their grandmother –

Me and my sister, Lorna.

met my grandfather, who was eighteen years her senior and spoke with a broad Durham accent.

When they travelled with the fair in the winter, Doris would make dolls to sell and apparently the other ladies became quite jealous of her artistry. She could 'turn her hand to anything', as the saying goes: she took photographs, developed and coloured them, became a hairdresser, a barmaid, she knitted and crocheted – a real Renaissance woman. After World War Two, the Colliery Exhibition was converted to electricity and became a permanent fixture at Seaburn Fairground until Ernest suffered a stroke. They sold the exhibition, but no one in the family knows who bought it and it's a mystery that I've never been able to solve.

When I was about 3 years old, we exchanged houses with the residents of number 4 Arthur Street as it had an extra bedroom and living room. Mum set to work and decorated the bedrooms with rose print wallpaper. We rented a black-and-white television set and I remember watching *Pinky and Perky* and *Watch With Mother*. My mother said that I could sing before I could talk, and would get me to perform for the family, singing the Connie Francis song 'Lipstick On Your Collar' (although I would say 'lickstick').

There was a teenager living next door called Marlene; I thought she was so glamorous with her backcombed, lacquered hair, full skirts, stiletto-heeled shoes and heavy make-up. I remember pestering her to paint my face and nails; my love of make-up began at an early age thanks to Marlene. The music of the day was the Everly Brothers, Elvis Presley, The Ronettes and Cliff Richard whose musical *Summer Holiday* I had just seen at the cinema in nearby Esh Winning. The Beatles were emerging with songs like 'Love Me Do' and 'She Loves You'. I was a sponge, soaking it all up.

There was a girl of my own age, Mandy, at the top of the street and a younger boy who would come calling for me to 'play out'. Our mums would give us threepenny bits (old money before decimalisation) and, unsupervised by adults, we crossed the road – and a railway line – to the post office where a world of sweets awaited us: Aztec Bars, Penny Arrows, Parma Violets, Floral Gums, Sherbet Fountains, Candy Cigarettes, Milky Ways, Bubble Gum,

her brother was brought up by other relatives. He was killed in the last few days of the First World War and her grandmother died shortly after, so Doris was alone in the world at the age of 17.

We believed that she had trained as a nurse and was lady-in-waiting to the wife of Sir Anthony Eden, the Conservative MP and British prime minister whose family resided at Windlestone Hall in County Durham. Though no evidence exists, it seems feasible and could account for her gentle, refined accent and sense of style, that she had clearly re-invented herself after such a tragic childhood. She would have been in her prime during the Roaring Twenties, stepping out in dazzling costume jewellery and chic tailored outfits, her light ginger hair styled in finger waves. I'm not sure how she

With my mother, Jean, and the tin bath, at 4 Arthur Street.

Black Jacks – I must have tried everything in that shop and could be bribed to do anything for my sister Lorna with a few 'Farties' (Smarties). I would plead to tag along with her and her friends but she would tell me to 'get lost' as I usually gave the game away when they were playing hide and seek.

Mandy and I fell out one day and I saw her sitting in her window pulling faces at me. I threw a stone at her, smashing the glass, then ran down the street and straight to my bedroom where I hid under the bed, awaiting the consequences. I could hear her mother angrily knocking on the door, informing my mother of the deed I'd just committed. I was never scolded or reprimanded, there was just the phrase 'wait till your dad gets home', and by the time he got home, the emotions of the incident had dispersed.

I can still remember my father, a solitary black figure, walking towards the house in the afternoon, having just finished a long shift in the coal mine. As he approached, I could see his black face, wet oilskin clothing, pit helmet and a bag carrying his 'bait box' – a colloquialism for packed lunch. My mother would dry his clothes on the oven door and he would get into a large tin bath of hot water and relax into the comfort of his home and family. I can only imagine the working conditions these miners faced. Packed into a cage that descended down a deep shaft into the dark, wet and dusty bowels of the earth. Crawling through small restrictive spaces to the coalface with the sound of heavy machinery echoing through the network of tunnels. It was hard labour with no relief, no amenities and no escape until the end of the shift. There would only be a few men down there on overtime shifts and my father said that you could hear the earth creaking, groaning and moaning. It was a unique shared experience that created a special camaraderie with the miners.

The environs of the colliery were a dangerous place for children to play. A system of rail tracks circled the village, using a ropeway mechanism to take empty tub containers to nearby drift mines. The tubs, filled with coal, would hurtle down an inclined tramway, using the force of gravity to take their payload back to the colliery. The only warning of their impending arrival was a vibration on the metal tracks that became louder and more intense as they approached. Before I was born, two 10-year-old boys were electrocuted whist playing on the roof of a colliery outbuilding – they'd reached for an overhead cable, and hadn't realised it was live.

Every Friday, I would walk with my mother to Esh Winning to visit *her* mother, known to me and Lorna as Grandma Coates. She'd had a hard life, giving birth to ten children and bringing up the seven who'd survived. My mother was fourth in the family, with Elsie, Ivy and Ethel above, and Percy, Thomas and Audrey below. There were already about nine grandchildren so my existence seemed to go unnoticed. I don't recall having any conversation with my grandmother and would sit in the front room with my magic painting book, keeping myself amused for the duration of our visits. She must have been ill, as she died as a result of untreated diabetes at the age of 63; I was just 5 at the time.

Mum's father, Granda Coates, was a retired coal miner, small in stature and, whilst stern-looking, was outgoing and enjoyed frequenting the local pubs. My mother described him as 'music daft'. When the older sisters were younger, Ivy went for piano lessons

Jean as a young performer.

and Ethel to dancing classes and they passed their knowledge on to my mother. The three sisters sang in harmony and by the age of 14, after school, my mother was part of a concert touring party, entertaining the troops who were stationed around the north-east of England during World War Two. My mother loved performing, and it's from this side of the family that I inherited my musical abilities.

After the war their father, acting as their music agent, sent Ethel and my mother Jean for auditions and my mother received an offer to sing with a big band; she was desperate to do it, but their father wouldn't split the sisters up. One of the songs in their repertoire was 'Sisters' by Irving Berlin, whose lyrics reflected sibling entanglement. They were offered a contract to sing and dance in the chorus line for the pantomime *Snow White and the Seven Dwarves* at a theatre in Stoke-On-Trent, so at 16, Jean and Ethel left Durham Station to embark on a new adventure. It didn't last long as Ethel struggled with rehearsals and it soon became apparent that she was pregnant. They returned home, my mother's hopes and dreams shattered. The disappointment was buried deep and she became emotional when she spoke of those times. She got a job as a shop assistant in Woolworths, tried to put it all behind her, met my dad at a local dance, got married and had kids.

Every year, on the second Saturday in July, the Waterhouses Colliery Brass Band assembled at the bottom of our street to make their journey into Durham for the Miners' Gala – or Durham Big Meeting, as we called it. Each colliery in the Durham Coalfield had a brass band and unique banner, representing the many lodges of the National Union of Mineworkers. The rectangular banners were usually made of silk, hung from a cross member with guide ropes for those carrying it. Each lodge would have its own slogan and the one for Waterhouses was 'Strength In Unity', with an illustration inspired by the Aesop's fable, 'The Bundle of Sticks'. We would cheer as they set off for Durham City, and then we would get the bus to Durham a few hours later to stand at the side of the road with crowds of people, while hundreds of colliery bands from the whole region paraded through the streets towards the racecourse, their personalised banners held proudly aloft. Young people laughed and danced through the streets, arms linked in chains, with party cowboy hats and plenty of beer. We would then make our way to the racecourse where speeches were made by the Labour Party and the trade union leaders of the day. It was quite a spectacle but, in all honesty, I was more impressed by the candy floss, helium balloons and hook-a-duck stall.

Soon it was time to start school. As my mother took me up the dirt track road to Waterhouses Junior Mixed and Infants' School at the top of the street, I asked her how much it was to get in. She thought this was funny and wrote to a women's magazine relaying the conversation and they printed the letter.

As I started school, Lorna was leaving to attend Durham Girls' Grammar School having passed the 11+, an exam at the time that determined your future life prospects at a young age. The headmaster of the school, Mr Pickard, was fairly young, progressive and modern. He had a Super 8 Cine camera and filmed all of the annual school trips to places like Lake Windermere and Flamingo Park Zoo, school events like sports day and the winter of 1965, when the snow drifts covered people's cars and were higher than the school wall. He involved the pupils in acting out sketches with dialogue handwritten onto white boards, and then he edited them into short films. We watched them at the Christmas Party, sitting on chairs in front of the screen, eating ice lollies in the middle of winter.

When I was about 6 we moved house to 41 North Terrace, which was one street away and even closer to the school. It still had two bedrooms but the cast iron range had been replaced with a tiled fireplace. My father converted the pantry into a kitchen with an electric cooker, and he installed a bath beyond the kitchen. It still had an outside toilet and a brick outhouse across the road which my father used as a workshop and later, he built cages to house rabbits which he had started to breed. (They all died, possibly of myxomatosis, a highly infectious, fatal virus that swept through the wild rabbit community.)

The view from the front of the house looked down the valley to the high outcrop on the south side, which was covered in hundreds of evergreen fir trees planted by the Forestry Commission several years before. To the front of the house were steps leading to a long steep garden with a lilac tree at the bottom. I once sat in this tree and observed a car crash. Afterwards, I collected pieces of broken glass from the windscreen, kept them in a brown suede pouch and imagined that they were diamonds.

My mother's sister Ivy and her husband lived about five doors away, and I would often visit to play their piano. I took a few lessons from a young lady in Esh Winning who said that I had a good ear for music, but I found it difficult to read music and would learn the pieces by heart and bluff my way through, turning the

School photo circa 1963.

page at the appropriate time. I soon gave up as I wasn't willing to put the practice in. Other distractions were coming into play.

The 1960s were now in full swing. The Beatles were on a roll with a string of hits and an air of positivity swept through the nation. We would look forward to *Top of the Pops* on TV every Thursday evening, seeing, for the first time, The Beatles, The Rolling Stones, Sandie Shaw, Dusty Springfield and a host of new young singers and groups, including American artists on the Tamla Motown record label. There was music everywhere – the records were playing, the radio was buzzing. It was uplifting, melodic and intelligent, and the music we were hearing evoked many emotions in the listener, from wistfulness to empathy to optimism. It made the previous decades of crooners and manufactured pop stars seem dull and pedestrian by comparison.

Winter in Waterhouses.

Me and Ann Ruecroft with our Tressy dolls.

With a friend on a school trip to Flamingo Park Zoo.

With a friend at Primrose Valley holiday park, Filey.

New fashions emerged, miniskirts and dresses, short angular hairstyles pioneered by young style icons like Mary Quant and Twiggy. Everything was colourful and bright in this exciting cultural explosion. Its energy was far-reaching and even infiltrated the hearts and minds of parents and grandparents. My mother, for example, had taken to wearing a green Lurex dress for special occasions and had a purple dress with black spots. I was impressed that the older generation were embracing the positivity too. My sister was wearing mustard and petrol blue suede coats and dressing like a mod. I had my hair cut short, inspired by Julie Driscoll, and Lorna would make me up with eyeshadow, painted eyelashes and pink lipstick. Ivy's husband bought a brand new metallic blue Ford Zephyr car with tail fins – the whole street turned out to admire it. (He left the clear plastic on the seats, prompting car sickness every time I rode in it.) This period of time presented a window of opportunity to a new world in which the working classes, women and young people could dream of a better future.

I was doing well at school academically, always top or second in the class, although I was a straggler when it came to sport or physical exertion. I only visited the headmaster's office twice. The first time was when I fainted in assembly. I could hear Mr Pickard's voice droning, about the forthcoming exams, when stars appeared in my vision and my surroundings were becoming blurred and distant. I woke up in his office as they were trying to bring me round. It was a frightening experience and I was anxious about going into assembly after that. The second time, I was summoned from class unexpectedly to his office and was asked to do numerous strange tests like throwing a ball of paper into a litter bin with my right, and then my left, hand, putting matches back into a box with my right and left hand, doing a written test with personal and hypothetical questions about my hopes for the future. I was perplexed as to why I had been singled out for this activity.

I was one of the 17,000 Pisces babies born in the week between 3 and 9 March 1958 to take part in a lifelong survey called 'The National Child Development

Bridesmaid at Waterhouses Chapel.

Study'. It was originally set up to study the high number of stillbirths and early infant mortality occurring at the time. Topics for study included medical care, health, home environment, educational progress, parental involvement, family relationships, economic activity and housing. It is the first and longest running data collection of a group of people from birth to death and has apparently been a valuable social resource. Every four years, I would have to take part and instinctively resented this. I managed to shake them off in my 20s, but they would catch up with me again in my 30s.

Two large families lived at each end of the street, the Halls and the Ruecrofts. I was friends with the Ruecrofts, mainly Ann and her older sister Carole. They had a younger sister who had been born with a deformity, her lower arm and hand were missing due to her mother being prescribed Thalidomide, a drug used to combat morning sickness during pregnancy. A prosthetic limb would be fitted and she would immediately smash it against the metal dustbins and

School photo, 1965.

At Easter, we would dye and paint boiled eggs and roll them down the bank of the fir tree forest. I've no idea why we did this; it was possibly a custom handed down through the generations where we made our own entertainment and had fun in the process.

During the school holidays, we would board a bus to Durham City, climb the narrowing staircase to the Cathedral Tower and sit on the edge of the turret, dangling our legs over the side. I remember one time Carole lost a shoe and had to hop home. We also used to visit Mr Openshaw's swimming baths at Lemington near Esh Winning. This retired miner had time on his hands and a vision to benefit the community, and he had built an indoor pool in his garden with changing rooms, a slide and grapevines growing across the glass roof, just out of reach of the noisy and excitable kids. This type of endeavour was very much of a time and place. I also remember this was the year a friend of the family took me to the cinema to see *Mary Poppins* and *The Sound of Music*; both musicals touched me on an emotional level.

Guy Fawkes Night was highly anticipated. Weeks before, preparations were made for the building of a bonfire on the field where the hay bales once ruled. We collected discarded wood, an old sofa, a tractor tyre and anything else that would burn, and kept the bonfire under surveillance until November 5th. We lit the fire and once it took hold it was time for the fireworks; as ever, there were no adults in attendance. On this particular occasion, the Catherine Wheel was pinned to a board and someone lit the touchpaper. Sparks were flying and it spun off its anchor with great speed towards the crowd. An older boy started to scream and roll on the grass and we laughed as we thought he was fooling around. The recent run of TV adverts had warned never to keep fireworks in your pocket as a stray spark could ignite them. The chances of that happening seemed remote but now we were witnessing a terrible accident as the fireworks exploded in his pocket, ignited by the Catherine Wheel spark. We ran to tell the grown-ups and he was rushed to hospital, where he remained for several months receiving multiple skin grafts.

break it to pieces, as I guess it was cumbersome for a young child to wear. We would play on the street, games such as hopscotch and hide-and-seek, or build camps on the field at the back of the houses with rectangular hay bales, when the grass had been cut. I would make clothes for my Tressy doll, whose hair would grow when the button in her stomach was pressed, and wind back in via a notch in her back. We would venture to the woods, full of bluebells, crossing the Deerness River to the south, and run for dear life when someone shouted 'the mummy's coming!', sparked by a rumour that a mummy was living in the woods. If there was a wedding at the chapel nearby, we kids would wait outside, knowing that it was customary for the groom to throw money out of the car window and we would scrabble around, picking up the coins and go straight to the post office to buy sweets.

The Murrays, Amble, Northumberland.

In winter, the silent street lamp shone its light onto the sparkling snow as we rode our sledges and made ice slides down the bank towards the main road. I was 8 years old in 1966 and things were beginning to change: it started in the summer, on the school playing field. We played a game called levitation where six people put their first two fingers under your head, feet and each side of your body and try to lift you into the air as you have your eyes covered. I was being lifted and heard someone say that it hadn't worked. When I opened my eyes, I saw faces crowding over me with an intense bright light (probably the sun) distorting my vision. This filled me with fear and freaked me out.

After that, I became frightened of the dark and had to have the staircase light on. I thought I could see faces on the wall or the door moving which I suspect was the product of an overactive imagination and part of the growing up process. It didn't help that Lorna would say things like, 'how do you know it's really me?' She had started to go for nights out in Durham and I would lie awake, listening for the last bus and her footsteps walking along the street. One evening, I saw the end sequence of a black-and-white TV programme called *Tales of Mystery and Imagination*, shot inside a coffin with a woman scratching, clawing and screaming at the closed lid. I had seen programmes about Count Dracula and was terrified that he would come into my bedroom. I lay in bed with my arms crossed over my chest. I didn't sleep for six months.

My parents were becoming concerned as my health was deteriorating and I was developing painful boils in my armpits. They took me to the doctor who referred me to a child psychiatrist and I couldn't tell them what was disturbing me as I didn't really know. Even now, I have sleepless nights where my brain just won't switch off as random thoughts race through my head. Perhaps this is how my brain developed at the time. I told them that I was stressed about having to give out the school registers each morning. He asked my parents if they were arguing or fighting. They weren't.

I was unaware of the dark cloud that had hung over Waterhouses since before I was born. After the nationalisation of the entire UK coal mining industry in 1947, Durham County Council had prepared a development plan in 1951 that graded all mining settlements into Categories A, B, C and D. Waterhouses had been placed into Category D which meant that there would be no future investment or development, it would be allowed to decline to the point of uninhabitability, left to die, be actively killed, demolished, and the population moved into new housing. This was a controversial policy at the time, led by a Labour council, where economics, as usual, were given precedence over the lives and desires of ordinary people. One of the streets had already been demolished before my sister was born and was left as a visual reminder of what was to come, with high weeds growing out of the rubble and a solitary wooden hut at the centre of the wasteland belonging to the local cobbler. In 1966, the miners finished their final shift and the coal mine closed.

I was a quiet and sensitive child and my sleepless nights were possibly connected to the unexpressed anxiety within the household. My father was now without a job and our home was under threat. Through a friend, he managed to find work at the Royal Ordnance Factory, an ammunitions manufacturer in Birtley about fifteen miles away.

We'd always had a car, going on family holidays to places like Butlins in Filey, Primrose Valley Caravan Park, trips to the seaside, Whitley Bay, Seaton Carew, Crimdon Dene, Amble on the Northumberland coast, Rhyl in Wales and the North Pennines. We would go to Hexham Races and Air Shows in the region as my father loved aeroplanes. He was an expert car mechanic and would often be underneath a vehicle in the back street with friends gathered around for the 'craic' – banter. There was nothing unusual about having an oily car engine in our living room.

I became introverted and didn't want to play out anymore. I'd grown accustomed to spending time alone and amused myself with arts and crafts – painting by numbers, 'Touch Tapestry', building Airfix models of aeroplanes and making flowers from brightly coloured crêpe paper. TV programmes had transformed into colour and shows such as *Batman*, *The Monkees*, *Bewitched*, *Lost in Space*, *Thunderbirds*, *The Jetsons* and *The Man From U.N.C.L.E* were more than enough to hold my attention. I was a deep thinker and inquisitive – my mother used to say that I wanted to know 'the far end of a fart and which way the stink blows'. I was an easy target and the butt of Lorna and my father's jokes. Having no sense of humour, I would pack a suitcase and wait at the bus stop before realising that, at 8 years old, I was unable to survive in the world, and I'd sheepishly go back home. During school holidays, I stayed with Nana Murray in Langley Park. At 65 years old, she was now crippled with rheumatoid arthritis and found it difficult to walk. She was quiet and composed and would teach me to crochet. I always enjoyed being in her company and resonated with her more than anyone else, but she never spoke about the past.

My father re-joined the National Coal Board as a structural engineer, repairing colliery machinery at Tursdale Workshops, about twelve miles from Waterhouses and seven miles south of Durham. The travelling became difficult, especially in winter, so I found myself being taken to one depressing pit village

Waterhouses Wood, 2014. Photograph by Paul Harvey.

after another to decide where I'd be happiest living. The move wouldn't affect Lorna as she was already travelling to school in Durham. The house in Dean Bank, Ferryhill, had a fluorescent light in the kitchen – that's the only thing that swung it for me.

We left Waterhouses in the spring of 1968. There was no going back. The council systematically forced the residents from their homes and quickly demolished the whole village, even digging up the foundations so that no trace of its existence would ever be discovered. The operation wasn't even slum clearance since the buildings were sound and in a beautiful, desirable location, a short commute to Durham. The colliery and village were erased from any future maps and the open space covered in topsoil into which fast-growing trees were planted. No commemorative plaque ever appeared, and the planners hoped that their shameful Category D policy would be forgotten, just like the 114 mining settlements they had destroyed. But the memories would remain in the hearts and minds of those of us who lived there, as we had no choice but to move forward into the next chapter of our lives.

# THUNDERTUNES

The last flakes of confetti fall
Like leaves upon the ground
And thundertunes ring out into the air
Without a sound
As thieves lie next to dead men
In these empty halls
And the last trace of tradition
Disappears behind the walls.

Thundertunes inside my head
Warning, warning...

Second hand experience
Is difficult to learn
You know that once you leave here
You can never return
There's nothing in existence
Nothing can be brought to mind
As these memories are washed away
Are worn away with time...

It looks just like a wilderness
Where have the houses gone?
No banners and processions now
The people have moved on
Some to distant places
Some have not gone very far
As these memories are washed away
Are worn away with time...

Posing in my wig, 1976. Photograph by Cindy Stern.

# CHAPTER TWO
# LOVERS OF OUTRAGE

**I was 10 years old, a child on the cusp of adolescence, a stranger in a town that was on a downward spiral.** Ferryhill, situated on the Great North Road between Durham and Darlington, was a much bigger place than I had been used to. I was totally unfamiliar with its layout and didn't know a single person that lived there. Our house at 4 Barrington Terrace, Dean Bank, opened on to a main road and was surrounded by identical rows of colliery houses. The local coal mine had closed two years before our arrival and the whole area seemed bleak and depressing.

In the spring term of 1968, I started at my new school, Dean Bank Junior, which was situated at the end of my street. Wearing short hair and a pale yellow dress with a brown satin bow, I felt conspicuous, shy and vulnerable as I was introduced to the class. The kids had all known each other since childhood and I felt like an alien who'd just landed. The atmosphere was very different to Waterhouse's and I sensed that I would have to rely on my instincts and adapt quickly to survive. After school, I hung out with the Dean Bank kids and was shocked to see them stealing sweets from the general dealers and entertained the thought that this new area I'd moved to was evil and corrupt. I was befriended by a girl of my own age, only to be delivered to a gang of older girls who'd taken a dislike to me and were waiting in ambush in the park to beat me up.

Naturally, I stopped going out after school but didn't tell my parents what was happening. It wasn't just me who was feeling out of place: my usually upbeat mother had abandoned her jaunty trilby hats and sense of style as if she didn't want to stand out from the crowd. She was struggling as she didn't know anyone and had been uprooted from her friends and family – none of whom came to visit with the exception of her youngest brother, Thomas. She'd managed to get a part-time job in the clothing factory canteen, but said that the women weren't very nice. My father, meanwhile, was visiting the Working Men's Club each evening for a few hours to meet up with his workmates. Feeling increasingly isolated and unhappy, Mum started developing psoriasis, an autoimmune skin disorder caused by stress.

I began the final year of junior school in a different class with people I didn't know. A tall, thin boy called Robert Blamire sat in the next aisle. He seemed aloof, reserved and composed and was smartly dressed compared to some of the ragamuffins in the class. His family owned the local printing works. I was intrigued and would pick fights with him to get his attention. A girl from another class, Sharon, made moves to befriend me; she didn't seem to have any other pals – and neither did I – so we naturally gravitated towards each other. I sometimes went to her house after school. She lived in a bungalow on the other side of town. Her parents were market traders and I would occasionally go to Bishop Auckland to keep her company while they worked on the market stall. It wasn't long before we were shoplifting – make-up, green glitter eyeshadow and false eyelashes. At Easter, we stole large chocolate eggs and bags of raisins from the local supermarket, hiding them under our coats; we were lucky that we never got caught. Sharon was obsessed with horses and was reading a series of fictional books called *Silver Brumbies of the South*. She had the idea that we should play truant from school to go and see these horses. We would have a long way to go as they roamed the Snowy Mountains region of Australia but I stupidly agreed. I was easily led and quite possibly depressed.

That Monday morning I set off for school as usual, but bypassed Dean Bank and headed straight to the bungalow where Sharon was waiting. We spent the morning cooking a vegetable fry-up – adding sugar, vinegar and Smarties for fun. Around lunchtime, we spotted a man on a scooter approaching the house and guessed that it was the school board man, coming to drag us back to class. As he knocked on the door, we hid under the kitchen table, laughing and keeping out of sight until he'd gone. We knew we were in trouble, so we did what any wayward kids would do – we decided to run away.

Leaving the house with nothing but the clothes we were wearing, we walked down Banky Fields to an area known as 'Doggy Wood', which led to the bottom of Steetley Quarry where trains on the main railway line from London to Edinburgh hurtled past at 100 miles an hour. There were large pools of quarry waste, some were semi solid with cracks on the surface which we walked upon. I remember jumping into a pool that appeared smooth and solid but was slurry, like quicksand, sucking me down. Sharon grabbed my arm and managed to pull me out – tragedy averted. I was up to my neck in mud so we smeared more on our faces. We were oblivious to what was happening at home.

School had finished for the day and the police had been informed of our disappearance and were driving around the streets with loudspeakers. It was starting to get dark so we decided to hide in the barn of a farm on the other side of Dean Bank where a girl from my class lived. The police were gathering recent photographs from our families in preparation for the local evening news broadcast. We passed my house via the back street and by the time we reached the farm it was already dark. Hiding behind an outbuilding, dogs started to bark, the farmer ran out, grabbed us and informed the police who took us back to our homes. The adventure was over and now we would have to face the music. I didn't feel worried and just allowed events to unfold. My mother cried at the sight of me, filthy, hungry and tired. I was questioned by the police, bathed then put to bed. The next day we were hauled separately to the headmaster's office and were forbidden from ever seeing each other again, at school or at home. I never did see her again.

My spirits were lifted when a letter arrived in the post to say that I had been offered a place at Ferryhill Grammar School; my previous school record must have been taken into account. I was relieved that I wouldn't be going to Broom Secondary Modern on the council estate, where my life wouldn't have been worth living – I was still being bullied by those older girls who attended that school.

The grammar school was a total contrast to the old Victorian Dean Bank Junior. It was a new modern building on two floors with a quadrangle and its own swimming pool, which was impressive. The bright sparks from the surrounding area attended and were known locally as 'Grammar Puffs'. Perhaps there was some resentment as we looked incongruous in our strict school uniforms, or maybe they just thought that we were entitled softies. It was a different world and a strange sight to see the teachers in assembly floating down the aisle of the school hall and up to the stage, wearing black gowns and mortarboards. I was in the final year group of the grammar school system. From the following year, the school became comprehensive.

I felt confident in the first year and found a friend, Pat, who was fun. We would take the French teacher's small bottle of whiskey from his desk drawer and run around the class with it while the other kids kept watch for the arrival of the headmaster when it all became too boisterous. Pat left at the end of the year when her family relocated so, once more, I was on my own.

I retreated into music, which has always been the soundtrack to my life and, by 1970, I was listening to *Pick of the Pops* with Alan Freeman on the radio every Sunday evening. I preferred the soul music of 'I Want You Back' by The Jackson 5 and 'Give Me Just A Little More Time' by Chairmen of the Board to heavy rock. I had also been given a record player by a friend of my mother's and had a copy of *Motown Chartbusters Volume 3*, which I played constantly. My birthday was approaching and I asked my parents for an acoustic guitar, something I was yearning for. They bought me a second-hand Spanish guitar with nylon strings, an instrument I took to instantly – my mother said that I just picked it up and played it. The neck was wide for such small hands but with the aid of a book borrowed from the library, I managed to learn all of the basic chords and, with practice, reached a point where I was able to join them together. A couple of other girls at school also had acoustic guitars, so we would get together at lunchtimes and play the song 'Leaving On A Jet Plane' by Peter, Paul and Mary in unison. We would sing a verse each and break into a three-part harmony in the chorus and performed this song at an event for the older pupils after school, which seemed to go down well.

Dean Bank Junior School, 1969. Back row, seventh from left, Robert Blamire. Third row, second from the left, me.

I found out that a youth club had started once a week in the Miners' Institute opposite my house and plucked up the courage to go there on my own. I was wearing a suit that Lorna had made for me with her new sewing machine – a turquoise skirt and bolero and a white shirt with a frill down the front. She had now left school and was working at Durham County Hall and had never had to engage in the day-to-day life of the local community. I was hoping that the bully girls wouldn't be there but I caught a glimpse of them in the cloakroom and stayed in the main hall where there were plenty of other people. The very sight of me seemed to stir up hatred and animosity, even though I barely knew them and had done nothing to provoke their attacks. I was different and didn't fit in and this was somehow a subconscious threat to them.

These incidents were sporadic so I didn't tell my parents as I hoped they would just fizzle out in time. One Friday afternoon, they were waiting for me to get off the bus after school so I stayed on till the next stop. As I got off the bus, my friend Dawn's grandmother saw them tussling with me and my cookery basket and reported the incident to my mother who, up to that point, had no idea what I'd been going through.

There was a group of older boys, about 16 or 17 years of age, who hung out at the youth club playing pool. They dressed in Levi or Wrangler double denim, jackets and jeans, and had longish hair. One of them, Peter Lloyd, approached me and began chatting. He seemed nice enough, gentle and shy but I wasn't looking for a romantic relationship – I was only 12, even though I may have looked older. He'd already left school and

Camping in Scotland.

More camping adventures.

Posing atop the Ford Anglia.

Camping in platforms.

was working at Fishburn Coke Works as an apprentice electrician. I stopped going to the youth club when my brand-new navy leather jacket was stolen from the cloakroom, but it wouldn't be the last I saw of Peter, who started calling at our house after he'd been to college on day release from work.

Peter's main topic of conversation was music; he was buying all of the weekly music papers – *New Musical Express*, *Melody Maker*, *Sounds* and *Record Mirror*, and studied them like a gambler weighing up the form of a winning racehorse. T. Rex were riding high in the charts with 'Ride A White Swan', and Peter bought me the single 'Hot Love' for my 13th birthday. He would show me photos of Rod Stewart in the music papers and try to copy his haircut. He was a big fan, and already had the album *Every Picture Tells a Story* before 'Maggie May' became a hit later that year.

Once or twice a week after school I'd visit Peter at his parents' house on the council estate on the east side of town. This was where I would be introduced to his latest vinyl acquisitions, which included *The Yes Album*, *Electric Warrior* by T. Rex, and at the end of that year, *Hunky Dory* by David Bowie. Peter was spending all of his wages on records on a weekly basis, and I was listening to music that I may not otherwise have come across. You could lose yourself for hours, taking in the sounds of the vinyl records, and this was the attraction/distraction of continuing to see Peter. He didn't make sexual advances towards me so I felt safe in his company. It was more like an innocent friendship where our love of music was the unifying factor, but my parents were becoming concerned about me hanging out in his bedroom and apparently had a word with his parents about my age. They trusted me and I never betrayed that trust.

I was still young enough to be going on holiday with my parents; the blue Ford Anglia was packed to the gills, the roof-rack piled high with camping equipment. We toured the west coast of Scotland, but the following year, when asked where I would like to go, I said London. I was aware that there was a big wide world out there beyond the confines of these claustrophobic pit villages: the capital seemed more exciting to me. The trusty Ford Anglia set off down the Great North Road and we

camped in Chigwell, Essex, which was still a fair distance from the city. We got the train into London several times and visited as many of the usual tourist attractions as we could. This was the first time any of my family had visited London and my parents were shocked at the price of everything. My father told an ice cream vendor that he wanted to buy the ice cream – not his van!

As a young teenager, I was still developing my own identity against the backdrop of chart music: 'Nothing Rhymed' by Gilbert O'Sullivan and 'My Sweet Lord' by George Harrison resonated with me at the time. I had a copy of Carole King's *Tapestry* album, which I played to death. I began cutting my own hair, which got shorter and shorter as I tried to match each side up. I would visit a shop in Bishop Auckland called Jack Sackville's where I bought a pair of narrow Levi jeans and a fishtail parka coat, and would wear a v-neck sleeveless Fair Isle tank-top over a shirt. Pop and rock music was tribal and what you wore reflected what you listened to. A group of kids at school were Led Zeppelin fans: they wore Afghan coats, had long hair and the overpowering smell of patchouli announced their arrival wherever they went.

My attitude to school was to just get through it; my school reports usually said that I was 'easily distracted'. I chose art as one of my options and was in a class with Vaughan Oliver (later the in-house designer for 4AD Records). I didn't really engage in school life and Peter was my only social contact out of school. I realised that I had no friends of my own age and at one point tried to break away from his influence, but he looked sad, so we just carried on as usual – there was nothing else going on. His friends seemed to have disappeared, possibly along the well-trodden path of jobs, Working Men's Club, alcohol, football, girlfriends, marriage, children and all the way through to old age and death. This was the traditional direction that life was supposed to take for working-class young adults in the 1970s, but Peter was focused on the latest developments in the world of music and, somehow, my own destiny was intrinsically linked with his.

We started going to see bands, the first being Yes at Stockton ABC Theatre in October 1971. I was impressed by their musicianship and could never have envisaged myself being in a band. It seemed like something beyond the realms of possibility. We saw Status Quo on the *Dog of Two Head* tour at Darlington Civic Theatre – the loudest sound I had ever heard. Newcastle City Hall was our main go-to venue, an hour-and-a-half bus journey from Ferryhill where we encountered T. Rex, struggling to be heard over 2,000 screaming girls stood on their seats.

At the start of 1972, the miners went on strike over a pay dispute between the National Union of Mineworkers and Edward Heath's Conservative government. The strike lasted around seven weeks and was characterised by violence on picket lines, power cuts to save electricity and a three-day working week. My father was on strike but I didn't fully understand what was going on. I had been disappointed at Christmas when money was tight and all I got was a new coat, which I needed anyway. (I usually found Christmas to be disappointing, mainly because I had asked for a bike on several occasions and it never materialised, but this year was especially grim.) The power cuts brought a glimmer of excitement as the house was plunged into darkness and the glow of flickering candles illuminated the room.

David Bowie's brilliant performance with his band The Spiders from Mars on *The Old Grey Whistle Test* eclipsed the mundane realities of everyday life, and I found myself filled with hope and excitement. Bowie looked unusual: tousled short hair, thin white face, peculiar eyes, crooked teeth and a beaming smile. He wore a tight colourful outfit and was sexy in an unconventional way, articulate, a great performer, singer and songwriter – full of life and vibrancy. He was like a beacon of light that connected directly to me and the misfits of my generation and became our main musical focus as the year progressed. We witnessed his transformation into a rock'n'roll star when he appeared on *Top of the Pops* with the release of the single 'Starman', closely followed by the album *The Rise and Fall of Ziggy Stardust and the Spiders from Mars*. We had seen him playing live for the first time in June 1972 at a half-full City Hall in Newcastle. We were near to the front of the stage and I thought that I saw him change

costume in the middle of a song. Magician! By the time we saw him again a few months later at Sunderland Locarno, things were really hyping up. We went there in the afternoon, hoping to catch a glimpse of the star at the soundcheck and saw him leave in the back of a black limousine, bright orange hair, the white-haired guitarist Mick Ronson by his side. This was a standing gig with much more rock'n'roll energy: bare chests, snow-white tan, leather bomber jacket with fur collar, tight 'jean jeanies' and boxing boots. We were totally smitten.

I tried to get a Bowie cut at the local hairdressers but my hair was too wavy, I didn't have straighteners and Crazy Colour wasn't yet available so a dark-red, semi-permanent dye was the closest I could get. The next time we saw Bowie at the City Hall, I stepped out of the house wearing silver satin trousers which I'd made myself, a silver velvet bomber jacket with batwing sleeves from a shop called Bus Stop in Newcastle, metallic bronze knee-length platform boots and I'd streaked my hair with silver hairspray. The sun was shining and reflected off my outfit and I felt elevated, a glowing departure from my normal self, a bold statement getting on to the number 46 bus. Bowie gigs were exciting events, full of drama and theatre. The house lights went down, the darkness punctuated by the red glow of amplifier lights as the silhouette of a roadie with a torch signalled last minute checks. The audience bristled with anticipation and excitement and when the intro music ('Theme from *A Clockwork Orange* (Beethoviana)' by Wendy Carlos) started to play over the PA system, the crowd erupted in a wave of euphoria at the sight of the band walking onstage.

Bowie introduced us to the music of Jaques Brel, Lou Reed, The Velvet Underground, New York Dolls, revived the career of Mott the Hoople with 'All the Young Dudes', produced Lou Reed's *Transformer* and the soon-to-be-released *Raw Power* by Iggy and the Stooges. Roxy Music debuted the same year with 'Virginia Plain' and their album *Roxy Music*. Their music was unusual and featured an oboe and synthesisers, original avant-garde rock with strange lyrics and singer Bryan Ferry's meticulous, quivering vocal delivery. Visually, there were elements of the 1950s fused with

Posing about like Bowie, 4 Barrington Terrace. Photograph by Cindy Stern.

colourful futuristic sci-fi. We saw them for the first time at Newcastle City Hall and I'll always remember seeing Brian Eno on synthesiser, sporting blue eyeshadow and a black feather bolero. Meanwhile, T. Rex still dominated the singles chart alongside the bubblegum glam-pop of Gary Glitter and The Sweet. The film of the year was *Cabaret*. What a time to be 14!

We were still going to see progressive rock bands like ELP, Jethro Tull, Led Zeppelin, The Rolling Stones and The Who, but these bands now seemed jaded and uninspiring compared to Bowie or Roxy Music. In 1973 Peter and I made several trips to London; we had tickets for Bowie's Hammersmith Odeon concert in the July

when Bowie destroyed his alter-ego Ziggy Stardust, announcing that this would be last show they would ever do. I didn't really take it in at the time but many fans were left shocked and devastated. We saw a kohl-eyed Lou Reed with a mop of curly black hair at the Crystal Palace Bowl, and we were in attendance for the first ever performance of the *Rocky Horror Show* with the original cast at the Kings Road Theatre. Inside the venue, usherettes dressed in 1950s style stood perfectly still and I thought that they were mannequins until I saw one coming towards me as I sat in my seat. I was terrified and jumped onto the knee of the stranger sitting next to me. There was an explosive sound as the usherettes ran towards the stage and scaled up scaffolding towers – it was a spectacular start to the show. The costumes pre-dated punk, with Tim Curry in the role of Frankenfurter wearing a tight rubber corset, skimpy underwear, fishnet stockings, suspenders and lashings of gothic make-up.

I was looking forward to seeing the Kings Road as I'd imagined it to be the centre of cutting-edge fashion, but I became more and more disappointed as we'd walked the whole street from Sloane Square and I hadn't seen anything that I liked. We were about to turn back when we saw a tiny shop window displaying a black leather jacket with the words 'Let It Rock' written with studs across the back. The shop seemed mysterious and we lacked the courage to go inside, although we would return a few years later. We visited the Biba store in Kensington, housed in an art deco building over several floors. Feather boas, pill box hats and leopard-skin print clothes blended into the subdued brown and plum decor. I was already wearing Biba Foundation Creme make-up and had a large black Biba paintbox with beautiful coloured eyeshadows. I was fascinated by fashion and was a loyal subscriber to *19 Magazine*: the epitome of style for any 1970s working-class teenager interested in the latest trends.

Before the end of the year, Peter and I had seen the New York Dolls at York University, as the music press had already primed us for their arrival. They were almost like cartoon characters, with singer David Johansen resembling a camp Mick Jagger dressed in a pale turquoise jumpsuit with feather boa. The guitarist Johnny Thunders, with his pale face and black backcombed hair, looked ill, almost as if he could throw up on stage at any moment. The music was raw and primitive, and a sense of danger and violence filled the room. The audience hated them, throwing hard plastic glasses, one of which hit me on the head. I'd never seen such a hostile reaction. A sign of things to come.

While we were still going to see bands and listening to new music, my own musical and artistic compulsions were bubbling away under the surface. I pestered my mother until she agreed to order an Eko six string acoustic guitar from her friend's Grattan's catalogue

that was to be paid for in weekly instalments. Peter had a cousin whose boyfriend was also in possession of an acoustic guitar, so we got together and learned a few songs, including 'Andy Warhol' by Bowie, Cockney Rebel's 'Hideaway', 'Sandy' by Bruce Springsteen and 'Celluloid Heroes' by The Kinks. We performed a couple of times at a folk night in a nearby pub and we went down well. It gave me a small taste of performing in public, but we didn't take things further.

I first met Gary Chaplin in November 1973, when he hired a coach for the Roxy Music *Stranded* gig at the City Hall. Gary was in the same school year group but attended Broom Secondary Modern where I suspect he was one of the few people interested in music. He reached out to people he knew at our school and managed to fill the coach. He was also helping out at the 2J's travel agent shop in the village, who had now started selling records as well as package holidays – this was like a magnet for Peter. Gary soon joined us in Peter's bedroom where we immersed ourselves in the newly released debut album by Cockney Rebel, *Human Menagerie*. The music was strange, with violin as a featured instrument and some tracks like 'Sebastian' were heavily orchestrated. Steve Harley's voice was unusual, his attitude, rebellious and their camp nuances and glam outfits ticked all of our boxes. We spent hours in that tiny bedroom, listening to the latest record releases. We were transported to other worlds through the music, lyrics, and visual presentation. It was inspiring and influential on a deep level.

I was fifteen and working every Saturday morning in a bakery at the end of our street, but this changed when one of the girls from school got me a job on Friday nights and all day Saturday at a supermarket in Newton Aycliffe. I was put straight on to the checkouts and in those days, each item had to be entered on the till by hand – no barcodes. There would be endless queues of shoppers and I would get home after 9 p.m. utterly exhausted, and would dream all night of entering numbers. I didn't last long as I found it too stressful. I got a Saturday job at the local supermarket in Ferryhill; this was easier as all I had to do was take items off the shelves into the back of the shop, remove

With Steve Harley of Cockney Rebel, circa 1974. Photograph by Cindy Stern.

the old price tags and replace them with increased prices with a labelling gun. I spent my meagre wages on clothes and make-up.

The miners went on strike again at the beginning of 1974 and it was almost a repeat of the previous strike, with a three-day working week and power cuts. This time, however, it triggered a general election in which the Conservatives were defeated and the Labour Party took power. The coal mining industry was now in steep decline and the National Coal Board were encouraging miners/tenants to buy their own homes at a percentage of the market price and guaranteed mortgages. My parents weren't interested in the scheme and applied for a council house on the other side of town. They were offered 129 Raby Road, a two-bedroom house which, by a strange twist of fate, was located directly

opposite to where Peter lived and just along the road from Gary Chaplin. Lorna had left home to go to teacher training college so I had a bedroom to myself for the first time in my life. One wall was painted Biba brown with a sepia-coloured poster of Greta Garbo. I had an orange candlewick bedspread, leopard-print carpet and a straw peacock chair.

Peter and I were attending Cockney Rebel gigs with Be Bop Deluxe as support whenever we could. I'd wear a lightweight bottle green suit with a fitted jacket and pencil skirt which I wore with a cream blouse, red beret, red flower in the lapel, silver lurex tights and pale pink ankle strap platform shoes which I'd dyed red. I was smoking St Moritz and Sobranie Russian cigarettes, which came in different colours; I thought I was very cool and sophisticated.

Gary had been teaching himself to play guitar and assembled a band called Image Fatale, a phrase taken from the lyrics of the Cockney Rebel song 'Mirror Freak'. Members included Robert Blamire (that tall, thin kid I'd pestered at Dean Bank Junior), Steve Jacobs and Steven Tarn, all from my school year group. They practised but didn't play any gigs and the project fizzled out. Gary was influenced by Bill Nelson, the guitarist from Be Bop Deluxe who were supporting Cockney Rebel. When we went to see the band at Bracknell Sports Centre, they seemed less than friendly at the soundcheck and I somehow thought that it was my fault; we didn't realise until afterwards that we were actually witnessing the demise of the original line-up.

It was my final year of secondary education. I'd taken no active part in any aspect of school life and couldn't wait to leave. There were two ways of looking at my situation: either I'd been led astray during my teenage years, or I'd actually received a top class education in contemporary music of the 1970s. I was travelling around the country with Peter following Cockney Rebel whilst sitting my O-level exams. I was lucky that my parents were easy-going and never pressurised me, allowing me the freedom to find my own way and make my own mistakes. I left with 7 O-levels and had been accepted onto a Foundation Course in Art and Design at Darlington College of Technology. As well as doing drawing, painting, ceramics and textile design, I'd signed up for A-levels in Art and English Literature and extra O-levels in History of Art and Biology. I soon dropped English Literature as I couldn't relate to Shakespeare or Chaucer; I was reading J.G. Ballard, George Orwell, Aldous Huxley, Graham Greene and Raymond Chandler in my spare time. The other students on the course were a nice set of people, mainly from Darlington, and the first year was enjoyable and fun. I took a Saturday job in the cobblers on Post House Wynd where I served customers and cut keys.

A band called Fox had appeared on the scene with a single called 'Only You Can'. The singer Noosha had an interesting, nuanced voice which was different to other female singers in the charts, like Kiki Dee and Tina Charles. Her understated persona and 1920s sense of

style appealed to my own. I mimicked her voice as I sang along to the record but never thought for one moment that I too could be a singer in a band. We decided to go and see them at Victoria Palace in London and got the coach with a couple of friends, somehow managing to get backstage after the show. We helped ourselves to the band's rider, which prepared us for the long night ahead as we had nowhere to stay. We slept on bench seats around Victoria Railway Station and in the doorway of the British Airways building on what was a freezing cold night. We thought nothing of making the long trip to London to experience new adventures.

Unconventional female voices were making their way into my consciousness via Peter's non-stop quest to discover new music. I liked 'Casablanca Moon' by a band called Slapp Happy, whose singer Dagmar Krause reminded me of Nico from The Velvet Underground. I'd heard 'Piss Factory' by Patti Smith and later that year, her debut album *Horses*. I didn't always understand what she was singing about, but I liked her guttural vocal delivery, freedom of expression and the fact that it was like nothing I'd heard before. I admired the way she dressed, understated and masculine with a white shirt and tie. She exuded a confident, strong and independent attitude.

Our final trip to London that year was to see Bruce Springsteen at the Hammersmith Odeon. Most of the gigs we were attending were in large venues with big crowds and I was seeing things from a fan's point of view. The artists and performers seemed to be from a different world – a million miles away from my own everyday life.

By the second year of college, quite a few students were leaving to get jobs, and I too decided to quit; I had no ambitions to go to university and I wanted to earn some money. After my exams, I secured a six-month temporary job at Darlington Library where they were converting the existing system into Plessey electronic bar codes. I performed general library duties, checking books in and out and arranging books on the shelves into alphabetical and numerical order, fiction and non-fiction. I would venture into the dark, musty Victorian basement on my own with a trolley-load of books and insert a barcode sticker into each. I could sometimes hear things rustling or moving about which set my heart racing, and I would make a hasty exit. I dreaded being asked to spend time in this claustrophobic space. The job itself was tedious and I couldn't see myself making a career out of working in a library. Some of the staff, mainly old spinsters who had worked there for years, were as dry and dusty as the books in the cellar.

When my employment came to an end at the library, I secured a full-time job as a clerical assistant in the Legal Department of Sedgefield District Council in Spennymoor, a ten-minute bus ride from home. Ironically, the solicitor's main activity was the conveyancing of National Coal Board houses to their new owners: ex-miners. The ownership of thousands of houses in the area was transferred to the private sector, an activity that intensified with the mass sell-off of council houses to sitting tenants, orchestrated by Margaret Thatcher when she became prime minister a few years later. My job entailed keeping folders in order and filing completed transactions into the deed storeroom, where I sometimes loitered with a girl from another department who'd started at the same time as me. An older lady who chain-smoked and whose young son had just been on an episode of *Jim'll Fix It* sat on the opposite side of the desk. The highlight of the day was when the clattering tea trolley arrived in the morning and afternoon with cakes and biscuits, which did nothing for my waistline. One day each week, I went to Durham Technical College to study Local Government. I opened my own bank account, not realising that this was the first year that women were allowed to do so without permission from their father, or through having a joint account with their husband.

In early 1976, Peter and I read a live review of a gig at London's Marquee Club in the *NME* by writer Neil Spencer. The headline read: 'DON'T LOOK OVER YOUR SHOULDER, BUT THE SEX PISTOLS ARE COMING', accompanied by a photo of the singer Johnny Rotten looking suitably deranged. On one of our trips to London, we thought we'd spotted him on the underground – his spiky orange hair and light blue Teddy Boy drape jacket were unmistakable. We'd followed him down the Kings Road to a shop called

'Sex', which was in the same location as 'Let It Rock' from a few years earlier. As we entered the shop, there was no sign of Johnny Rotten, but Peter struck up a conversation with Malcolm McLaren, their manager, about the Sex Pistols while I just stood there feeling timid and shy. Rubber clothing and fetish items were displayed on the walls, an old 1950s jukebox stood in the corner of the room with records such as 'Psychotic Reaction' by Count Five and 'Shake Some Action' by the Flamin' Groovies. The shop assistant, Jordan, looked stunning with a backcombed blonde beehive, black make-up strips across her eyes, a rubber dress and stiletto-heeled shoes. I felt decidedly ordinary, even a little afraid, so I lurked in the background. Malcolm took Peter's phone number and rang him a few months later to ask if we knew of any venues in the north-east of England where the Sex Pistols could play.

We started to go and see a band called Doctors of Madness who'd appeared on our radar when their debut album *Late Night Movies, All Night Brainstorms* had just been released by Polydor Records. Their theatrical glam rock style appealed to us; there were echoes of Cockney Rebel, with violin a prominent part of their sound, and their lyrics were inspired by the American writer William Burroughs. The singer Kid Strange, tall and thin, wore a shiny jumpsuit with thigh-high boots, had bright blue hair and eyes painted onto his eyelids so that his eyes looked open when closed. He played a custom-made guitar in the shape of the word 'KID'. He sauntered onstage at Scarborough Penthouse with a cigarette in his mouth, but when it was time to play the guitar and sing, it stuck to his lips and blew his cool as he tried to spit it out. I don't know why I remembered this brief, amusing incident – perhaps it was the first time that I saw through the illusion of a performance and realised that these entertainers were no different from myself.

Peter's record buying impulses were intensifying, almost becoming an addiction. At least once a week, he would make the three-hour round trip to Newcastle to visit Virgin Records, especially if there was a new 'must have' record due out. Hearing the Ramones album on the day it was released was a revelation. The short

In a straitjacket with Kid Strange (Doctors of Madness), 1976. Photograph by Cindy Stern.

songs with simple barre chords and no guitar solos were in stark contrast to the intricate musicianship of progressive rock. They sounded irreverent, with humorous lyrics like 'beat on the brat with a baseball bat' and 'now I wanna sniff some glue'. Dressed in scruffy leather jackets, ripped jeans and dirty sneakers, all four members had adopted the surname Ramone as if they were a band of brothers. It was primitive, energetically intense and contained all of the elements that would be the blueprint for 'punk', a word that was entering our vocabulary, a buzzword that conjured up feelings of excitement and rebellion.

In May 1976 we were at London Victoria train station when David Bowie stood in an open-topped black Mercedes and did his infamous wave, widely interpreted as a Nazi salute, as part of his promotion for the brilliant *Station to Station* album. Speaking as an eyewitness, I honestly thought that he was waving at the crowd and didn't interpret it as anything sinister. Later that month, we went to see the Sex Pistols for the first time at the most incongruous location: Sayers nightclub, a small venue at the end of a row of garages in Northallerton, Yorkshire. It was a Wednesday night, Peter's 22nd birthday and we were there with a couple of friends who had a car. There were about thirty local people sitting at tables waiting for the 'turn' to come on. As the band launched into their first song, the audience were taken aback by the powerful onslaught of their raw and aggressive sound. Johnny Rotten was compelling as a vocalist and performer, spitting out his angry, confrontational lyrics to songs such as 'Pretty Vacant' and 'No Feelings' with a sneering whining voice and insolent stare. The band wore clothes from Sex and Johnny wore a pink drape jacket with a black collar and an Iggy t-shirt. I noticed he had cigarette burns on his forearm. The whole gig was an aural and visual assault and when they left the stage after about forty minutes, the regulars were in a state of shock. We knew that this untamed energy, capable of cutting through inertia into another dimension, would lead to something, although it was unclear at this point just how completely it would change our lives.

We saw the Pistols again two nights later at Middlesbrough Town Hall supporting Doctors of Madness – an interesting combination. The Pistols were on fire that night and made the theatrics of Doctors of Madness look pretentious and silly. It was as if a seismic shift had taken place, the young upstarts, with no respect for anything, had stolen their thunder, rifled through their luggage and nicked their belongings in the dressing room while the headline band were on stage. It was sad to see as the Doctors were nice people, but the Pistols, who had nothing to lose, were burning anyone that crossed their path. Peter and I were hooked, our friends less so, and that night there would be a parting of the ways: our friends continued to follow Doctors of Madness and we placed our allegiance with the Sex Pistols.

The next time we saw them was at the Screen on the Green Cinema in London on 29 August 1976. The show didn't start until midnight so we went to the Hope and Anchor pub just along the road to kill some time. As midnight approached, we headed back to queue outside, and, as I observed the rest of the line, I felt decidedly underdressed in a plain white t-shirt, black narrow trousers and black cropped hair: there were more than a few flamboyant characters posing about self-consciously. Our seats were near to the front so we had a good view of the evening's antics. A DJ played records on the stage and a small group of fans couldn't wait to get up there, dancing about and basking in the attention. One dark-haired girl was particularly noticeable in a black shiny under-bra, her small breasts exposed, tight shiny knickers, fishnet tights, black patent thigh boots and a Nazi armband. Siouxsie Sioux.

Manchester band Buzzcocks were on first; it was possibly only their third or fourth live performance. Singer Howard Devoto was an unusual sight: he had a receding hairline, wore a red shiny jacket and leather trousers and delivered his vocals with confidence and intensity. The guitarist, Pete Shelley, looked faintly ridiculous in black leggings, a long pink jacket and had sawn off half of the body of a cheap guitar, as if to show contempt for the instrument. Their music adopted a buzzsaw guitar style and the songs were well formed, interesting and catchy, with titles such as 'Breakdown', 'Times Up' and 'Orgasm Addict'.

Next up was a very early performance of a band called The Clash. We'd already heard of them through their association with the Pistols and their manager Bernie Rhodes. The singer Joe Strummer was intense and wore a brown suede jacket with pieces of broken mirror stuck to it. Paul Simonon on bass and guitarist Keith Levene (later to join John Lydon in PiL) looked like twins. Both were tall and thin with blonde short hair and were wearing paint-splattered shirts, ties and jackets, and their movements seemed to be synchronised. Another guitarist stood to the right of Strummer: Mick Jones, deadly serious in his intentions and he had everything to play for. They were amateurish, tuning up at full volume between songs, which had titles such as 'London's Burning' and '1977'. It was pretty ramshackle but the energy, attitude and excitement more than made up for the lack of musical proficiency.

It was time for the Pistols to hit the stage; they were well practised by now and delivered a powerful set which included a couple of new songs: 'Anarchy In The UK', and 'Lazy Sod'. Johnny Rotten was distracted when he banged his tooth on the microphone and was searching around for his dental crown between songs. It was all very chaotic and a far cry from all of the 'professional' bands we'd seen over the years, but we felt part of something that was embryonic, new and exciting.

Punk music is often remembered as being played at breakneck speed, but at this point in their careers, these bands were not especially fast-paced as they were frankly still struggling to play – the Ramones were much faster and tighter. Charles Shaar Murray reviewed

Early punk days, 1976. Photograph by Cindy Stern.

the gig for *NME* and slated The Clash saying that they 'should be speedily returned to their garage, preferably with the motor running, which would undoubtedly be more of a loss to their friends and families than to either rock or roll'. The established music journalists were finding it difficult to get their heads around this new, irreverent, nihilistic musical form. It was making them feel old.

Meanwhile, back in Ferryhill, Gary had been practising his guitar with enthusiasm. In the March of 1976, on my 18th birthday, he'd entertained us at Peter's house with an acoustic guitar and enjoyed the attention. His playing was improving and later in the year he bought an Antoria gold top electric guitar and amplifier and was keen to put a band together. He asked me to be the singer and I agreed

without hesitation, even though I'd never sang in a band before. Gary then recruited Steve Jacobs from his previous band on drums and Alan Hetherington on bass. Gary was now working full time at Durham County Hall and each week, after I'd finished my day release at Durham Technical College, we would get together at a church hall in Durham for a band practice. Robert Blamire, whom I'd not encountered since our school days, was in attendance and I still sensed some shyness in our communication. Although he'd been in a band with Gary before, his present role seemed to involve borrowing his brother's small PA system and transporting it, along with the rest of the musical equipment, in the back of his yellow Ford Escort estate. We would play songs such as 'Pills' by the New York Dolls, 'Roadrunner' by The Modern Lovers and the Patti

*Backstage with Eddie and the Hot Rods, wearing my wig. Photograph by Cindy Stern.*

Smith version of 'Gloria'. Our playing and confidence improved each week and Gary organised for us to play this set of covers at our old school, although I don't recall us having a band name at that point.

We soon realised that we needed to start writing our own songs and, by the end of 1976, we were concentrating on getting a set together of original material. Most bands in our local area were 'proper' musicians and played chart cover songs around the working men's clubs, or were heavy rock or blues bands. There were phrases like 'paying your dues' or 'earning dough'. We had nothing in common with this muso world and were totally isolated in our own environment. Any women involved seemed either to be chicks, groupies or backing singers, but this was soon to be turned on its head. Punk rock was our saviour and

we were beginning to feel the urgency to make our own contribution to 'the cause'.

Pub rock, a back-to-basics musical reaction against progressive and glam rock, had briefly taken hold of the music scene but by the time it reached the north-east, we were already seeing bands like Dr Feelgood playing in large venues like the City Hall. Smaller venues in the area began to open up and the Rock Garden in Middlesbrough became the place where we would see new emerging bands like Eddie and the Hot Rods, the Vibrators and The Damned. It was up-close and personal, and I always stood right at the front of the stage – one step away from being up there myself.

Meanwhile, the London-based music industry was becoming increasingly threatened by the growing interest, momentum and confrontational attitude of

Punk poseur with wig.

Punk attitude.

Pensive punk.

Daft punk. Photographs by Cindy Stern.

'punk rock', this rebellious subculture headed by the Sex Pistols. With the age old adage of 'keeping your friends close and your enemies even closer', EMI, one of the UK's largest record companies, signed the Sex Pistols, only to drop them after three months as they were too hot to handle. A&M Records picked up the gauntlet – the contract was terminated after only ten days. The band were making a mockery of the music business and exposing its inner workings to the public. The BBC realised that the existential threat of energy building up among Britain's disaffected youth was potentially explosive, and while they refused to play punk rock music on their mainstream channels, they utilised the portal of the *John Peel Show* as an avenue for new upcoming bands to reach a wider audience. The Damned's 'New Rose' was the first punk single out of the gate on the independent Stiff Records, closely followed by the Vibrators 'We Vibrate' on RAK Records. The programme's live session format became legendary: bands, some of whom had never been in a recording studio before, would record four songs in a day at Maida Vale, the BBC's own hallowed studio. This made for unpredictable, edgy and compelling listening.

John Peel was a lifelong music fan and embraced the energy and enthusiasm of this new generation. The mainstream media on the other hand, wanted to quash it before it could further influence the nation's youth. The Sex Pistols' appearance on the Bill Grundy show would become legendary, largely because guitarist Steve Jones was goaded by the presenter into uttering the words 'you dirty fucker' on live TV at teatime. This was the perfect opportunity to demonise punk. The entire nation was outraged, tabloid front pages were dominated by the story and the Pistols instantly became Public Enemy No. 1. While it gave them mass exposure, the incident severely impacted their upcoming *Anarchy In The UK* headlining tour, with The Clash, Johnny Thunders and The Damned in support. Many of the dates were cancelled by local authorities, or targeted by religious freaks who believed that Satan himself was in attendance as they sang hymns and prayed for the souls of all those concerned.

Peter and I had travelled to Leeds in the hope that the Polytechnic show would go ahead that evening. In the afternoon, we somehow found ourselves in Johnny Rotten's crowded hotel room along with members of the support bands and other hangers-on. The atmosphere was tense and anxious as the bands waited for confirmation as to whether they would play that night. They were also at the centre of a media storm. Word came through that the gig was on, and the bands had so much pent-up energy that they almost blew the roof off the Poly later that evening. There had been talk of The Damned wanting to leave the tour to do their own gigs, and this was seen by Malcolm McLaren as a breach of solidarity. He kicked them off the tour a few days later, calling them 'punk traitors'. There was no room for sentiment in punk rock. These were serious times and highly charged, emotionally.

At some point in late 1976, Peter and I became engaged to be married. I don't remember him proposing to me or me suggesting that this was a good idea. I was 18, he was 22 and I suspect that we were entangled in an unspoken social tradition. If you have been with the same person for a long period of time, it's expected that you follow the path of engagement, marriage and having a family. We'd been kicking about together for six years – the whole of my teens – and music had been the main focus. I didn't analyse the situation at the time and just went with the flow; I was oblivious to the fact that this was a statement of intent, a commitment that could have consequences further down the line. I was also unaware that my life was to move in a different direction that, at this juncture, was impossible to envisage.

It was to be quite a year. I had turned 18, had my first full-time job and had witnessed the birth and subsequent explosion of punk rock, which proved both an inspiration and a massive turning point for me. I was engaged, had joined a band as a singer and frontperson and, through that, had unknowingly reconnected with a person who would be of creative and emotional significance throughout my life. It was as if all of these factors had conspired to push me out of my comfort zone and into new and unchartered territory.

Overleaf: In the crowd at Leeds Polytechnic, Anarchy Tour, 6 December 1976. Photograph by Graham Wood.

## LOVERS OF OUTRAGE

Prisoners of disguise
Your sentence is never through
What do you see when you look in the mirror?
Hidden identity
It's all a fascination
All your imagination
Light up the stage for the lovers of outrage
Let them try something new.

Painted puppets, clockwork clowns
Painted lips that make no sound
Time to think and ask anew
Is it them or is it you?

Let them go, set them free
Let them be who they want to be.

Shattered and vacant eyes
Looking behind the glass
Change back at midnight, reality in sight
Time will erase the mask
It's all a fascination
All your imagination
Light up the stage for the lovers of outrage
Let them try something new.

Paul Harvey painting, 1977 (Ferryhill).

Penetration, 1977. Photograph by Rik Walton.

# CHAPTER THREE

# SILENT COMMUNITY

In mid-January 1977, we were offered a support slot with Slaughter and the Dogs at Middlesbrough Rock Garden, although our band was still in its formative stage with Steve Jacobs on drums and Alan Hetherington on bass. We didn't have a name and hastily called ourselves The Points. In terms of our repertoire, there were possibly a few covers, but mostly we were now playing early versions of our own songs.

We had nothing to lose and were confident and excited to be playing in front of an audience. Slaughter and the Dogs wouldn't let us share the stage so we had to set our equipment up on the floor in front of the stage. Even at this early stage of punk, some bands were vying for their own top dog position and adopting a competitive attitude. We weren't fazed, and our performance was full of energy and bravado. When we saw them a few weeks later in Darlington, one of their songs bore an uncanny resemblance to one of our own and when we confronted them, an altercation almost ensued. Hey, this was punk!

We were just starting to get things going when Steve was offered a full-time job in a bank, which he sensibly took, but this left us without a drummer. Steve sadly died of leukaemia a few years later. Alan was replaced by Robert Blamire on bass, which seemed logical as he had played with Gary before and was already involved with the band, helping out with equipment and transportation. Gary knew a 16-year-old drummer called Gary Smallman, whom we auditioned at the local scout hall. Gary Smallman turned up with his older sister and brother-in-law, who said that I sounded like Kiki Dee. I took this as a compliment. Gary's older brother (who didn't accompany him to the audition) was a 'proper' musician, earning decent money playing in working men's clubs. I doubt he approved of Gary joining a 'punk' band.

Robert's brother wouldn't lend us his PA system anymore, so we pooled our cash resources and bought a small PA, bringing it back from Newcastle on the number 46 bus. Once a week at the Miners' Institute we started working on more new songs: Gary would play his guitar ideas, the band would join in and I would experiment with melodies over the top of the music, without lyrics. We had no recording equipment so I would have to memorise the musical arrangements and write some lyrics for the next practice to fit with the music. This is how all of our early songs were composed. They were short, primitive, noisy and punky with titles such as 'I'm Nobody', 'In the Future', 'Silent Community', 'Duty Free Technology' and 'Firing Squad'. The Clash were writing about urban landscapes, tower blocks, hate and war. I was writing about my own environment, which was a cultural vacuum – 'nothing to do and nothing to say, the silent community is here to stay' – and I was observing the state of society from a Northern 18-year-old girl's viewpoint. I had to dig deep and extract ideas from thin air, from within myself, from the knowledge I'd gained so far. I'd never written lyrics before and didn't find it easy. The words for the song 'Don't Dictate' consisted of one verse, repeated twice with a simple chorus. It was more of a personal than political statement, saying that I wanted to do things in my own way. I only realised a few years later that it was some form of double negative as I was dictating to you not to dictate to me.

We were at the very beginning of a steep learning curve. While some might have considered a young woman fronting a punk band as unusual, even scandalous, my gender was something I didn't even think about. I was the singer, I wrote the words, fronted the band and wanted to do the job to the best of my ability. The music, creativity and challenge was my main interest and motivation. I had no intention of seeking male approval or placing myself in the role of a sexual object, and I considered myself an equal member of the band, presenting myself on stage as asexual so that the music would speak for itself. As far as I am aware, both the band and the audience could see that I was a fully integrated member and I didn't feel pressurised to flaunt my sexuality to further our aims. The dynamic

First band photo, Ferryhill Miners' Institute, early 1977. Photograph by Cindy Stern.

of a female fronting a group is very different to an all-male band and I had be strong and stay true to my own ideals at all times. Vocally, I was influenced by Johnny Rotten's sharp, angry delivery and Patti Smith's cool push out, where the energy of the vocal seemed to originate from somewhere deep inside of the body. But ultimately my own voice came through loud and clear, and also naturally gravitated towards singing in tune, transcending the cliche that punk vocalists sang off-key, sometimes deliberately.

Buzzcocks had just released their self-financed *Spiral Scratch* EP on their own New Hormones label, and London's Rough Trade, a record shop and distributor, was ready and waiting for the new movement to gain momentum. There was still a long way to go and at this point, the major labels were still the main outlet. The Clash, who'd struggled to get through their set five months earlier, had now signed to CBS, a major US record company, and had upped their game massively. There were cries of 'sell out' from fans who believed that punk should remain against the system. The Clash were one of the most prominent bands of the punk era who espoused its ideals and doctrines, but the majors still dominated the industry and independent labels were in their infancy, with limited distribution and resources. The Clash, by signing to CBS, extended the reach of punk into the wider world and would have struggled to survive if they'd attempted to go it alone. They paved the way for many bands who followed in their wake. Something was happening – there was a sense of excitement in the air and we wanted to be part of it.

We needed to make a recording of our songs but there were no studios in the area. An eccentric local DJ and electronics wizard called Ray Kelly, an older friend of Robert's, offered to bring his reel-to-reel mono Ferrograph tape recorder to one of our practices. He set up the equipment using upturned pool tables as sound baffles. We played the songs live and hoped for the best. The recordings were primitive but captured the energy and enthusiasm of the band and we somehow managed to get some cassettes duplicated.

The band still didn't have a name that we were all happy with and it was becoming a matter of urgency. One evening, inspiration struck as we sat in Peter's bedroom with Gary Chaplin. A fanzine on the wall caught our eye. The cover bore the word 'Penetration' in a shattered typeface, a reference to a song by Iggy and the Stooges. It was decided in the spur of the moment – we had no long term plan – the future was unwritten and anything was possible! Some of the punk characters had adopted pseudonyms like Johnny Rotten, Captain Sensible, Sid Vicious, Rat Scabies, Poly Styrene and Siouxsie Sioux. This was nothing new in music. Many artists had changed their names to a monicker that caught the public's attention, defined their brand and protected their personal identity. I think the punk names were derived more from nicknames, a sense of fun or possibly to evade detection from the social security system but they certainly defined the flavour of the genre. We toyed with the idea briefly, as Gary became Gary Grant or Whizz Kid, Robert was R and I was just Pauline. In a few early live reviews of the band, journalists took to calling me Pauline Noname, which I didn't like. In the end, we all just decided to stick with our given names.

Peter and Gary took cassette copies of our roughly recorded demos to Pete Brent, owner of Newcastle's Listen Ear record shop, and Andy Worrell, manager

at the Virgin record shop in Newcastle, who then forwarded it to Virgin Record's Head Office in Vernon Yard, London. They sent copies to Jonh Ingham, a journalist at *Sounds*, and Stuart Joseph at Rough Trade (both managers of the newly formed Generation X). In a bid to get the band some more gigs, a copy was sent to Andy Czezowski who was putting on bands at the Roxy in Covent Garden, London, which at the time was becoming a central location for punk in the eyes of the media. They sent a copy to Rui de Castro, a Portuguese entrepreneur who had set up a small independent punk label called Warm Records. Buzzcocks' manager Richard Boon in Manchester was contacted to see if there were any support slots available. We looked up to Buzzcocks as an authentic punk band – and they were Northerners – so we felt that we had something in common. Kindred spirits.

The first response came back in the form of a photocopied recording contract from Rui de Castro of Warm Records. There was no way we were going to sign it: we'd only existed as a band for five minutes and we were keeping our options open. He was keen to approach the Roxy who were recording live shows for the forthcoming album *Live at the Roxy*. We were offered a date supporting Generation X on 9 April but didn't want to be recorded – it was our first proper gig with this line-up, we were still developing as a band and not being part of the London crowd made us cautious. Rui had organised an event for the following evening at Bonham Carter House in Gower Street with The Adverts and a band called London, with Jon Moss on drums (later of Culture Club).

Viewing the London scene from a distance of 260 miles through the lens of the music papers, perception and reality didn't always match up. We held the Roxy in our minds to be some sort of mythical place and were really excited to be playing there. Seven hours in the back of a Luton-style box van with Ray Kelly driving, sitting on equipment that was sliding about, wasn't the safest or most comfortable way to travel. We distracted and amused ourselves with Ray's portable battery-operated record player with Buzzcocks' *Spiral Scratch* and the recently released 7" 'White Riot/1977' by The

Clash. Gary Smallman would sing 'nights in the cellar' instead of '1977', mimicking Joe Strummer's serious and impassioned voice. Our spirits were high, or at least they were until the batteries ran out and we reached our destination, which was an inevitable let-down – it wasn't Disneyland.

A stylish individual with blonde hair and leather trousers, whom we would later discover was Steve Strange (later of Visage), was standing outside the club, smoking a cigarette. He was friendly, being a polite Welshman – some of the London punks weren't so charming. Andy, the club's owner, was downstairs in the basement venue, which was small and dark. There was no PA system but luckily we'd brought our own primitive set-up, although, as the support band, we weren't expecting to have to supply the sound system for the entire evening's entertainment. Generation X arrived like rock stars in the making and complained that the PA was a Mickey Mouse operation. They took over the small dressing room, being the headline act, and we had to prepare for our debut performance in a cramped narrow corridor behind the stage. We were nervous before going on. The venue was packed with punk scenesters, poseurs and members of prominent bands, casting their cool, critical eyes over the night's proceedings.

I was wearing a black shirt, a black leather jacket which I'd studded myself, black trousers with zips held up with a thin piece of rope, black eye make-up, black lipstick and black nail varnish. We played with our usual intensity and commitment. How would we fare in the metropolis? Halfway through the set, Ari Up from The Slits shouted 'you're too stiff!' to which Ray retorted, 'so would you be, love, if you'd sat in the back of a van for seven hours!' We seemed to go down well, getting through our set without any major setbacks. Robert was approached afterwards by Glen Matlock, who'd recently been ejected from the Sex Pistols, and was asked if he would join his new band The Rich Kids, to which the answer was 'no'. With all of the activity, we'd forgotten to put Rui from Warm Records on the guestlist and he was refused access to the venue, missing our set. He wasn't too happy about that.

We stayed at a flat in Walthamstow that belonged to a friend of Ray's, arriving late at night, sleeping on beds, sofas or the floor, before heading the next day to our gig at Bonham Carter House in Bloomsbury. As we arrived at the venue, we were oblivious to the fact that the show we'd been booked to play, along with The Adverts and London, was an after-match reception for 600 Portuguese football fans. We and the other bands helped ourselves to the food on the tables as we thought it was for us. When the guests arrived, they were horrified that three punk bands were to be the evening's entertainment and accused Jon Moss of disrespecting their country by allegedly wiping his hands on the Portuguese flag. We were ejected from the building before we could even play a note and our equipment was thrown out onto the street. On the plus side, we received our first-ever press/publicity coverage when both *Sounds* and *NME* reported the incident with the headline 'PUNKS IN PORTUGUESE SOCCER FOUL-UP'.

We supported London band the Vibrators at Middlesbrough Rock Garden and Seaburn Hall, a large venue on the north-east coast, who had started to promote punk gigs with bands such as The Jam. There were no other punk bands in the area so we were the obvious choice. The Vibrators were making headway on the front wave of punk with the single 'We Vibrate', a John Peel session, a recent support slot to Iggy Pop and the imminent release of their first album *Pure Mania*. They were a lot older than us, accomplished musicians and for this reason, we didn't consider them to be authentic punk but they were gracious people and treated us with nurturing respect.

Gary and Peter were making regular trips to Listen Ear record shop in Newcastle and sounding out the owner Pete Brent as a prospective manager. All of the bands had managers – the Pistols had Malcolm McLaren, The Clash were managed by Bernie Rhodes, Buzzcocks had Richard Boon, The Adverts, Michael Dempsey, The Damned, Jake Riviera – all of them mavericks and chancers with limited financial back up. Peter (Lloyd) was well placed for the job but was purely a music fan with no knowledge of the music business and didn't have the self-confidence or bravado

The Roxy, London, 9 April 1977. Photograph by Cindy Stern.

to take on the challenge. Long-haired, moustachio'd Pete Brent, on the other hand, was older than us and had a few tenuous links with the music industry. His typically Seventies style: shirt, waistcoat and flared trousers, represented the old guard, but perhaps we thought he was well positioned and credible enough to take us to the next level. We were clueless but starting to become ambitious. He sometimes attended our practices in Ferryhill, and on one occasion brought along a writer called Kev Anderson, who wanted to interview us for his fanzine *Deviation Street*. We were starting to get noticed and were accessible to those inspired by punk and its DIY ethos.

In Newcastle, a few other punk acolytes began to make themselves known to us: a group called Speed, fronted by Johnny Isis (Brown) (later of the Band of Holy Joy), and Raw (local hairdresser Mark) who'd organised a gig at The Canteen, Newcastle University

on 4 May. On 6 May we supported Cherry Vanilla, the New York performer associated with Andy Warhol and David Bowie, at Newcastle Polytechnic Green Bar. Her backing band were The Police, who played a set of their own material and were experienced musicians. We made quite an impression as we were young, fresh, authentic and fearless with a hard-line punk attitude. Miles Copeland, Cherry's manager, owner of Step Forward Records and brother of The Police's drummer, sent one of his scouts to the Miners' Institute to see us practise and when he produced a cassette tape recorder to capture our essence, we refused to play and sent him away! We had a deep mistrust of these people and were very protective of our music at this stage. Apparently both Miles Copeland and Bernie Rhodes approached Gary regarding management and unbeknown to the rest of the band, he turned them down as he was informed that Copeland's father was head of the CIA. We only found this out years later and it would appear that Gary was running the band with a tight, secretive grip.

The Sex Pistols' provocative single 'God Save the Queen' had just been released and was instantly banned by the BBC. The fact that it was the Queen's Silver Jubilee year, and that the lyrics seemed heretic in nature, served to fuel the fire that the Pistols were a threat to the nation. The Clash, meanwhile, were on their nationwide *White Riot* tour with Buzzcocks, Subway Sect and The Slits; we saw them at Edinburgh Playhouse and other venues in the North. Each person's contribution to the anti-establishment punk cause, whether as a fan or as a creative, was like molecules of energy rushing about, turning up the heat.

Our own persistence was paying off and we were asked to play at Manchester's Electric Circus on 29 May with Buzzcocks, punk poet John Cooper Clarke and Warsaw, aka Stiff Kittens (later Joy Division). We travelled three hours south-west and pulled up to the venue, an old cinema standing alone in a large area of bleak wasteland. Feral children appeared from nowhere and pelted us and our van with stones and bricks. We managed to get into the venue unscathed. It was scruffy inside but had become home to the punk community, as no other venues in the city would entertain such outcasts. Howard Devoto had already left Buzzcocks by this point but he came to the show, dressed in an overcoat with a manbag over his shoulder and a book under his arm. (I didn't catch the title.) We thought he was pretentious at the time but he was no fool; he could already see beyond punk and was on his own creative path. A three-piece band called The Worst were also in attendance and I'd never seen anyone so dirty: they looked like they'd just emerged from underneath a car, covered in oil and with what looked like glue stuck to their faces.

We played our set and tried to impress. It was reviewed by Paul Morley for the *NME*, who wrote that Penetration 'seemed nervous and oddly angular except for the faintly erotic boilersuit-clad chick singer who aimed hard for psychotic stares' and Ian Wood for *Sounds*: 'this band are killers. There's a she-vixen of a singer with a great voice and a guitarist with a

Bowie and Ronson. Photograph by Rik Walton.

superb feel for dynamics'. We were delighted with these reviews. That same week, a full-page article appeared in *Sounds*, with the headline: 'ANARCHY IN COUNTY DURHAM... IT'S THE PITS', written by Phil Sutcliffe, a regional journalist who was involved in the north-east music magazine *Out Now* and a weekly music show called *Bedrock* on BBC Radio Newcastle. He looked like a long-haired hippy but had shown genuine interest in our progress and championed the band from the beginning. He was perplexed as to 'how they can make savage music, making established bands like The Damned and The Clash look like next week's fossils, when they come from the backside of beyond, Ferryhill Co. Durham'. We didn't like the constant references to Ferryhill as it made us feel uncool, like country bumpkins, and we were unaware at the time of our power and potency and the real barriers we

Innocent punk. Photograph by Rik Walton.

were surmounting connected to our upbringing and environment. We were also much younger than most of the people we were coming into contact with, and still retained an air of innocence and naiveté. We looked up to the London bands and lacked confidence in ourselves, possibly due to the notion that the capital looked down on the rest of the country as being generally backward and uncultured.

It was difficult to find any decent clothes to wear onstage that were new and original, so I bought four white shirts from a charity shop and dyed them different colours for each member of the band. Robert's was green, Gary Smallman's was yellow, Gary Chaplin's blue and, for my own, I took off both sleeves, dyed them dark red, dyed the main body green, then re-attached the sleeves. I bought some fabric paint and painted geometric designs onto each shirt – a tradition

that I still return to when I am stuck for something to wear on stage. It was less of an artistic statement and more of wanting the band to present themselves as a cohesive unit. I enjoyed these creative pursuits that carried on from my childhood and art school days.

On 6 June 1977, Pete Brent had hired the Guildhall in Newcastle to coincide with the Queen's Silver Jubilee celebrations. As a Listen Ear Promotion, he'd invited The Adverts from London, Warsaw from Manchester and local band Harry Hack and the Big G to play alongside Penetration. The general public believed punk should be stamped out and Gary Chaplin was chased down the street in Ferryhill as a result of the growing animosity. However, the audience for punk was expanding as young people realised that this was their time. Punk was alienating previous generations, it was exciting, rebellious, social and it was opening minds to

Johnny Rotten's jumper. Photograph by Ray Stevenson.

new possibilities. Warsaw were on first and their music was standard punk, showing no indication that they would soon transform into the deep and thoughtful Joy Division. Harry Hack played a great song called 'I Hate the Whole Human Race'. The Adverts were an authentic punk band with a great collection of songs in their arsenal; they'd just recorded a John Peel session and released their first single 'One Chord Wonders' on Stiff Records. As for us, we were improving every time we played, although a new song like 'V.I.P' could easily trip us up with its quirky time signatures. My parents were away on holiday at the time, so we invited The Adverts to stay at our house in Ferryhill. I could never understand what bass player Gaye Advert was saying, as she spoke so fast. All she can remember of that night was that I made her a banana sandwich!

Decca Records briefly took an interest in us but nothing came of it. Things started to happen when Virgin Records got in touch (after eventually listening to our rough demo) and offered us recording time in an eight-track studio called Virtual Earth in Swiss Cottage, London. We were placing our trust in Pete Brent, who was now involved in handling our 'business affairs', and he arranged for Virgin to pay our travel and accommodation costs. Up to this point, we'd organised everything ourselves and weren't making any money (in fact, it was costing *us* money) and any of the small support fees we received went towards making up the shortfall, so this new development was welcomed. We still had day jobs, except Gary Smallman who'd just left school, and we saw it more as an adventure than a moneymaking concern.

We set off for London in two cars. Robert transported our equipment in the back of his estate car with one passenger and the rest of us travelled with Pete Brent. About twenty miles into our journey, just south of Newcastle, we picked up a friend of Pete's: an unassuming older man with spectacles and a tweed overcoat. He had nothing with him except a large plastic carrier bag. As the journey progressed, he revealed the contents of the bag, which was a huge slab of dope with weird letters and shapes stamped onto it. I'd never seen dope in my life. We dropped him off on

the outskirts of London then checked into the motel at Scratchwood Motorway Service Station where we would be staying for the next few nights.

We'd never been into a recording studio before and took the engineer's advice on how to set up the equipment. Nine songs were recorded in total, including new compositions 'Race Against Time', 'Never Never', 'V.I.P', 'Don't Dictate' and 'Free Money', a Patti Smith song which had become part of our live set. Each song was played live with minimal overdubs and once the music was recorded I had to sing on my own, over the top of the music, in a vocal booth, to ensure audio separation and clarity of sound. We'd never heard ourselves so clearly, and I cringed at the sound of my own voice when it was isolated over loudspeakers during the mixing process. The recording captured the fizz, energy, spirit and progress of the band in late June 1977. Virgin took possession of the recording and we awaited their response.

While we were in London recording the demos, we visited Sex, which had now changed its name to Seditionaries. The shop had been refurbished and was more clean-cut, with white walls and upside-down murals of London street scenes. Jordan was still there but now her blonde hair was teased into tall sharp spikes and her make-up consisted of angular black lines filled in with red. She was wearing the clothing that the shop now sold. The rubber and fetish items had almost disappeared and had been replaced by fabric bondage suits, screen-printed t-shirts, boots, trousers and hand-knitted mohair jumpers. There were subversive twists to each design; inside-out, straps between legs and each piece of clothing was unique. We splashed the hard-earned cash from our day jobs and I bought a black bondage suit, a cowboy cock t-shirt and a pair of Spiderman boots. Gary bought a blue parachute top, a pair of skinny red trousers with see-through plastic pockets and a mohair jumper. Peter already owned an 'Anarchy' shirt, a 'Destroy' t-shirt and a white short-sleeved shirt with red-and-pink print motifs. These items of clothing were objects of great beauty and cultural significance to us. We wore them onstage and further pledged our allegiance to punk and the Sex Pistols.

**Who's On Where**

• **PENETRATION**
in Manchester

• **500...**
in Sto...

PRAIRIE OYSTER: Islington, London...
O. BAND: Pier Pav...
JALN BAND:...Liskeard, Cornwall...
DAVE BERRY...under-Lyme...
AUTUMN...
KURS...

Friday 28th April
at the
NASHVILLE ROOMS

**PENETRATION**

**VORTEX**
...MONDAY
...TILL 2am
AT CRACKERS · 203 WARDOUR ST, LONDON W.1.

MONDAY 1st
Generat...
the Lurkers
Geoff Travis
Stee L pulse
arT...

TUESDAY 2nd...
GeneRation X
PenETRation
SCREWdriveR
...Curious & The Strangers
...king enquiries DAVE WOODS 01-734 8181.
Extn 315 Licensed Bars 2am

DJ: Geoff Travis
Admission £1
(EACH NIGHT

**100 CLUB** 100 OXFORD STREET, W
Monday March 6. 7.30       01-636 0933
**ADAM** and the          Tuesday March 14
**ANTS**                  **THE STUKA**
+ The Hotpoints           **SORE THROAT**
Monday March 7            Monday March 20
**WIRE**                  **PENETRATION**
+ The Bleach Boys         + **DICK ENV...**
Cheap Bars + Chinese Food!!  Tuesday March 21
                          **THE TROGG...**

WEST STREET
BRIGHTON
Top Rank
'Suite

Friday 24th – tickets at the door
**PENETRATION**
+ PIRANNAS + DJ PETER FOX
Friday 24th – THE DYAKS

Page 44—Melody Maker, July 30, 1977

**marquee**
90 Wardour St., W1      01-437 6603
Sat. 30th July, Sun. 31st July. Mon. 1st August,
**the Vibrators**
Penetration & D.J.

**PENETRATION**
+ THE MIX
Monday April 3rd: ROLL UPS
(Beside White Hart Pub)
Licensed bar 8 pm to midnight
Nearest tube: Hendon Central 266 767
Enquiries 01-959 7324
Monday March 27th

STRAIGHT MUSIC PRESENTS
**BUZZCOCKS**
**SIOUXSIE & THE BANSHEES**
**PENETRATION**
**ROUNDHOUSE**
CHALK FARM, N.W.1
**SUNDAY 11th DECEMBER at 5·30**
To advance Roundhouse Box office, Tel. 267 2564...
...Ave. W.1 Tel 439...

**MUSIC**
Page 58—MELODY MAKER, June 17, 1978

FULLERS TRADITIONAL ALES
**THE NASHVILLE ROOM**
Thursday March 2nd
**PENETRATION**
+ THE SCREENS
Friday March 3rd
**FLYING SAUCERS**
+ GINA & THE ROCKING REBELS
Saturday March 4th
**SUBWAY SECT**
+ THE LOUS
Sunday March 5th
**WRECKLESS ERIC**
Monday March 6th
**DAVID LEWIS** + THE YOUNGSTERS
Tuesday March 7th
**THE BOYFRIENDS**
+ THE INMATES
CORNER CROMWELL ROAD/NORTH END ROAD, W...
(Adjacent West Kensington Tube)   Tel. 01-603 6...

**marquee**
90 Wardour St., W1      01-437 6603
OPEN EVERY NIGHT FROM 7.00 p.m. to 11.00 p.m.
REDUCED ADMISSION FOR STUDENTS AND MEMBERS
Thurs. 15th June (Adm. 70p)       Mon. 19th June (Adm. 70p)
**THE AUTOMATICS**              **TYLA GANG**
Plus support & Ian Fleming      Plus support & Jerry Floyd
Fri. 16th June (Adm. £1)         Tues. 20th June (Adm. 75p)
**CHELSEA**                     **AFTER THE FIRE**
Plus support & Ian Fleming      Plus support & Joe Lung
Sat. 17th June (Adm. 75)         Wed. 21st June (Adm. 70p)
**WARREN HARRY**                **PENETRATION**
Plus support & Ian Fleming      Plus support & Jerry Floyd
Sun. 18th June (Adm. 75p)        Thurs. 22nd June (Adm. 70p)
**THE SOFT BOYS**               **THE AUTOMATICS**
Plus support & Mandy H          Plus The News & Ian Fleming
Hamburgers and other hot and cold snacks are available

**READING FESTIVAL**
AUGUST BANK HOLIDAY WEEKEND

**VORTEX**
AT CRACKERS · 203 WARDOUR...
MONDAY, AUGUST 1
**GENERATION**
**THE LURKERS**
**ART ATTACK**
STEEL PULSE
TUESDAY, AUGUST 2
**GENERATION X**
**PENETRATION**
**SKREWDRIVER**
...Y CURIOUS & THE STRANGERS
...TRAVIS — ADMISSION BOTH NIGHTS £1
...Booking: Dave Woods 01-734 8181.

...MES POLYTECHNIC
...wood St.,
Woolwich, SE18

**Eric's** LIVERPOOL
9 MATHEW STREET LPOOL 2    051-236 7881
Members Notice
DECEMBER DATES                        members    guests
Fri 16th  Howard Devoto's MAGAZINE    75p       £1-00
          with special guest John Cooper-Clark
Sat 17th  PENETRATION                 75p       £1-00
          with special guests THE FALL

**ROCK GARDEN**
Middlesbrough 241996
TONIGHT
Double Punk with
**SLAUGHTER AND THE DOGS**
Plus THE POINTS
Admission £1.
SATURDAY
**PINK FAIRIES**
Tickets £1.25 from usual agents.
Starting Thursday, January 20,
and every Thursday,
7-10.30 p.m.
TEENS DISCO
14/16s  50p

Saturday March 4th
**THE BUZZCOCKS**
+ PENETRATION + THE SLITS
Licensed Bar
Non Students Welcome
Doors op...

ROXY

THE ROXY CLUB

GENERATION X + PENETRATION *

april sat. 9

fri 15 the CORTINAS + the MODELS

mon 18 WAYNE COUNTY + the ADVERTS

fri 22 SLAUGHTER AND THE DOGS + the LURKERS

sat 23 SIOUXSIE AND THE BANSHEES +

fri 29 CHELSEA + the PREFECTS

sat 30 BUZZCOCKS + MENTAL

41-43, NEAL STREET, COVENT GARDEN, LONDON W.C.2.
836-8811

THESE ARE OUR ONLY NEW-WAVE GIGS & POSSIBLY THE LAST. THANK-YOU & GOODNIGHT.

On the way home from our studio session, we found out that Penetration and Harry Hack and the Big G had been banned from the Newcastle Festival due to take place the following day on 1 July. As the venue director Mr Stratham explained, 'I just don't want punk rock anywhere near my theatre'. The other fourteen bands on the line-up, which included Scratchband, Hot Snax and Junco Partners, played as planned, while we were banished with Harry Hack to play an afternoon show at the Polytechnic canteen. The *Evening Chronicle* wrote 'Ignore them and they might go away', while the more sympathetic *Sounds* reported that 'Penetration, wrecked by over-night trip back from London, looked ashen and angry, knew they were below par and hated it, [but they] still burnt holes in the stage'. Yes, we were tired and angry and channelled this energy into a blistering performance that became a full frontal attack on the audience. A David Bowie lookalike called Neale (Floyd) Cooley and his girlfriend Susan – herself a dead ringer for Debbie Harry – were in the crowd. Apparently they lived a couple of miles from Ferryhill, and had become friends with Gary Chaplin and started to turn up at some of our other gigs.

We were asked to support Elvis Costello and the Attractions and Generation X at Huddersfield Polytechnic on 29 July. Elvis had emerged from the London pub rock scene and was part of the Stiff Records roster. His 'Less than Zero' single and debut album *My Aim Is True* had just been released, garnering extensive press coverage. Costello's persona was akin to Buddy Holly with short, coiffed hair, oversized spectacles, shirt and tie and tightly fitted suit. The term 'new wave' was being applied to bands who were riding the punk wave but wanted to distance themselves, as they were serious, respectable artists. Elvis fitted into this new genre perfectly.

Generation X insisted upon having their own dressing room at the Polytechnic, so Elvis Costello and his band allowed us to share theirs. The venue was large and drew a big crowd, it was a safe environment for the curious to check out punk rock. We went on first and played with our usual gusto. Some people at the front had read the tabloid press and began acting out,

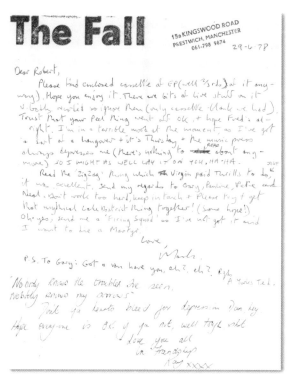

Mark E. Smith letter to Robert, June 1978.

pogoing and spitting which was starting to occur more frequently. If you told them to stop, they would do it more, so you had to try and dodge the gob. I was dragged into the audience by over-enthusiastic punters, and had to be pulled back out by Pete Brent. By the end of the set, my new black parachute top was covered in spit (my mother washed the disgusting article) and Elvis didn't fare much better. They gobbed throughout the whole set and at the end, he came back into the dressing room beyond furious. I remember him brandishing a bottle and threatening to go back out and 'smash their fucking heads in'. If this was a sign of approval by the audience, it was a funny way of showing it!

The following day, we were back in the van, driving to London for a two-night support stint with the Vibrators at the Marquee Club in Soho and a support with Generation X at the Vortex the following night. We then had a day off to drive home, then we were back over to Manchester to play at Rafters with The Fall supporting. They were there with their manager,

The Electric Circus, Manchester, 29 May 1977: Buzzcocks, Penetration, Warsaw and John Cooper Clarke. Photograph by Kevin Cummins.

Kay Carroll, an older lady who was forthright and intimidating. When Tony Wilson, the smartly dressed Granada TV presenter, called in to see us during the soundcheck, Carroll verbally attacked him, with 'fookin' Tony this and fookin' Tony that'. We didn't know much about Tony Wilson as we weren't from Manchester but there was obviously rivalry between the local bands and he was in a position of power with his music TV shows to favour one band over another. We'd already met The Fall, who were around the same age as us, on a previous visit to the Electric Circus where they were keen to play us a cassette on our van's tape-player. It was a recording they'd just made at a local studio which included the tracks 'Industrial Estate', 'Psycho Mafia' and 'Bingo-Master'. The guitar, drums and organ were offset with deadpan vocals, original lyrics and we were most impressed.

Fall frontman Mark E. Smith got on well with Robert and had sent him a copy of the cassette with a letter inviting him to go fell-walking on the Pennines to look for mushrooms! They never got round to it.

We went straight onto dates with Doctors of Madness, who'd invited us to support them on the Northern and Scottish dates of their early August tour. It was a strange turn of events that we had started off as fans of the band and now here we were sharing a stage with them. A year ago, I wouldn't have been able to predict this current situation, but in the present it felt perfectly logical, as if it was all supposed to be this way. As well as this tour, we had a number of our own dates to honour, and we had almost used up our allocated annual leave from our day jobs. My work colleagues had witnessed the band's energetic take-off over the past five months and had seen me turn up for work at nine

The Vortex, 2 August 1977. Photographs by Mick Mercer.

in the morning after having only returned from a gig at 5 a.m. with no sleep. I'd also stopped eating before gigs, as the nerves kicked in and I was sometimes sick afterwards due to the amount of effort I'd put my body through, singing and performing. We weren't used to this strenuous activity.

Still, it was gratifying that we were getting good reviews for our live shows, and mentions in the national and local press increased as the band's profile continued to rise. As a person, I felt I hadn't particularly changed, but I noticed that people were looking at me differently as we became more well known. In the press, they would usually print a photo of me, which is common with the lead singer – I had no control over that. It was strange to see myself as a separate entity that bore no resemblance to my everyday life: the person and the performer. I was still living with my parents, engaged to be married and the band was taking over our lives.

The next time we visited the Electric Circus in Manchester, we were to be filmed by Granada TV for the second series of the music programme *So It Goes*, presented by Tony Wilson. I'd seen the Sex Pistols on the show the previous year, and they'd given a stunning, confrontational performance. Tony realised that he was in a unique position to capture and document live shows of the upcoming bands in the burgeoning punk scene, never mind the fact he was putting his own reputation on the line. When we arrived in the afternoon there was a great deal of activity in the venue as the film crew were setting up, so we sat in the van. The Jam, who were also to be filmed that evening, arrived with brand-new expensive flight cases and smart mod suits, but they didn't speak to us or even acknowledge our existence. Although The Jam were the same age as us, they'd had much more playing experience, having worked the club circuit of their hometown of Woking, and they were tight and

Grandad Punk's t-shirt.

professional. We, on the other hand, had only been playing together for a short time, had never been filmed before and were quite nervous as we took to the stage wearing our Seditionaries togs. As we launched into 'Don't Dictate', giving it our all, some moron in the crowd started to flick beer from a bottle aimed right at my face. It was disconcerting and annoying and I tried to dodge the spray. He carried on with more intensity and now I was getting really angry. I tried to grab the bottle from him but couldn't quite reach, so the crowd piled on top of him and he was never seen again. It made for great and exciting footage and Tony reckoned that the Pistols and Penetration were his favourite film clips from the *So It Goes* series.

We visited Granada TV to view the edited footage. As we were entering the large glass-fronted reception, Ian Dury and the Blockheads were on their way out. As they got to the main door, they all turned around and shouted 'Penetration Rule OK!', which we thought was

a fantastic gesture. We were asked if we would like to visit the set of *Coronation Street*, a soap opera that I'd watched regularly since being a young child. Naturally, we jumped at the chance as we were all *Corrie* fans. We were shown around the Rovers Return by the fictional character Eddie Yates (Geoffrey Hughes), a binman in the long-running storyline. We didn't carry cameras in the days before mobile phones, so these are memories in the film footage of my mind.

Behind the scenes, we were encountering some bumps in the road. Robert had met up with friends in a Newcastle nightclub, got drunk, danced on the tables and fallen off, smashing his right hand on a broken glass which had damaged the tendons and required stitches. We'd started rehearsing at a community centre in nearby Bowburn and considered recruiting John Evans (with whom I'd played in the folk club) to stand in on bass. Robert would have none of this and insisted on playing with a painful and damaged hand. We failed to turn up for a meeting with Pete Brent and, what with this and the drama with Robert, he was angry and questioned our commitment. We were young, headstrong, immature and ambitious, he was busy with the shop and things were moving on at a rapid pace. It was time to part ways, and my father accompanied us to Pete's office above the shop and backed us up as we severed the connection.

The Boomtown Rats had cancelled a gig in Dundee and we were asked to be a last-minute replacement. We transported the gear in Robert's Ford and my father's Austin Maxi estate. My father was proudly wearing a blue t-shirt with 'Penetration' printed along the front which one of his work colleagues had had made for him. As we got out of the car, an old lady across the road pointed at him and shouted 'Grandad Punk!' which made his day. We were supposed to support The Jam at Maxims in Barrow-In-Furness but they cancelled so we headlined instead. We always went onstage and gave a full-on performance and this gig was no exception. Not only did we win over the audience but the promoter was highly impressed. He got on the phone the very next day to one of his contacts in the music industry, John Arnison at Quarry Productions in London, and raved about the band. It wasn't long until John contacted us and expressed a keen interest in becoming our manager, even travelling to Ferryhill to meet us in person to make his case. This serendipitous turn of events came at the perfect time: we'd been doing everything ourselves, but it was becoming harder to keep things going on our own. We were delighted with the outside interest and hoped that this would relieve the burden and open up more opportunities.

John, who was at least five years older than me, was baby faced and sly-eyed behind his spectacles. Quarry, the company he worked for, was based in Hammer House, Wardour Street, Soho, the old headquarters of Hammer Films, best known for their horror movies. Quarry managed Status Quo, Irish blues guitarist Rory Gallagher and Graham Bonnett, a singer and James Dean lookalike with ever-present aviator shades. John also managed Jenny Haan's Lions, the remnants of Seventies rock band Babe Ruth. Quarry was an organisation of many parts: they had a publishing company, a promotions company, a merchandise operation and they even hired out limousines. John and the head of Quarry publishing, David Oddie, drove to Ferryhill and tried to persuade us to sign a contract. We were offered a production deal which meant that they would take 25 per cent from every source of income: recordings, songs, live shows, merchandise and anything else you could think of. We sensed that this was bad but were focused solely on the band and the music and justified it to ourselves, joking that 'if we were going to get ripped off, we might as well get ripped off professionally'. We tried to ignore the contract and hoped it would go away but John had procured a booking agent from the magic circle of the close-knit music business, and multiple headline gigs were being lined up for November and December.

It was a crucial point for the band. We couldn't continue living two separate lives and the far-reaching decision was made to give up our day jobs (including Peter Lloyd, my fiancé, who wasn't even in the band). Life really was a gamble but we were young and optimistic enough to take a leap of faith. Luckily we were all still living with our parents and were

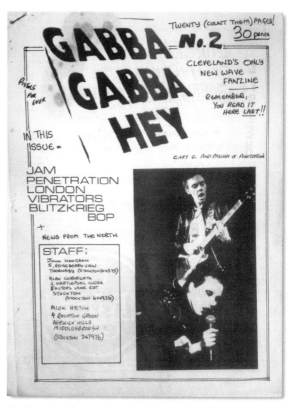

*Gabba Gabba Hey* fanzine, number 2, 1977. Courtesy of Kevin Mckimmie.

cushioned to some degree, but now we had to make a living from the band and, from our experience so far, this would be challenging. Quarry were going to put us on a wage of £30 per week (including Peter Lloyd) but we still hadn't signed the contract and had not even taken it to a lawyer to check out the legalities. It was a big step to take. My mother said, 'Do you think you're good enough?' which was a strange thing to say and immediately put doubts into my mind. She was perhaps worried about us giving up our jobs and entering the entertainment industry knowing from her young singing days that it was a dirty game. Or perhaps she just thought we weren't good enough. In typically rebellious style, I said, 'Well, if they want to sign us, we must be'. We were being drawn into the heart of Tin Pan Alley, home of the music business, sex shops, gangsters and drug dealers. We were minnows in shark-infested waters.

Virgin Records got back in touch and were now liaising with John Arnison. They offered us a one-off single deal for the song 'Don't Dictate'. We were disappointed as our hopes and expectations had been to get an album deal, although realistically we'd only been playing together for five months. We didn't particularly like the song and felt we'd moved on with new output, like 'Life's A Gamble' and 'Lovers of Outrage', both written after the recording of the demos. But we had no external overview and time was of the essence. It seemed imperative that we should release a record to keep up the momentum and catapult us to the next level. We dealt with Simon Draper at Virgin and I have no recollection of signing a recording or publishing contract.

We were booked into Pebble Beach Studios in Worthing on the south coast, a popular studio at the time: the Stranglers had laid down demos here and it was also the studio The Adverts had used when recording their second single 'Gary Gilmore's Eyes', which had just been released and was heading towards number 18 in the UK singles chart. Mike Howlett, bass player from the hippy band Gong (also on Virgin), was assigned production duties. He was one of Virgin's in-house producers so we didn't have much choice in the matter. We mischievously wondered if he would turn up with a tea cosy on his head – these Fair Isle woolly hats were part of Gong's 'look'. (Disappointingly, he didn't.)

Mike was personable and thorough, arranging the musical components to get the best out of the song. 'Money Talks', the B-side, was recorded during the same session but with less attention to detail. We gained more experience from the recording process and were very happy with the results. However, when we saw the artwork for the cover, we thought it was terrible. Blue background with darker blue felt pen scribbles, a torn black-and-white photo with the backs of what looked like soldiers, torn photos of ourselves on the reverse... it just seemed like a cliché of what someone thought punk should be. We'd left it up to Virgin and this was the result. We had no knowledge of how the music business worked and realised that many aspects were out of our hands, and that was something we'd have to get used to.

Our reputation locally was enhanced considerably when we were offered a prestigious support slot for the Stranglers at Newcastle City Hall. The Stranglers had been building up a following and securing their place in punk rock since 1976, when they supported the Ramones and Patti Smith at the Roundhouse. They had signed with United Artists later that year and had two Top 10 albums – *Rattus Norvegicus* and *No More Heroes* – in the UK Charts in 1977. For us, it was a landmark moment to see how far we'd come since forming the band and playing our first gig at the Roxy only six months before. It was surreal to be performing on the stage of the City Hall where I had sat in the audience so many times and witnessed all of the great bands and artists who had passed through this iconic venue. We were still only 19, and Gary Smallman was just 17. It was a lot to take on board, but we took it in our stride.

Our episode of *So It Goes* was due to be screened. Of the fifteen independent television stations, only three were prepared to air the show because it was, apparently, 'too extreme for [their] viewers, [showing] punk rockers pouring beer over a girl singer' and 'a fan hurling a bottle at a group then being beaten up by several punks around him'. There was definitely something threatening about punk to the general public, according to the national media at the time. Yes, it was high-spirited, with teen hormones raging, and it was an outlet for anger and frustration, but the constant putdowns in the media failed to address why this was happening in the first place.

On our trips to London we would call in at Virgin Records in Vernon Yard, and it was really exciting when copies of our new single 'Don't Dictate' arrived. To hear it on the radio for the first time on the *John Peel Show* was both nerve-wracking and thrilling. It sounded quieter in volume compared to other records but at least now our music was reaching more people. The reviews were good. *NME*'s Charles Shaar Murray wrote: 'Set to a wild mutation of Alice Cooper's 'I'm Eighteen' riff, singer Pauline Noname howls defiance in a suitably spiky/sensitive manner'. In *Melody Maker* Ian Birch described my vocals as 'positively clear and colourful'. We were optimistic and had high hopes, but

Backstage. Photograph by Ray Stevenson.

through his radio sessions in a bid to pressurise major labels into signing them. We hadn't been offered a John Peel session, even though we had released a single. I felt that we were disadvantaged being based in a north-east ex-mining town, but we were in no position to up sticks and move to London – nor did we want to. All the same, there was nothing going on around us. Newcastle was a small city with no local scene and there was only Phil Sutcliffe writing for *Sounds* who had any link to the London-based media. Manchester was a much larger city with media links through Tony Wilson, Paul Morley and the clutch of bands breaking through, headed by Buzzcocks. We were so far north – true north – that every time we played, it cost us for van hire, fuel and accommodation if we were too far from home, and we'd generally arrive tired having spent most of the day travelling. The London-based bands were on hand for press interviews, impromptu photo sessions, local prestigious gigs, networking and were part of a much larger musical landscape that could generate random opportunities. We always felt like outsiders who were up against it, although whenever we played in London, we were welcomed with open arms by the growing number of fans coming to see us.

Nevertheless, we outsiders were resourceful: we borrowed money from our parents and bought a second-hand brown Ford Transit van that had previously belonged to the Gas Board, and we installed a row of bus seats behind the driver and passenger seat. We boarded the space behind these to make room for our equipment and fitted a cassette-player and speakers. For some reason, I painted the front panel dashboard, the roof and interior doors in red gloss paint, perhaps to personalise it and make it feel more like home. There were at least thirty gigs booked all over the country during November and December, so we were going to be spending a lot of time in it.

One of the stand-out gigs was at the Vortex in Wardour Street, supporting Johnny Thunders and the Heartbreakers. Their junkie reputation and doomed glamour preceded them and the venue seemed darker than usual. Their friends, Sid Vicious, Nancy Spungen and members of The Only Ones hung out in the dingy

there was still no way the record would get played on mainstream radio with a band name like Penetration and a rabble-rousing title like 'Don't Dictate', plus Virgin had shown no long-term commitment to the band; after this single, there were no further plans. Still, the song appeared on writers' playlists in the national music papers and Virgin were quick to include it on the ten-inch *Guillotine* compilation, which featured other signings including The Motors, XTC, Roky Erickson and X Ray Spex's 'Oh Bondage Up Yours!'. They'd already had their money's worth.

Many of the newly formed punk bands were scrambling to secure major recording contracts. Buzzcocks had signed with United Artists, The Jam were with Polydor Records. Siouxsie and the Banshees and The Slits were being championed by John Peel

Hitting our stride. The Vortex, 23 November 1977. Photograph by Paul Slattery.

dressing room. I'm assuming that heavy drugs were in abundance though we weren't offered any – we were there for the music, not the drugtaking – but we somehow fitted in. Johnny Thunders tripped over and mocked Robert's bass guitar case, which had been constructed by Pete Dewhirst (a fellow North-Easterner from Middlesbrough who was living and working in London as a joiner). It was built in solid wood, was really heavy and looked like a coffin. Pete helped us out as a roadie whenever we played in London and eventually became part of our permanent crew. Jane Suck, a young, nihilistic punk writer for *Sounds* reviewed the gig and said 'the voice is orgasmic – Patti Smith with singing lessons.' As we were loading our van outside afterwards, we noticed Sid and Nancy standing nearby, and they asked if we would give

them a lift. Of course we would! It's not every day that you have punk's terrible twosome riding in your van. Robert was driving, the two Peters were in the front, then there was me, Sid, Gary Chaplin and Nancy, who sat on Gary Smallman's knee, crammed into the back seats. We set off and as we were driving around Marble Arch, Sid demanded that Robert open the driver's side window and he threw a bottle out which smashed all over the road. He gobbed on the roof of the van and we dropped them off somewhere. We left the spittle drip on the roof, where it crystallised over the next few months, and we marked it with a circle in black felt pen and the simple caption, 'Sid's Gob'.

We were spending a lot of time in London and usually stayed at the ABC guest house in Sussex Gardens. The owner got used to us. At breakfast it was always, 'one egg or two?' It was always late when we got back from gigs and we were living on Kentucky Fried Chicken as it was the only place open for food. One evening, we went to a nearby takeaway and bumped into Wayne County (now known as Jayne County), the American performer who was in London for gigs with Wayne County and the Electric Chairs. When we told Wayne where we were staying, he said, 'you should stay at the Madison, it's great. It's where we always stay and it's really cheap!' So on our next trip to London, we booked the Madison at the end of Sussex Gardens. What a flea-pit! It stank of air freshener and there were about ten beds crammed into one room, all with woollen blankets and old curtains for bedding. We all piled in there, Kev Anderson was with us on the trip, and in the morning, the room smelled rancid, mainly due to Pete Dewhirst's sweaty feet and the bones of last night's Kentucky Fried Chicken. We returned to the ABC.

Gary Smallman and I were cigarette smokers and I remember getting through countless packets of Rothmans King Size or Benson and Hedges between us, but none of us were drinkers. Gary Smallman would have a few beers after a gig, but Robert or Pete Dewhirst were driving and Peter and Gary were more interested in scoping out record shops. On our days off, I would look for clothes. My Spiderman boots had been stolen from a dressing room and the parachute top had been ripped, so I found replacements at Acme Attractions on the Kings Road, who were now selling Seditionaries clothes. Don Letts, the DJ at the Roxy, was working there.

In those days, you could still park the van outside Quarry on Wardour Street without any restrictions so I would look around Soho and Oxford Street. There were sellers who set up shop fronts on Wardour Street and with dodgy microphones they would tout their wares and throw in other items with the purchase. Gary Smallman had seen a cuckoo clock that he wanted to buy to take home for his mother. There was a cheap tool set and digital watch included in the bargain. He had paid a full week's wages for it but when he got it back to Quarry, it didn't work so he took the tool set and dismantled the clock. Unable to fix it himself, he tried

to take it back the next day, but the ad hoc shop had, inevitably, vanished. If there was anything glamorous about being in a band, I had yet to find it.

Peter's dad, a talkative cockney, found out that there was a flat to rent above the local pet shop in Ferryhill, and he saw this as an opportunity for Peter and I to move in together. It was assumed that we would be getting married as we were already engaged. I didn't give it much thought as my attention was on the music and progress of the band, but there were unforeseen events playing out both in the background and the foreground. As the realities of our involvement with Quarry began to dawn, Gary Chaplin started to distance himself from the band and would make regular trips to the Senate, a bar in Newcastle where he met a new set of friends. He would bring girls back to Ferryhill and they would sleep on my bedroom floor as his parents were strict and wouldn't approve. When we picked him up for gigs, he appeared in full make-up and what looked like his mother's clothes. His arrogant attitude had re-surfaced and he seemed disinterested in writing new songs – we didn't know what was going on but kept our focus on moving forward.

We still had plenty of gigs in the diary and played the Nashville, a pub rock venue in West Kensington which had opened its doors to punk the previous year. It was a cold Sunday night and the gig was reviewed in *NME* by Steve Taylor who gave us the worst write-up we'd had so far – a full page with the headline: 'PENETRATION SHOW PROVES DEAFENINGLY AWFUL'. This didn't deter a group of fans who'd turned up from Hounslow and decided that we were their band. Members of the 'Hounslow Mob' were to subsequently follow us around the country, attending as many of our gigs as possible. They were a nice bunch of lads, good-humoured and friendly. A young lad called Gary hitchhiked around the country and we would let him sleep in our van. We weren't aware of his personal circumstances but he always had a smile on his face. A confident cockney called Tom Bennett also attached himself to the band and became friendly with Robert. When we were back in the North, Robert's mother realised that there were people sleeping in

The Vortex, 2 August 1977. Photograph by Mick Mercer.

the van, and insisted that they came into the house, providing them with clean beds and hot food.

As well as playing smaller venues like the Nashville, we had the opportunity to play larger places like the Roundhouse in Chalk Farm, North London. Throughout its long history, this iconic venue has hosted bands like Pink Floyd, The Rolling Stones, The Doors, Jimi Hendrix, the Ramones and Patti Smith to name but a few. We were to play there on a bill with The Worst, Siouxsie and the Banshees and Buzzcocks. At the soundcheck, I tried to say hello to Siouxsie but she blanked me, and later, as she was doing her ballet warm-up exercises in the corridor outside the dressing room she studiedly ignored me. Backstage awkwardness aside, things were looking up: we'd been on tour for at least the past five weeks and, while we were tired, we were on good musical form and we

got an encore, which was unusual for a support band. Siouxsie and the Banshees went on after us. I don't know whether Siouxsie saw me as a rival, but I was no threat as they had many advantages.

Soon after our Roundhouse triumph, we headed across the country to play a gig at Eric's, a basement venue in Liverpool, who were hosting many of the emerging punk bands. We were supported by The Fall. On a previous visit, the hotel we were staying at had TV sets chained to the walls, something I'd never seen before. The following evening we were playing at Belle Vue in Manchester with the same line-up as the Roundhouse – Buzzcocks, Banshees and The Worst. The Elizabethan venue was a large hall, situated on the site of Belle Vue Zoological Gardens, a leisure complex that had grown from humble beginnings in 1836 as the first privately owned zoo, to become the

Late '77. Photograph by Ray Stevenson.

third largest in the UK. At its peak, it included an amusement park, an exhibition hall complex and a speedway stadium. Its closure had taken place only a few months before this punk gig. Although many of the animals had already been sold off, a few lions and tigers remained, pacing angrily back and forth in their small restrictive cages.

It had been a turbulent and eventful year, 1977. We'd formed a band, written our own songs and played numerous gigs up and down the country. We'd released an authentic punk single, garnered positive reviews from the music press, given up our day jobs and attracted professional management. We were gaining a dedicated following and as the year came to a close, Jon Savage summed up what we'd achieved in such a short time and against all the odds. In his full-page article for *Sounds*, bearing the heading 'THE FUTURE IS FEMALE', he wrote:

'Forced to travel to London for management, record company, gigs, press... a young 19/20 punk band with remarkable freshness, excitement, invention within a form debased so quickly, so deeply... a cliché in blaséd-out London but outside – people keep the faith'. Paul Morley, in a piece for *NME*, ended with the words 'Don't let anyone kid you. Penetration are one of the best bands in the country'.

# SILENT COMMUNITY

There's a lot of freedom
But not enough choice
Habits never change
And there's only one voice
Fifty odds under 25's
Are past the caring age
What will have to happen
Before this place can change?

Nothing to do and nothing to say
The silent community is here to stay
Opinions exhausted but healthy and needed
Wake up to the future
You can't overlook it.

Frightened to speak
Yeah, freedom of speech
Means nothing to most
And trouble if you preach it
Punished for speaking
And praised for the silence
Pent up emotions or modern day violence

Shout if you want to
Fight if you need to
Hesitations surging into view
Secret societies encouraged but untrue
Just say something
We all want to hear you.

# GUILLOTINE

**THE MOTORS** You Beat The Hell Outta Me. **PENETRATION** Don't Dictate.
**THE TABLE** Do The Standing Still. **AVANT GARDENER** Strange Gurl In Clothes.
**X T C** Traffic Light Rock. **ROKY ERICKSON** Bermuda.
**POET & THE ROOTS** All wi Doin Is Defendin. **X RAY SPEX** Oh Bondage Up Yours.

## TEN INCHES OF MUSIC FOR £2.99

The eight track, ten inch rock, punk, new wave, dread,
humour sampler with the blood red jacket.

# IS REAL SHARP

From Virgin Records.      The Good Taste People.

**ORS** You Beat The Hell Outta Me. **PENETRATION** Don't Di
**LE** Do The Standing Still. **AVANT GARDENER** Strange Gur
**ffic** Light Rock. **ROKY ERICKSON** Bermuda.
**THE ROOTS** All wi Doin Is Defendin. **X RAY SPEX** Oh Bonda

## NCHES OF MUSIC FOR £2

# ENJOY BEING A GIRL...

...s Debbie Harry

MUSICAL EXPRESS

*Poly Styrene, Gaye Advert, and Pauline say:*

## SO DO WE!

**Left column (NME):**

...US ARTISTS
...e (Virgin)

...bird, is it a plane, is
...ee, eepee, single or
...nch discomix? No,
...a inch 33⅓ rpm
...ack

.../compilation from
...Records.

...unpleasing gimmick,
....99 an intriguing
...pricey) proposition for
...rning punter, seeing
...e's the top sides of
...aimed singles here,
...cuts of more than
...nterest to the curious
...ctor. What it adds up
...cy cross-cut of new
...recycle their one-offs
...at and a chance for
...vertising the wares of
...re permanent signings.
...rly, two of the most
...cuts are by groups
...n't get full contracts
...company — The
...th "Do The Standing
...l Penetration with
...ictate."
...able's offering
...the accolade of *NME*

...The Week when it
...sed last year; it's
...ggable, an inventive
...outing into territory
...by Syd Barrett, Roxy
...d oh, I dunno . . .
...ation are younger,
...nstream punk,

though their "Don't Dictate"
makes nonsense of the popular
notion that all punk is frantic
buzzsaw three chord wonder
stuff; it's a haunting,
atmospheric single reminiscent
of early Jefferson Airplane if
anything, a comparison helped
by their well-voiced lady
singer.

Well-voiced in a different
and less melodic way is Poly
Styrene of X Ray Spex whose
music maybe doesn't yet match
up to her personality, stage
presence and lyrical wit. The
Spex get their
legendary/best/only "Oh
Bondage Up Yours" here.

Roky Erikson is a weighty
name to drop among
knowledgeable rock critics but
the ponderous "Bermuda"
doesn't suggest why; a leaden,
old fashioned heavy metal
yarn.

The cut from Poet And The
Roots' reggae twelve incher is
of far greater importance.
Black poet Lynton Johnson
intones his "All Wi Doin' Is
Defendin'" over a stark

*Neil Spencer*

**SOUNDS**

## VARIOUS ARTISTS
'Guillotine'
(Virgin VCL 5001) ***½

THIS IS a not very big review
for a not very big record.

Virgin have collated eight
tracks to present a trendy ten
inches of fun packed pleasure to
illustrate some of their highly
rated singles that you slower
moving merchants may have
missed out. This is what ya get
for your money: (£2.99 in fact),
The Motors' 'You Beat The Hell
Outta Me', direct power 'B' side;
Penetration's much lauded and
much loved in this office 'Don't
Dictate'; the equally acclaimed
classic 'Do The Standing Still' by
The Table; and Avant Gardener's
'Strange Gurl In Clothes' which
terminates side one.

XTC — 'the pride of
Swindon' — offer the only real
collector's item here with 1.40
minute's worth of 'Traffic Light
Rock', the strange world of Roky
Erickson is explored in
'Bermuda', contrasting with the
Jah poetry from 'All Wi Doin' Is
Defendin''. As a curtain closer
they could find no better track
than X-Ray Spex's 'Oh Bondage
Up Yours!', their healthy anthem
that explores an area wider than
that immediately apparent.

There's not a dud among 'em
and for anyone without a
majority of the singles represented
here, a useful and space saving
purchase to get the lot in one foul
swoop.

*DAVID BROWN*

**Record Mirror**

## Small but irresistible

VARIOUS ARTISTS:
'Guillotine' (Virgin VCL
5001).

THE QUESTION on just
about nobody's lips at
the moment is, are 10
inch records about to
make a comeback?

The answer is, possi-
bly, but not at this price
(£2.99).

'Guillotine' is a
worthwhile record, but
too expensive, when for
a quid extra you could
buy a full - price album
of original material
(this is all re - releases).

Still, for those that
have pockets deep
enough and tastes
diverse enough, 'Guillo-
tine' is no waste of
money. There isn't a
lead balloon among the
eight tracks.

Featured are people
with weird names like
Roky Erikson (late of
the Thirteenth Floor
Elevators), Avant Gar-
dener, Poet and The
Roots, and The Table
plus the slightly better
known Motors, XTC, X
Ray Spex and Pene-
tration.

The Motors' 'You Beat
the Hell Out Of Me' is
better than anything on
their debut album,
punch drunk and heavy,
very Status Quo.

Penetration, no longer
with Virgin, contribute
'Don't Dictate' which
has a too - catchy chorus
that's been driving me
spare all week. The
girl's got such a husky -
beautiful voice.

'Do The Standing Still'
by The Table is not the

musical pun you might
expect. Stilted but
interesting, insistent
chorus again.

Aren't these run-
downs **tiresome?** That's
the frustrating thing
about samplers — not
that they're fragmented
but that they're so
tedious to review.

Ah well — might as
well get it over with.

'Strange Gurl in
Clothes' is by Avant
Gardener who appar-
ently spent his child-
hood conversing with
sheep. Least memo-
rable track here.
'Traffic Light Rock' by
XTC appeared pre-
viously on a Record
Mirror free EP. It was
the best cut on that and
it's the best cut on this.

Roky Erikson whose
previous band (see
above) are apparently
"legendary" comes a
close second with the
sparse and tough
'Bermuda' while Poet
and The Roots contri-
bute a decent enough
reggae jig with lyrics
from rent - a Marley.

Finally X Ray Spex
modern classic - 'O
Bondage Up Yours'. Bit
MOR for me. No, really,
no seriously now, I love
it — Spex at their best
with crazy lyrics, lovely
Laura Logic on sax and
Poly letting rip with her
amplified sparrow - fart
voice. Absolutely round
the bend but irresistible.
Which could be said of
the album as a whole. It
could even be said of the
price. Can' you resist?

*TIM LOTT*

**...uillotine**

**Melody Maker**

VARIOUS ARTISTS: "Guillotine" (Virgin VCL 5001).
Features tracks by: the Motors; Penetration; the
Table; Avant Gardener; XTC; Roky Erickson; Poet and
the Roots; X Ray Spex.

**Bottom-left column (Melody Maker):**

...LEY assort-
...of odd out-
...singles from
...ot an album,
...n-inch, eight-
...mmick, which,
...or just 21-and-
...nutes, is a cut
...l rip-off. No

...a is okay — un-
...bscure or under-
...ems by all the in-
...new acts at the
...this just doesn't
...unless you reckon
...half out of eight
...score.

...ms first Pene-
Don't Dictate has
...rown on me since
...se a couple of
...go, more for its
...n its lyrics, though
...aren't noticeably
...er.

...Pauline is the focal
...casionally and very
...tely touted as the
...Patti Smith. She's not
...in that class of
...out she deals with
...infinitely more con-
...here than as the
...he turns into live.

It's the best track here
apart from "Oh Bondage Up
Yours!" the first song Poly
Styrene wrote for X-Ray Spex,
which is just as piercingly,
eccentrically amazing as it
ever was with that so-simple-
but-still-stunning sax riff and
colourful satire. It'll surely be
remembered as one of 77's
most essential singles, demon-
strating for posterity that
Roxy-punk did have its (admittedly tiny) Department of
Humour and Charm some-
where amid the power,
pace and passion.

Giving the Table's "Do
The Standing Still (Classics
Illustrated)" a measly half a
point might be unfair, but
it's not a complete success. A
quirky little animal with

bubble-bass and surredelic
wordage, it's closer to Syd's
Floyd than the present mainstream, especially for the way
in which the tune chooses to
descend. Space-age tackiness
worth salvaging.

As for the rest . . . "You
Beat The Hell Outta Me" is
an apposite nomen for the
Motors' contribution, the flip
of their most recent sunk-
without-trace single, "Be
What You Gotta Be." The
sheer sledgehammer weight of
this is unbearable — feeling
it pressing down on my pulp
potential head is not an experience I feel like repeating.
Besides, with those macho
vocals and pseudo-melodies,
harmonies, this attempt to
cloak HM in pop's fancy dress
... Forget it, and seduce the
singles you fancy. — C.B.

Sandpiper Club (Wednesday).

D146 1754 LONDON T 13

PENETRATION MARQUEE CLUB 90 WARDOUR ST
W1

PENETRATION RULE OKAY
            IAN THE BLOCKHEADS

W1 90 BLOCKHEADS

TS0 TG0S LNAZ

299858 P0 WD G

# CHAPTER FOUR

# PENETRATION RULE OK!

**When the first edition of *Sounds* appeared in the New Year with its predictions for 'The Faces Of 78' on the front page, Penetration were smack bang in the middle with what I thought was a pretty ugly photograph of me.** The other recommendations were The Pleasers, Rich Kids, The Slits, Magazine, Wire, Devo, Siouxsie and Steel Pulse. Despite the enthusiastic plaudits from *Sounds*, Virgin showed no sign of engaging with the band for further recordings and there were no other record companies in the picture. John proposed that Quarry would advance the money to record a follow-up single, 'Firing Squad', and lease the tapes, as it was important to keep the ball rolling. We'd already signed the management contract without having it looked at; we didn't know any music lawyers and we'd joined the Musicians' Union in the hope that they would point us in the right direction. They didn't. No recommendations were forthcoming and Quarry were putting us under pressure. They were now insisting we sign a publishing contract for the rights to our songs, otherwise the recording of the next single wouldn't go ahead. They had us over a barrel.

The date for my wedding to Peter had been set for 11 March, 1.30 p.m. at St Luke's Church, Ferryhill: it was almost like another date in the gig calendar, another pressure to add to the growing list. I pushed it to the back of my mind and under normal circumstances may have questioned my lack of enthusiasm and commitment to such a major life event. As it stood, I could see no way out of it and as usual, just went with the flow. There was too much happening with the band, too many things going on at the same time, no time to think. We were trying to get new songs together, Robert had come up with his first song, 'Movement', but Gary Chaplin was spending more time with his newfound friends in Newcastle, and to make matters worse, we'd received a call from Virgin Publishing to say that Pete Brent was instigating legal action, claiming that he had contributed to the writing of 'Don't Dictate'.

John Arnison and David Oddie from Quarry came to our gig at the Newcastle University canteen and were still pressurising us to sign the publishing contract. Pete Brent was in attendance in his role as DJ. I don't recall speaking to him as I was pretty disgusted with his actions regarding 'Don't Dictate' but he must have attempted to speak to the band as I describe him as 'dead greasy' in my diary.

For several weeks, we had been waiting for confirmation of a support tour with The Clash in Italy along with French all-female band, The Lou's. We were incredibly excited when we received the news that it was definitely on. Quarry would make all of the travel arrangements and John would accompany us. But for every piece of good news, bad news would inevitably follow. My diary entry for 20 January: 'We thought that Peter getting German Measles was the trouble of the day until Gary Chaplin rang to say he was leaving the group. J. Arnison says he must fulfil the contract before he leaves. Whatever happens, we must get to Rome!'

Gary didn't make it clear as to why he wanted to leave the band and only he knows what brought him to this decision, but we were pretty angry about it. When he told one of the bosses at Quarry that he was leaving, he was apparently informed that he 'would never work in this industry again'. Bands are fragile entities and nothing can be taken for granted – we were individuals operating within the confines of a shared experience, surrounded by external factors that were constantly in play.

Quarry had booked us into the Workhouse Studio on London's Old Kent Road to record 'Firing Squad' with Mike Howlett producing. Our sessions were to take place through the night from 10 p.m. till 6 a.m. as the recording rates were cheaper. On the day of the recording, we travelled to central London to do a photo session for *Vogue Italia*. I don't know if this was connected to our forthcoming trip to Italy but it seemed strange that four kids from Ferryhill were to appear in such a prestigious fashion magazine.

I somehow felt that we were imposters. We were still in denial about Gary's intentions to leave the band, and headed off later that evening to begin recording 'Firing Squad' at the Workhouse.

It was an ominous-looking building but the studio, owned by Manfred Mann, was becoming popular with the record companies. Ian Dury had apparently recorded his debut album, *New Boots and Panties!!*, at this location, taking advantage of these nocturnal sessions. We were used to late nights but recording through the night was a different ball game. Your body's biorhythms are all over the place and function differently than through the day. It was difficult to maintain a high level of concentration and focus but we managed to get through with sheer determination. Emerging from the dark studio into the daylight, there was no time for sleep and recovery. We had to organise our passports for the Italian tour and we were having difficulties with Gary Smallman's documents, as he was still only 17 and needed his mother's signature.

Back in the studio that evening, I tried to get the vocal done but got really tired singing through the night and gave it up as a bad job. By the third night, the vocals were completed and we mixed until 1 p.m. the next day when the track was finally finished. We had a gig that night at Middlesbrough Rock Garden but there were still problems with Gary's passport and he had to fill in forms and appear before a judge at Bow Street Magistrates' Court before we were able to make the long journey back to the north-east. The day after the gig in Middlesbrough, Gary, Peter and I got a train straight back to London to appear before the judge to get the passport. We were utterly exhausted.

The band drove down in the van that same day as we had a gig that night at the Nashville: a sold-out gig with queues around the block. We went down a storm and I wrote in my diary afterwards that the audience 'went mad and invaded the stage'. Everything was unpredictable and you just didn't know what would happen from one day to the next.

The Clash pulled out of the Italian tour at the last minute. We were still going, accompanied by The Lou's, and would apparently be the first punk band to

visit Italy. None of the band had been abroad before and had never flown; the only time I'd ever been airborne was on a pleasure flight in an old Shackleton with my father at one of the air shows when I was young – I loved it. The day after the Nashville gig, we drove straight to Gatwick Airport only to find that our flight to Rome was delayed by four hours due to bad weather. It was a small aeroplane with only about twenty seats and it was dark when it eventually took off. While we were glad to finally be in the air, it was a hair-raising experience. The black sky was lit up by flashes of lightning and the plane lunged, shook and rocked with the turbulence. As we approached the airport in Rome, the weather was so bad that the plane had to over-shoot the runway and land in Milan. We got there in one piece but had missed the first gig. We got to Rome the following day, and according to my diary, the city was 'generally poverty-stricken with graffiti (mainly communist) on every spare wall'.

We were booked to play the Piper Club, a discotheque famous in the 1960s for its rich clientele. Now it was, from my diary entry, 'like some surreal dream, people dressed like puppets and dancing to disco music'. Halfway through our set, a very large man was lifted onto the stage; he was apparently the mascot for the local football team. He resembled a Weeble.[1]

We travelled north by coach over the beautiful snow-covered Alps to a place called Reggio Emilia, where two people from Venice had travelled especially to see us. The venue was a flash disco with lighting under the floor. Italian disco was an emerging musical genre, evolving from underground dance, pop and electronic music with bands like Chrisma (Krisma) leading the way. There was a punk influence in their presentation, with cool and sexy dance routines, and at this point in time, the two genres existed in strange juxtaposition.

Ancona on the Adriatic Coast was our next port of call and, again, the venue was an upmarket disco. We did an afternoon show to about twenty people and I wrote in my diary, 'is Italy ready for punk rock?' In the evening I added, 'audience reaction negative. Lousy.' The hotel we stayed at was huge and right next to the

1. Weeble: A child's egg-shaped toy with the advertising catchphrase 'Weebles wobble but they don't fall down'.

Press cutting. Courtesy of Kev Anderson.

beach but we were the only people staying there, as it was winter and out of holiday season. This made it a bit eerie, like *The Shining*. Some of our band and The Lou's raided the kitchen and spat into jars of seafood. Gary Smallman was being friendly with The Lou's, and Gary Chaplin intimidated him with some snide comment which infuriated Gary S, who said, 'either he goes or I go'. Chappy's arrogant attitude was becoming intolerable to us all. Fate intervened when the promoter announced the following day that he had run out of money and we had to go home.

When we got back to London, I searched the shops and found a cream boucle suit, knee-length skirt with long-sleeved top and a cream beret for my wedding outfit. I didn't want a conventional bridal dress and had left all of the other arrangements to my mother and Lorna, as I was too busy to get involved and the date was fast approaching. We picked up the tapes of 'Firing Squad' from Quarry and returned home on the train, some of the band having already set off in the van in heavy snow. We found out that Gary C had been

gossiping about the band around the village, and this was the final straw. He was obviously planning his next move and, unbeknown to us, was in negotiations with Carol Wilson at Virgin Publishing to sign over his share of the songs. We still had a couple of gigs to do with him and now just wanted him to go. Gary's last gig was at the University of London, where Black Slate topped the bill and Patrick Fitzgerald supported. We dropped Gary off at his parents' house afterwards and that was it – he was no longer in the band. We would have to move on.

We contacted Neale Cooley, who had been following the band with his girlfriend Susan as a fan. We knew that Gary had been teaching him the songs, and although he'd never actually played in a band before, he certainly looked the part: black spiky hair, black jacket and tight black jeans accessorised with badges and chains. Robert went through all of the songs with him and he seemed to be picking it up quickly, he just needed to play with the full band. We rehearsed two or three times a week, leading up to a string of

Neale joins the band. Photograph by Paul Slattery.

dates booked for early March. Quarry had persuaded Virgin Records to get involved with the release of 'Firing Squad'. Neale, at this point was covering Gary Chaplin's guitar parts for our live set. Gary had been my songwriting partner but had been reluctant to engage in working on new ideas for quite some time. We didn't know how this aspect of the band would progress in the future and perhaps Gary hoped that it would all fall apart without him.

We visited Neale's parents to explain what was happening with the band, as he would be giving up his job at his father's roofing business. It was a high-risk situation for all of us; there were no guarantees. We had a 7" single due to be released, management, an agent constantly supplying gigs and we had just been offered the support slot on the Buzzcocks'

Entertaining Friends tour, which was due to start in early May. I suggested that Neale use his middle name Floyd as a stage name as I thought it sounded good. All of the foundations had been laid the previous year to get us to this point and he was joining a band that was already up and running. With no previous experience of any aspect of what this entailed, he would be diving in at the deep end. The Nashville in London was his first gig and it was poorly attended due to lack of publicity, which was probably for the best as we were all a bit nervous.

The wedding was due to take place in nine days time – we had another seven gigs to play before then and I still didn't have a wedding ring. More stress! I felt a cold coming on with a throbbing throat when we played Cleethorpes Wintergardens and I had to go straight to

Wedding, 11 March 1978.

bed with mugs of Lemsip after the soundcheck. On my 20th birthday, we played Norfolk College, King's Lynn and, after the final gig at Lancaster Polytechnic, we got home at four in the morning, the day before my wedding. I was physically exhausted, emotionally numb and felt that my life was out of control and there was nothing I could do about it.

Quarry had provided one of their limousines for the big day, a light blue metallic Bentley with a chauffeur. Gary Chaplin had been asked by Peter to be best man before he had left the band, which made things a little awkward. My diary entry for the day said, 'Got up 9.30. Took things easy. Church at 1.30. Service was nice. All aunties etc went back to mam's house. We stayed till about 10.30, went to the Eden Arms for the night.' Not exactly over the moon for what is supposed to be the

happiest day of your life! Phil Sutcliffe attended the wedding and later wrote in a full page article for *Sounds* that 'the vicar, a popular gent with one and all, turned from the formal litany of the service to some closing comments which ran something like: "Of course there are lots of people now who want to share in your future. Personally I wouldn't trust them as far as I could throw them."' All eyes turned to John.

The following day, we travelled back to London with John in Quarry's Bentley. We stayed in Sussex Gardens and went to see *ABBA – The Movie* and The Only Ones at the Marquee. This was essentially my honeymoon. I did an interview with Adrian Thrills, picked up some singles from Virgin then got the train home. Five days later, we were back out doing gigs again at Birkenhead Mr Digby's, where I was sick after the set and we

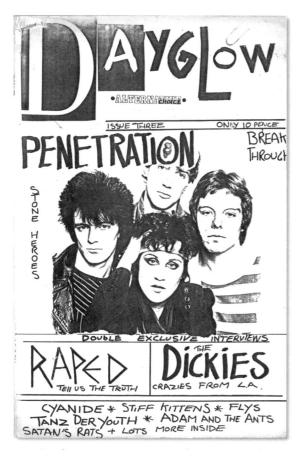

*Dayglow* fanzine, 1978. Courtesy of Andy Cunningham.

who I had my photo taken with; this was printed in *Sounds* the following week. There was always something happening. We had gigs in Plymouth, Brighton and Nottingham which was reviewed for *Sounds* by Stephen Gordon. 'The Hounslow contingent, a group of about seven totally committed followers, are justified in their devotion,' he wrote, 'because even now, Penetration cruise several streets ahead of the opposition, and with Floyd fully worked in, they'll be unstoppable'. We'd managed to replace a founder member, make the musical transition and get away with it.

I wasn't happy with the vocals on 'Firing Squad' and felt that I could do better, so we returned to the Workhouse Studio, re-did the vocals for both the A- and B-side 'Neverr', erased Gary Chaplin's guitar solo on 'Firing Squad', which Neale, who hadn't been in studio before, replaced with his own rendition. The tracks were remixed and the single was ready to go.

We had about a month off from gigs, time that was mainly spent writing new material. We still didn't have the keys to our new flat so I was living with my parents even though I was married. It was as if nothing had changed. When I eventually signed the publishing contract with Quarry, I was named as Pauline Lloyd, which came as a bit of a shock – I hadn't even contemplated the fact that my name and signature would change. With so much going on with the band, I wasn't thinking straight and couldn't keep track of everything. We were writing or rehearsing every day and Neale was coming up with good song ideas as he was fresh to it all. He contributed 'Stone Heroes' and 'Future Daze', where I re-wrote some of his lyrics to fit the melody, and Rob presented the musical idea for 'Vision'. I was under pressure to get all of the lyrics finished before we embarked on the Buzzcocks tour, as we wanted to move forward creatively with the band but it was difficult to concentrate as there were always people visiting. In my diary I noted that 'Kev stayed last night. Neale and Susan came through, but I had words to do so went into Peter's bedroom all afternoon.' Susan had been coming to all of the gigs since Neale had joined the band, so we were carrying an extra person in the van and an extra expense for hotels. Sometimes Kev

travelled straight home, getting back at five in the morning. At the time, I showed no outward signs of my inner turmoil. We were away most of the time so I didn't interact with my family and it would take something drastic for my true feelings to be revealed. I focused on the band instead. We played the Middlesbrough Rock Garden the following night: the venue was packed out and we received nothing short of a heroes' welcome.

We were back in London again on 20 March for a gig at the 100 Club. A band called Dick Envy were supporting, whose female singer Vermillion got into a cat fight with Jane Suck, who was reviewing for *Sounds*. Jane was an unpredictable character and, according to my diary, 'made a fool of herself'. The Adverts and Patti Palladin (an American singer from the duo Snatch) were there and also Steve Jones from the Sex Pistols would come for the ride. Since Gary had left the band, I became the first point of contact for the management and it was becoming a heavy responsibility.

We travelled back to London, went for a meal with Simon Draper and press officer Al Clark from Virgin: 'it seemed like a peace offering', I noted. The van broke down in Wardour Street but we got it fixed in time to play Leeds F Club and Liverpool University, which was the first date of the Buzzcocks tour. 'Firing Squad' was released the same day with a plain black sleeve and Penetration logo, and the reviews were good: 'Pauline's voice is smooth and taunting, the back-up liquid and urgent,' wrote Ian Birch for *Melody Maker*, while Alan Lewis at *Sounds* loved 'the streamlined, honed-down headlong rush of sound they make'. I always had high hopes when our records were released. John Peel played it and gave positive comments, although it wouldn't be played on any of the mainstream radio channels: the sound was too spiky and the subject matter too weird for the masses, but it was our sound and creatively authentic to us. Of course, it made no impression on the charts, which were dominated by the usual suspects: The Bee Gees, ABBA, Elton John, Rod Stewart, Barry Manilow, Eric Clapton and Chicago. We existed in an alternative reality and a breakthrough was highly unlikely. We were a punk band, and authentic punk was still a no-go with the general public, so we would have to carry on doing it the hard way – playing live and building up a following, which was, at times, exhausting and dispiriting. Virgin had taken out a few half-page ads in the music papers but had very little commitment to the band since Quarry had paid for the recordings. We had no idea what the deal was. We were still on £30 per week and Quarry were paying for all of the merchandise and collecting the profits.

The tour with Buzzcocks raised our profile as we were playing large venues to big crowds and were introducing ourselves to new people. We were now fairly tight and proficient due to the amount of regular gigs we were playing. Neale was integrated into the band and we had added three new songs to our repertoire. Some nights we kept Buzzcocks on their

'Firing Squad' record sleeve. Design by Rocking Russian.

toes and quite often got called back by the audience for an encore. We didn't get much chance to interact with the headline band as we were travelling separately and staying in different locations but we usually got to watch their show every night and it was great to see them going from strength to strength. They had progressed dramatically since their *Spiral Scratch* EP. Punk was beginning to soar in an upward trajectory and we felt that our own efforts were an integral part of that process.

We had three days off in the middle of the tour, so we collected the keys for the flat and painted it out. The day after we moved in, I started to feel unwell with an aching mouth and sore throat. I woke up in agony with 'a pain worse than toothache inside my chin'. I went to the dentist and discovered I had an abscess at the root of one of my teeth. I was prescribed penicillin and painkillers, and I felt even worse the next day. We were due to play our first headline sold-out show at Newcastle City Hall the following day, so I went to the doctors again at 8 a.m. on the day of the gig. Nothing could be done and there was no chance that the gig would be cancelled as we couldn't let the fans down and the show represented a landmark for the band.

100 Club, 20 March 1978. Photograph by Paul Slattery.

was clearly neglecting my health without even realising it. Adrian Thrills came to the flat after the City Hall gig to interview us for a full-page feature in the following week's *NME*. With the title 'Fluffy Slippers And Bondage Strides' he described me as having 'angular features and matchstick-thin arms'. Luckily, there was no drink or drugs involved.

The Buzzcocks tour continued to Bradford St George's Hall and Bracknell Sports Centre (where I'd seen the original Cockney Rebel split up) and Southampton Top Rank and then back home for some days off. I just wanted some rest but there was a constant stream of visitors at the flat – friends, family and band members. We played Middlesbrough Town Hall and some of us set off for Birmingham the next day in John's car. A sense of chaos was building, compounded by the news that the van had broken down and the rest of the band were stranded in Middlesbrough. We had to cancel the Birmingham date for that night. Everything was done on a shoestring budget and a wing and a prayer. The night before the Roundhouse, the rest of our entourage and equipment arrived in Robert's yellow Ford Escort Estate car and his mother's blue Simca van. I was beginning to question, in my own mind, what was the point of all this stress and hassle but we still had everything to play for and pressed on, full steam ahead.

On 28 May, I wrote in my diary: 'A beautiful sunny day today. Went to the Roundhouse for one (o'clock) and really that was far too early. Sat out in the sun all afternoon. Trouble started at soundcheck time. Alternative TV were billed as being on first but they started a fuss about going on second. We said we would go on first – it was stupid to go on and on arguing. We did really well. Went down great. ATV followed us and after three numbers left the stage with showers of abuse and tins!' ATV's petulance had backfired.

We were making the seven-hour journey to London at least once a week. We returned from the Roundhouse and were back in London two days later. Buzzcocks had gone to Ireland and we had two of our own gigs at the Rock Garden in London and High Wycombe Town Hall whilst calling in at Virgin and doing an interview with Chris Brazier for *Melody Maker*. I was feeling really

Virgin were also coming up with journalists in tow, so I suffered the pain and toughed it out. Halfway through the set, the abscess burst which at least gave some relief, but clearly I wasn't looking after myself. I possessed pent-up nervous energy, was a worrier and never thought about healthy eating. My diet consisted of Greggs[2] cheese and onion pasties, sweets and chocolate, Vesta chicken curry, Findus cod in butter sauce with Cadbury's Smash, motorway services junk food, Kentucky Fried Chicken, chips and cigarettes. I would sometimes be sick before and after gigs. I was going to bed at four in the morning after travelling back from shows and the singing and performing in themselves took a lot of energy. On days when my period started, I would feel pretty ill but just had to get on with it. I had lost weight and was looking good but

2. Greggs Tyneside bakery was founded in 1939.

The Nashville, 24 April 1978. Photograph by Paul Slattery.

tired and in one diary entry I wrote, 'I really hated being onstage tonight. I couldn't get enthusiastic about it and it was like a job'. The disillusionment and reality of my situation was making its first appearance. We had a day off in Edinburgh and went to see The Only Ones. 'Had a bit of trouble with the disc jockey and local band The Skids' (the diary doesn't say what the trouble was) and after the final date of the tour at Glasgow Apollo, the biggest place we'd played so far, we parted company with Buzzcocks.

Word had filtered through from Virgin, via Quarry, that they thought we needed another musician to augment our sound before they would consider offering us an album deal. There was no specification as to what type of musician, we thought perhaps a keyboard player, but we were all aware of our situation. There wasn't

exactly a massive pool of suitable musicians in our local area and Gary Smallman suggested Fred Purser, a guitarist from Newton Aycliffe. We needed to sort this out as soon as possible as things were moving at a hectic non-stop pace. Gary rang him and brought him to the flat the next day where we were all in attendance. He seemed like a nice chap, didn't exactly look the part with a mop of curly longish hair but we auditioned him a couple of days later. 'He's a good guitarist and could only make us better', I wrote in my diary. Fred's influences were more jazz-based and his playing was intricate and technical, adding another layer to the sound. It would keep Yes fan Gary happy to have another 'proper' musician in our ranks.

That weekend, we were booked to play a matinee show for under 18s and an evening show at Eric's in

Fred joins the band. Photograph by Paul Slattery.

Liverpool, so we took Fred with us, not to play but for him to see what we were about. The day after, we met in the flat to go through the song arrangements – we had a gig at the Marquee in three days' time and hoped to get Fred worked into the band with just two days' rehearsals! We'd only met him a week ago but there was no time to lose and Fred's entry into the band was as quick as that. Virgin were coming to the gig to see us to decide whether or not to sign Penetration for an album deal.

We set off on the long journey to London. Neale wasn't too happy that there was no room in the van for Susan now that we'd added an extra band member but there was nothing we could do about it. When we arrived at the venue, there was a telegram waiting for us from Ian Dury and the Blockheads which simply said 'Penetration Rule Okay'. Our spirits were lifted immediately and we were thrilled that they had gone out of their way to show such support and encouragement. To our amazement, the gig was sold out and they were turning people away, resulting in trouble outside of the venue when angry fans tried to break the doors down. This ultimately led to us being banned from the iconic venue. It was packed to the gills and Quarry and Virgin had turned out in full force. No one knew anything about Fred and he was in at the deep end, as we all were, since we'd never played with him before. Tensions were running high. It was a boiling hot night, 21 June, Midsummer Solstice. Everyone was gasping for air.

People were shocked when we went onstage with a new guitarist who didn't look like a punk. Bodies were sprawled onto the foot-high stage. It was like a sauna but we pushed on through our set. Halfway through, Gary was flagging on the drums and walked off into the dressing room behind the stage. This ramped up the tension into a whole other level. Robert went off and made Gary come back on and we managed to finish the set. Tempers were flaring in the dressing room immediately afterwards and Robert and Gary were fighting in the corner. Word was filtering back from the fans to say that they didn't like our new addition, as they perceived him to be a heavy metal guitarist. And into this mayhem walked Simon Draper, Virgin's A&R, to say

that they had decided to go ahead with the album. This gig was another turning point, a watershed moment for the band. It had been a long time coming and we had surmounted so many hurdles and obstacles to get here. It marked the end of a phase and the beginning of a new one. We were relieved that Virgin had finally committed to the band but we didn't have time to celebrate another milestone or even pause to take a breath.

We called at Virgin offices the following day to collect any new releases and drove home as we had a gig at Sheffield Limit Club the following night. The following morning, the van wouldn't start yet again so we were late in getting away. According to my diary, 'Neale was in a huff and got the train with Susan because he "didn't want to inconvenience you lot!"' The following night, when we played Manchester's Rafters, the van broke down completely. The AA came to the rescue but nothing could be done so the van was stranded in Sheffield and we had to hire one to get to Manchester. Even though we had management, the day-to-day running of the band was left up to us, mainly Robert who, along with Pete Dewhirst, was the only driver in the band. After long drives, Robert played bass onstage and we all took this for granted like the selfish bunch of immature individuals that we probably were. Susan invited someone from Selby to the gig and we ended up trawling around North Yorkshire trying to find where he lived, dropping him off like some 'taxi service'. We got home at 7.30 in the morning. Both Peters had to go back to Sheffield a few days later to return the hire van and pick up our own. Then we were back to London a few days later for a one-off gig at the Royal College of Art. This time, we travelled without Susan in the van, which gave us a little more space on that long and uncomfortable journey down south. Neale wasn't too happy, but, as I reflected in my diary, 'neither are the rest of us when it's crushed'.

We played a Rock Against Racism gig at Coventry Locarno, which was headlined by Black Slate who borrowed our backline. These events were becoming popular and promoted multi-culturalism in music and the arts against a backdrop of institutional racism. Inevitably, right-wing fascists turned up in the form

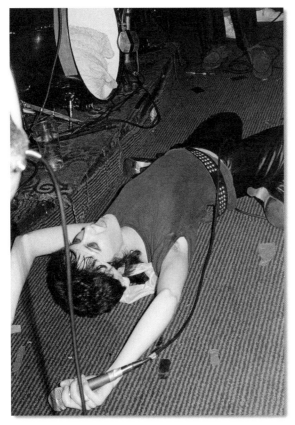

The Nashville, 7 July 1978. Photograph by Paul Slattery.

the live backing track recorded pretty quickly and spent time re-recording guitars in the usual way. It was Fred's first time in the studio with us and he took it in his stride. The vocals were recorded without too much stress and it was all mixed and completed by 11 p.m. Nice work. We didn't meet John Peel at the time but were just thrilled to be getting a session on his show. At the time, he had a captive audience for emerging new music and was very influential.

We played a small pub in Cheltenham the following night, but the strain was beginning to show. I wrote in my diary that evening: 'Feel really tired and am starting to lose enthusiasm and edge. We need a rest!' But rest wasn't on the cards: the next day we were back in London for a meeting with Virgin's Simon Draper to discuss the album, which producer we would use and which designer to commission for the album sleeve artwork. We went into a small video viewing room to watch Devo's latest offering and Sid Vicious was sitting there on the sofa looking a mess. There were injection trackmarks on his hands and arms and he was spitting at the TV screen repeatedly. He was demanding that the girls in the office go out to get him some padlocks and chains – I don't know what he wanted them for but the staff were terrified of him and duly obliged. Before long, we left and headed to the Nashville where we had a gig that evening. There was trouble at the gig: about 600 people were queueing around the block and the capacity was only 300. They'd admitted about 100 people when an underage girl who had been refused entry apparently attacked the manager with a bottle. They locked the doors, prompting the people outside to try and break them down. The police were called. We played to the 100 people who'd managed to get in but were banned from ever playing the Nashville again. We were beginning to get a reputation in London for trouble at our gigs.

During the month off, I had to sort out the band's accounts, as we were still responsible for presenting these to our own accountant. It was another heavy burden and I worried about our financial situation. Peter's grandad was a retired accountant and checked my work before it went to the band's accountant. On the

of skinheads who paid their money and only seemed interested in stirring up trouble. There were groups of them in attendance and I noted in my diary that there was a 'funny violent atmosphere'. We had started to notice that more were turning up at regular gigs; this would escalate over the next few months. Our view from the stage gave us a good vantage point from which to observe subtle changes in the audience.

The following day, we travelled to the BBC studio in Maida Vale, excited to be recording our very first John Peel session. We got to the studio at 2 p.m. and began recording at 3 p.m., four songs in total: 'Movement', 'Future Daze', 'Vision' and 'Stone Heroes'. Bob Sargeant was producing with two recording engineers at hand. Mike Howlett came along to offer moral support and Adrian Thrills turned up. Because we were playing live constantly, we were able to get

Russell Mills' initial design ideas for *Moving Targets*.

road, we had an envelope each day that recorded things like van hire, train fares, petrol, PDs (*per diems* – £2 per day each for food) and some wages. We may have picked up some of the fees in cash after a gig and this would keep us afloat to pay for hotels and fuel. Quarry picked up everything else, other gig fees, merchandise, etc. and paid money into the bank for the wage retainers of £30 per week – £210 to be distributed to the five band members and two road crew. It sometimes didn't arrive and I had to hassle them for the money. All I know is that we were constantly broke and lived hand to mouth, just about managing to pay the rent on the flat, food and incoming household bills. It didn't seem to matter how hard we worked – and we were working really hard – we just never seemed to get anywhere financially.

We wrote a couple of new songs for the album in our time off from touring, including 'Too Many Friends',

a jazz-tinged song with an unusual bassline. Fred and Robert wrote the music, and I wrote the lyrics and melody line. Another song that came out of this time was 'Reunion', a reflective song based on Neale's musical idea with my lyrics and melody. Neither of these songs could be classed as 'punk' in any shape or form; we were still expanding our musical horizons and didn't really fit with anything. Fred came up with an idea that sounded like 'My Sharona' by American yacht rock band The Knack. I didn't like it. I tried to write words for it, and even gave it the title 'Dark Hearts', but never completed the lyrics. We attempted the song once as an encore and I still didn't like it, it was just a direction that I didn't think we should be going in.

Virgin had been in touch to let us know that the album artwork was ready for inspection so we hired a car and drove down to their London office: these were

Painted shirt at the Roundhouse. Photograph by Ray Stevenson.

the days before fax or e-mail, when life was conducted in 3D reality. The artist/designer Russell Mills, known for his Brian Eno record sleeves, had created 25 separate illustrations that would make up the artwork for the first Penetration album. Each panel was beautifully hand-painted in bright colours and reflected the theme of the album's title *Moving Targets*. The title came from a conversation I'd had in a dressing room with a guy who was trying to wind me up and was calling the single 'Firing Squad' 'Moving Targets'. The phrase must have lodged itself into my subconscious as it popped into my mind: it seemed perfect for the album.

The sleeve was looking wonderful – we now had to make the music to match. We were booked into Matrix Studio at Little Russell Street in early August for eleven days to begin the recording of the album. Mike Howlett was producing again with Mick Glossop (known for his studio work with Van Morrison) co-producing and engineering with an assistant. We were in good, experienced hands and put our trust in the professionals. Eleven tracks were to be recorded in total: the best songs from our live set and three new songs: 'Too Many Friends', 'Reunion', and 'Nostalgia', a Pete Shelley song that was presented to us as a demo tape by Carol Wilson at Virgin for our consideration. We recorded the song before Buzzcocks, and were able to make our own unique interpretation of it. The backing tracks were played live as usual and Mike Howlett listened out for the best takes. By the end of the eleven days, all of the drum tracks were recorded and we'd started on guitar overdubs. The recording of the album was interrupted by gigs at Middlesbrough Rock Garden, a headline show at the Lyceum in London and Reading Festival.

When we got home from the studio at 5.30 in the morning for the Middlesbrough gig, Peter's dad had introduced a new cat into the flat; when we'd first moved in, we took in an abandoned stray which died soon after and he replaced it with another cat, so now we had a pair to look after even though we were away most of the time. Someone would have to go there each day to feed them. Things were being done without consultation, that weren't of my own choice, and this made my life feel even more complicated and out of control. The madness continued but there was no way I could get off this high-speed train.

The Rock Garden that night was crammed. Our management had booked the Lyceum Theatre in a bid to avoid the fiascos of the Marquee and Nashville with people being turned away but this presented us with the opposite extreme: the venue was too big. Apparently 1,400 turned up but Adrian Thrills described the venue as being '(half-empty)' and our performance 'lacklustre' in his review for *NME* the following week. He was entitled to his opinion but I felt disappointed that we had been so trusting and had allowed him to get too close to the band on a personal level. We were supported by Newcastle band Punishment of Luxury, The Fall and Ed Banger. Some factions of the audience deemed that it was acceptable to throw cans at the support bands and there was an air of violence creeping into the gigs. Sham 69 were attracting groups of skinheads and the National Front were starting to rear their ugly head at punk gigs. We were paid £400 but no mention of the merchandise takings – and we'd sold a lot of t-shirts. Meanwhile, Pete Brent was still on our trail regarding 'Don't Dictate'; Gary, Robert and I had to visit a solicitor in response to his grievances. We'd come a long way from being carefree kids, seeing how far we could go in this game. We were getting somewhere but the fun element had disappeared and been replaced, from my point of view, with seriousness, professionalism, trepidation and uncertainty. In the beginning, we had nothing to lose, but now we were caught up in the demands of the business on one side and the fans on the other as we manoeuvred our fragile vessel through deep, dark, dirty waters.

Reading Festival beckoned. One of the oldest UK music festivals, this three-day annual event was held over the August Bank Holiday weekend and traditionally hosted progressive rock, blues and hard rock bands. In 1978, however, the organisers decided to designate the Friday to punk rock and new wave, inviting The Jam to headline and John Peel to DJ. Other bands playing that Friday included Pirates, Sham 69, Radio Stars, New Hearts, Autotomatics, The

Losers, Ultravox and us. 'Backstage is like a garden party,' I wrote in my diary. 'Beer tents, record company marquees and Virgin's Penetration caravan! Wow!' But trouble was brewing in the audience.

The bands before us got canned by Sham fans and drunken punters who were becoming restless. It was still light when we took to the stage and faced the biggest crowd we'd ever played to. A film crew were recording the event – including some of the songs in our set – for the film *The Kids are United*. I was expecting to dodge flying missiles but the crowd were obviously saving them up for Sham 69 who were on after us. We played with full commitment and got through our repertoire without too much drama. 'Now the work's finished, time for the partying!'

It was dusk when Sham 69 stepped onto the stage with Steve Hillage (considered a hippy by the punks) on guitar. The atmosphere was explosive and the stage was crowded with skinheads. Lead singer Jimmy Pursey was overwhelmed at one point and broke down in tears as he tried to control the crowd and keep the violence at bay. 'To end the day's festivities, Robert smashed up the Virgin caravan'.

Some of the band stayed for the whole weekend. According to my diary, 'Fred fell out with John Arnison and things were a bit heavy between them'. I spent the weekend arguing with Quarry Management who were trying to persuade the band to go on a tour of France with Rory Gallagher who was part of the Quarry set-up. I thought it was a bad idea, a punk band with a blues guitarist. I felt that it would be a waste of time and energy but none of the band backed me up as they were obviously fans of Rory and wanted to do the tour. And so it was arranged, and the dates added to our already hectic calendar.

We were back in Matrix Studio again for three days to do more work on the album. Neale was doing guitar overdubs and Fred did the solo for 'Life's A Gamble' which had been chosen as the single as Virgin must have thought that it was the most accessible and commercial track to become a chart contender. I was having trouble with the vocals in Matrix trying to get them to match up to my own perfectionist standards so we booked into Richard Branson's residential recording studio, the Manor, for one day with the two producers. It was a top-class, expensive studio in the grounds of his private Oxfordshire estate with the peaceful and impressive old manor house at the centre. There was a go-kart track and swings within the well-kept gardens. Several friendly Irish Wolfhound dogs lived in the house and members of staff were looking after the place. I don't think Branson himself was there but we'd met him before at the offices in Vernon Yard – our punk attitude had deemed him to be an old hippy. The Manor was impressive and I managed to get most of the vocals done in that one day. We were served a hot meal in the evening and stayed overnight in this exclusive abode. I imagined it to be spooky at night but found it to be cosy, warm and welcoming. In complete contrast, we returned to Matrix for the next four days to finish the album and switched to D.J.M. Studio for the mixing. Adrian Thrills, Jon Savage and Jane Suck arrived separately to see how things were shaping up. Jane seemed a bit calmer this time but I felt anxious about their first impressions of the album as these people had a certain amount of sway within the music press at the time, and we were at their mercy.

The album was completed. We had all put our hearts and souls into it. Again it was a massive learning curve and pushed all of our abilities to the limit. Robert, Gary and I had been through so much since the band had formed eighteen months ago. Neale and Fred had both entered on different timelines and we had all been under pressure from many different angles. It was a relief to get the record finished and we were proud of the results. It would now enter the public arena to be enjoyed, judged, praised, criticised, take on a life of its own and become part of rock's rich tapestry. For every triumph, there was always another battle to be fought. Virgin wanted to press the album on luminous vinyl which hadn't been done before and was a marketing ploy. We thought it was an unnecessary gimmick and were concerned about how it would affect the sound quality. We were persuaded and reassured that there would be no problem.

'Life's A Gamble' was released a week before the album as the mechanisms of the record company switched into gear. The reviews were a mixed bag: *Record Mirror*'s Steve Gett wrote, 'Surpassing all of Penetration's past releases, this has a strong chance of charting.' Jon Savage wrote in *Sounds* of the 'soaring vocals and a gorgeous hook, for which you're kept waiting a little too long' and *Melody Maker*'s Ian Birch appraised the single as 'a quality ROCK song neatly structured and paced'. The single reached number four in the 'Other' chart but only managed to reach 63 in the Official Chart and dropped like a stone, receiving virtually no airplay.

The album was released while we were on tour in France with Rory Gallagher. Rory was a thoroughly decent man and insisted that we stay in the same hotels as him and his band, paid for by him. They were usually Holiday Inns, a luxury for us. We thought of Rory as an elder statesman: he was only 30 at the time, but we were 20. He made us feel welcome, invited us into his dressing room, shared his rider and Rob even got to play his iconic, scratched and beaten up Fender Stratocaster.

It was a thirteen-date tour and most of the venues were large sports auditoriums, like aircraft hangers or large circus tents. Our first gig was in Lille and the audience hated us. They must have all arrived with packed lunches which they were willing to forgo as they pelted us with egg sandwiches and tomatoes, such was their instinctive reaction to our band. Still, it was an improvement on showers of greasy sputum. Unless you were there at the time, it's easy to overlook the animosity that punk generated. The following night was in Rouen and I wrote in my diary, 'We play at another exhibition centre – massive – and go on with plenty of fight after last night. We won some over – I'm sure.' Some of the loyal Hounslow boys had travelled to France to follow us and they slept in our van, which unfortunately was broken into while we were all in the venue, and their money stolen.

Break-ins aside, the tour was a marvellous adventure and the weather was beautifully hot and sunny for October. Our album was released on Friday 13th, the day we travelled to play in Dijon. I wrote, 'We've heard that the reviews for it are really good.' 'The gig is a massive sports stadium. Some punks there. Are

Girl on a swing. The Manor recording studio. Photograph by Cindy Stern.

we winning?' John arrived from London, armed with copies of the music papers; we'd made our first front page in *Sounds*, which showed a Chalkie Davies photo of me holding large dandelions in front of my eyes. The article was written by Garry Bushell, who had interviewed us in Ferryhill before the current tour, with photos by Paul Slattery whom we'd known since the early days of the band. It had been quite a journey, from zero to a hundred in just under two years, and we'd worked really hard and overcome many obstacles to get to this point. Even more significant was the fact that we had managed to do this whilst still living in a tiny village totally disconnected from the networking of the London music business. We had been supported by our families but we were still pretty much on our own and achieved things by the skin of our teeth. Financially we had no stability or security but we would push on regardless to see how far we could go.

The album was highly anticipated by both the fans and the music press who had a lot of influence at the time. We'd successfully passed the first hurdle, getting decent album reviews, but the glow-in-the-dark vinyl gimmick was, as we'd predicted, a disaster. The manufacturing process had created some type of static electrical reaction and the disc crackled and was distorted, interfering with the music and making it virtually unlistenable. We were fuming. Neale took it upon himself, without telling anyone, to write an open letter to *Sounds* about our 'shitty luminous disc' urging people to send it back to Virgin. We weren't too pleased but what he said was true. The damage was done as the record was already on sale in the shops. We were congratulated on our success in our hometown with a brick through our bathroom window. There could have been several reasons for this anonymous outburst. We had drawn attention to the place, criticised its social

*Sounds* front cover, 14 October 1978.

traditions and the locals had all read about punk in the tabloid press. Alternatively it might have just been a jealous individual who thought that we were getting too big for our boots.

We still had ten dates to play on the Rory Gallagher tour. At several shows the audience couldn't muster up more than six claps between them, and some people in the crowd behaved like morons, throwing cans at the end. I still didn't understand why we were even on this tour other than the management keeping us working every waking hour, or maybe just testing us to see how much we would tolerate. The last two dates were in a circus tent in Paris. Virgin sent someone over to take us out for a meal (which we were probably paying for) and arranged a day of interviews on the final date of the tour. We had two days to get back to England before our own 29-date headline tour for the album was due

to start. We had problems getting back as the road crew were stopped at the Belgian border because the equipment carnets hadn't been stamped. Some of the band travelled by train and others with John and we all managed to miraculously meet just as the hovercraft was about to depart.

*Moving Targets* entered the Official Album Chart at number 15, with *Grease – The Original Soundtrack* in the number one position. Quite an achievement for a band formed and fired by punk ideals, with no musical experience at the beginning. We had joined the punk cause hoping to change the world, and through our actions, determination and integrity, we had certainly made a small dent in the established order, encouraging many new bands in our wake. All the same, we didn't even have time to savour the moment of our chart success, because our tour began the day after we returned from France, kicking off at Huddersfield Polytechnic. Travelling with us was *NME* journalist Ian Penman, who would be with us for the next three days. But first, we had to sort out clean clothes and outfits for the next eight days before we could return home for four days off. We had no wardrobe mistresses or entourage to look after our personal needs. We were on the road so much that I had started to cut my own hair by making numerous small plaits tied off with sellotape, and I'd snip the ends with a pair of scissors. This process served to crimp my hair giving it more volume but it was sometimes hard to get the sellotape out, damaging the ends. Our time with Ian Penman resulted in an *NME* front page the following week, featuring a Pennie Smith photo of me, sitting in the Roundhouse dressing room with some of the plaits still in my hair, the sellotape yet to be cut off.

Our second date was at Eric's in Liverpool where we had to do a matinee for under 18s and a show in the evening which Adrian Thrills attended. As ever, there was a lot of spitting. John's Ford Granada was stolen and when the police found it and he went to pick it up, it had been stolen again! There was always something going on. We were totally unprotected and just had to deal with whatever was thrown at us. The old brown van with Sid's gob on the roof had given up the ghost and Quarry had provided us with a black limousine, which was more in keeping with Rod Stewart than a punk band. It was embarrassing to have such a vehicle and we were crammed in there like the Bash Street Kids with either Robert or Pete Dewhirst driving.

Next up was the Roundhouse in London. John's car was still missing along with a new shirt I'd recently bought. It was a big deal for us to be headlining this venue and a large crowd had turned up for the occasion. The night was marred by a few skinheads looking for trouble but was generally a success. After the show, Virgin had booked a set meal for 42 people at an expensive restaurant in Knightsbridge (again, we were probably paying for this ourselves) and Steve Jones and Paul Cook from the Sex Pistols and a few of their cronies turned up. They proceeded to throw food all over the place, crawling under tables and generally causing chaos. Peter had an argument with John and the whole evening ended on a bad note. I was starting to get pretty sick of this rock'n'roll circus. It was three weeks since we'd been home with another week to go and we were all feeling tired, cooped up in a stifling environment and tempers were beginning to fray.

We travelled to Bath to do a show with Buzzcocks and Subway Sect (who argued about the billing so we went on first), then went straight to Newport to do another gig at 11.30 the same night. 'By the time we finish this tour, we will be walking skeletons,' I wrote. I was feeling exhausted and frequently suffered from bad colds because of all the travelling, not eating properly, sweaty gigs, cold cramped dressing rooms, different beds every night and the amount of energy required for a performance wasn't being replenished as there was no rest or recovery time. We were all pushing ourselves, but how long could we keep this up? When bands get to a certain level, you would expect that things would be made easier but there was no one looking after our wellbeing. It would appear that we were being flogged to death.

We played Bristol Polytechnic, 'the audience were sensible – not spitting morons', then on to the Russell Club in Manchester where we met up with Tony Wilson. He took us back to Granada Studios, which killed some

*NME* front cover, 11 November 1978.

time as we weren't on until 11.30 p.m. 'The club was packed out and we went down really well. Manchester has always been a good place for us,' I observed in my diary. We drove straight home, getting back at three in the morning, pleased to be back as we'd been away for four weeks. It was my mother's 50th birthday and I hadn't even had time to buy her a present.

We might have had four days off, but that didn't mean we could stay in bed all day. My mother helped me get the washing done, then we were supposed to do an interview for *Look North* in the morning but they didn't turn up till 3 p.m. and knew nothing about the band, asking dumb questions. Phil Sutcliffe arrived in the middle of it all for an interview for his *Out Now* fanzine and, as ever, there was a steady stream of people visiting the flat. There wasn't a minute's peace before we were back in the van to do another nine

*Moving Targets* album sleeve, October 1978. Design by Russell Mills.

shows over the next twelve days. We were doing five gigs in a row, a couple of days off before we travelled home then another four in a row. We still had another eleven to do before Christmas. There were now usually interviews after the soundchecks, arranged by Virgin to promote the album. It was all becoming a blur, like being in the eye of a storm where you just can't see what's going on.

The Uxbridge University gig on 10 November was wild and completely packed. My diary reports that there were 'some nutters in the audience. Chaos. People flooding the stage. Some mad skins there. Girls shouting for Fred! Fred!' Everything was totally unpredictable and chaotic and we were often put in some dangerous situations. Northampton Cricket Club was packed and someone threw a pint of beer in my face. 'i was mad all the way through. Hated the audience'. Some of the gigs were becoming more violent and unruly. Chelmsford Chancellor Hall: 'Audience were great. Did two encores'. We could never tell how things would go. After the Chelmsford gig, we convened to the hotel bar where Fred, Robert and Neale struck up a conversation with a respectable-looking couple. When the topic turned to music and punk rock, the man claimed to be a professional songwriter having written the song 'Torn Between Two Lovers', which was written by Peter Yarrow (Peter, Paul and Mary) and Phillip Jarrell (both Americans). 'He was winding everyone up and John had a fight with him'. The next morning, we found out that the couple had been thrown out of the hotel as the man had beaten up his wife in the hotel room.

We had another four days off which were supposed to be for writing songs, but Fred was down with the flu, so I dyed a couple of shirts and painted on a white one. Back on the road, and Aylesbury Friars was always a good gig for us. We'd played there on the Buzzcocks tour and it had a big stage, a nice dressing room and held about 1,200 people. It was virtually sold out and we had Gang of Four from Leeds supporting us. It was a great, appreciative crowd and we played two encores. The hotel was near Luton and John had to stay with us as he'd left his briefcase on the car roof and driven off.

When he returned to look for it, it was gone, with about £300 and his house keys inside.

We had a few days off where I did an interview with some 'stupid bloke from the *Daily Express*' and we tried to work on new songs. There was always some distraction. Devo were playing at the City Hall and we went along but I found myself surrounded by fans asking for autographs which was flattering but also disconcerting: I didn't think of myself as 'famous' and was uncomfortable with all the attention. After the show, we were invited out for a meal with Devo as they were on the same label, although everything was such a whirlwind and I don't remember anything about it!

Then it was back to more live shows. We played Wolverhampton Lafayette, a small, cold club and didn't go on until midnight. 'Audience were horrible. Drunken sods. We shortened the set, the atmosphere was so bad'. There were usually interviews to do when we arrived at the venues. Birmingham Mayfair was up next and Neale and I went to BRMB Radio before our soundcheck. Again, we were on late, around midnight; none of this is normal or healthy for a human being's biorhythms: most people are tucked up in bed at this sort of time, not singing and shouting and charging around a stage. We were becoming more and more removed from a regular lifestyle. After the show, there would be some wind-down time and we would get to bed at maybe two or three in the morning, only to get up early to drive to the next venue. We lived on motorway food and there'd be nothing to eat after the gig as everywhere was closed, except Kentucky Fried Chicken if we were lucky. No caterers on tour in those days. It was a pretty rough existence, and I was starting to struggle physically but we were young and thought we were invincible.

We had a number of enjoyable shows in Croydon and Norwich and that lifted our spirits, but more drama was about to unfold during the long drive to Malvern Winter Gardens. As we approached a set of traffic lights on the North Circular, the brakes failed on the limousine and we crashed into a metal barrier on the central reservation. No one was hurt and we were all a little shaken but the car resembled a bashed up litter bin as we piled out onto the roadside, leaving our debris

The Roundhouse, 29 November 1978. Photograph by Paul Slattery.

and empty pizza boxes behind us. We should never have been travelling in this cramped and dangerous set-up. Quarry promptly provided a replacement limo but the heater didn't work and we froze all the way to Malvern, arriving at 9 p.m. and going onstage half an hour later. The weather was terrible so we cancelled Derby and made the long journey home for a local gig at Redcar Coatham Bowl and another four days off. We never had time to settle at home. As soon as we got back to the flat, visitors would start arriving and there was no time to relax or recover before we were back on the road again. There was certainly never enough time to concentrate on writing new material.

On 14 December, we travelled to London again in preparation for our performance on a TV show in Munich. We got a plane from Heathrow and arrived at the TV studio where we had to mime along to the

single 'Life's A Gamble'. I felt really embarrassed and compensated for this by running about like a mad woman. Afterwards, Ariola, the German record company affiliated with Virgin, took us out for lobster cocktails, and we retired to the Holiday Inn bar which was circular and boasted floor-to-ceiling fish tanks with evil-looking sharks swimming about. We returned the next day for a show at Cambridge Corn Exchange and were joined for the next two days by Chris Westwood, who was writing a piece on us for *Record Mirror*.

The last two shows on the tour were at Thames Polytechnic, where a mobile recording studio was hired to record the show, and Newcastle City Hall. Both were promoted by John for Quarry Productions, as he knew they would sell out and be guaranteed money-spinners. We were paid £400 for the Thames Polytechnic show

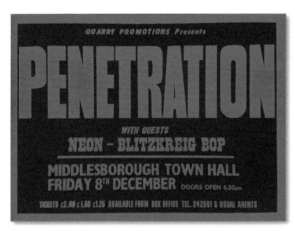

Middlesbrough Town Hall poster, 8 December 1978.
Courtesy of Jimmy Burns.

but I had no idea of any of the other fees we were being paid for the gigs we were playing. We were all still on £30 per week and were so busy that we didn't have time to question the financial side of things. John had roped in a couple of the Hounslow boys to run the merch stall and Tom went on to work for the company, becoming extremely rich in the years to come. The best piece of advice we were ever given was from one of the original partners in the merch company, who told Robert one drunken night that 'one thing you've always got to remember is that they're all fucking cunts'. We didn't know whether he meant Quarry or the whole of the music industry.

Our hometown gig at Newcastle City Hall would be the final date of the tour and also the year, and was completely sold out. Local bands Neon and Punishment of Luxury (whom John was looking to manage) were supporting. In the final bars of our second encore, we noticed that the City Hall bouncers were getting heavy-handed with some enthusiastic factions of the audience who'd ended up on stage. Chaos inevitably ensued. Some seats were broken – which we had to pay for – and we were banned from the venue. This was yet another example where our triumph was turned into a chastisement through no fault of our own. We'd hired a coach to transport our family and friends as this was a big occasion for us. We had gone from the beginning of the year, losing our

guitarist, adding two more, not knowing if we would ever release another record or whether the band would be able to continue, to releasing an acclaimed album that sat at number 15 in the charts, sell-out shows and a lot of hard work in between. This was a cause for celebration. We had a party afterwards at the Centre Hotel, I had too much to drink on an empty stomach and was sick in the coach on the way home.

Christmas was approaching and it was Robert's 21st birthday on Christmas Eve. We had a house full at the flat as usual, and then we went to Robert's house and had a party. When the music papers reached their year-end publication, our album *Moving Targets* was number six in *Sounds* between The Jam's *All Mod Cons* and Blondie's *Parallel Lines*, with *Give 'Em Enough Rope* by The Clash at number one; in *NME* we were at number 13 between *The Scream* by Siouxsie and the Banshees and *Shiny Beast* by Captain Beefheart. Bruce Springsteen's *Darkness on the Edge of Town* was at number one. John Peel played our radio session again and on the face of it, 1978 had been an extraordinary, extremely busy and successful year for the band. We had contributed so much of our energy to music, put our own personal needs to one side and made our small mark in the entertainment industry. Virgin were making plans for *Moving Targets* to be distributed in North America in the New Year and a five-week tour was being lined up for late May. It was all going so well, but did we have the personal energy reserves and enough of a solid foundation to consolidate our position, or was it all a castle built on sand, our hopes and dreams forever pursuing that proverbial carrot on a stick?

## MOVEMENT

Movement in the trees
And movement of the pendulum
Moving up the scale
We'll tango to the dance beat
Movement in the heart
And action on the battleground
Moving in the circles
Pushing through the crowd

Hey, baby we're moving

Caught up in a scheme
Mixed up in a moving dream
Music in the motion
Rhythm just repeats, repeats
Echoes multiply
And waves of sand are lost in space
Motion of the wheels
And pulling of the strings.

Moving to the music
Music and the avant garde
Moving out of reach
Well, can't get back you've gone too far
Justify the motion
Quicken up the dance beat
Movement in the heart
And movement in the feet

Hey, baby we're moving...

Opposite page: Bondage trousers and fluffy slippers.
Photographs by Chalkie Davies.

# ITS THE 1978 ZIGZAG POLL

## FEMALE SINGER
1. DEBBIE HARRY
2. PATTI SMITH
3. SIOUXSIE
4. PAULINE MURRAY
5. POLY STYRENE
6. NICO
7. ARI UPP
8. JONI MITCHELL
9. FAY FIFE
10. KATE BUSH

## SEXIEST PERSON IN ROCK 'N' ROLL
1. DEBBIE HARRY
2. SIOUXSIE
3. GAYE ADVERT
4. PATTI SMITH
5. PAULINE MURRAY
6. CHERRY VANILLA
7. TINA WEYMOUTH
8. ARI UPP
9. JOAN JETT
10. PAUL SIMONON
10. DAVID BOWIE

## UNKNOWN/ UNSIGNED BAND
1. SIOUXSIE & THE BANSH
2. THE SLITS
3. THE FALL
4. DOLL BY DOLL
5. POP GROUP
6. SUBWAY SECT
7. STIFF LITTLE FINGERS
8. THE ANTS
9. REZILLOS
10. PENETRATION

## HOT TIP FOR THE TOP
1. SIOUXSIE AND THE BANSHEES
2. PENETRATION
3. ONLY ONES
4. GRUPPO SPORTIVO
5. LURKERS
6. FLAMIN' GROOVIES
7. ALTERNATIVE TV
8. THE SLITS
9. THE BOYS
10. REZILLOS
11. BUZZCOCKS
12. STIFF LITTLE FINGERS
13. MAGAZINE
13. DIRE STRAITS
15. BLONDIE
15. STEEL PULSE
17. DEVO
18. DOLL BY DOLL
19. GEORGE THOROGOOD
20. JOHN LYDON'S NEW BA

## STEPPIN' OUT Sound

THE PERILS of Pauline strike again as Penetration make London's Nashville
Kensington (friday) on a tour tail-ender.

ORS
LE D
ffic L
THE F
NO

MUSICAL EXPRESS
new

# T-ZERS

## TRA-LA-LA

**L**ISTEN, SUMMER may or may not be still here — depending on whether you believe your calendar or your barometer — but sleepy London town still ain't no place for a street-fighting girl. At least, Kensington's rock and roll palace the Nashville certainly isn't — a conclusion arrived at by its manager **Dave Young** after a youthful person of the female persuasion clobbered him with a bottle after being refused admission to a **Penetration** gig there last Friday on grounds of being under-age.

Some 600 punters had showed up to clock the Newcastle punkos, and 100 of them had actually gained admittance when Young stopped the bottle. Fortunately, he wasn't cut up too fierce, but decided to close the doors there and then anyway. At which point the bodily wastes collided with the ventilation and the remaining punters (a mere 500 or so) broke down the doors, a violent penetration which led Young to holler cop in order to safeguard his premises against further rape.

Order was eventually restored, and after some persuasion Penetration played to the lucky 100, though they've now been informed that they're "too big for the Nashville" and won't be seen there again. After a similar incident at the Marquee a fortnight or so back, their warm-up-for-the-Reading-Festival gig has been blown out, and they won't be seen playing there again either. Can this mean stardom, we here at T-Zers ask ourselves...

# Taking trad punk into a new league

## Penetration
### NASHVILLE

THE LARGE and very spikey-topped contingent that packed The Nashville on Friday night was proof enough that, to stalwarts of the New Wave, the gig was of great importance.

In fact, many irate-looking souls were turned away at the door, and I doubt it'll make them feel any happier to know they missed a great show.

Penetration, who formed nearly two years ago after seeing The Sex Pistols, still have their roots very firmly in trad punk, but with so much variation as to be in a completely different musical league.

No great believers in a uniform stage presence, visually, the band's front-line is a very mixed bag.

The recently acquired lead guitarist, Fred Purser, looks almost reserved alongside Neale Floyd, who plays rhythm, and obviously shares Keith Richard's keen interest in a rosy complexion and the joys of prime physical health.

Far right, we have man / beanpole bassist Robert Blamire, towering above the crowd and working solidly with the concise drumming of Gary Smallman.

And out front is the inimitable Pauline, scampering around the stage, fetchingly clad in leathers, studded belt and a lurid yellow headband.

Their songs, except for "Don't Dictate", are nearer observations than criticisms, and so don't feel the need to over-assert their ideas with brainless chord-bashing and rebel yelps. "Lovers Of Outrage", "Life's A Gamble", and "Race Against Time" were all perfectly balanced, rising, falling and doubling time to follow the changes in the lyrics.

Pauline carries the whole show with her shrill, commanding vocals (especially on Patti Smith's "Free Money"), and her not-too-self-indulgent theatrics.

They seem to have mastered an exact mixture of a very raw live sound and Purser's supersmooth guitar solos. Very rarely do they become predictable, or lose a feeling of acceleration throughout the set.

On this level, playing small venues, and to crowds of converts, Penetration can do no wrong. Countless punk bands that disintegrated over the last few months would still be on the circuit if they had half the imagination of this lot.

I noted fresh graffiti on the much-abused khazi wall, which, I'd venture, was the modest artwork of the band's bassist. It read "Penetration — The Future Is Robert".

Exactly what the future is will be stamped with a little more permanence by the arrival of their first album.

**Mark Ellen**

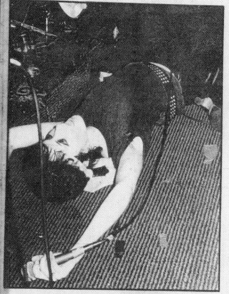

PENETRATION'S Pauline. Pic: PAUL SLATTERY

Page 8  SOUNDS  JULY 15, 1978

# JAWS

RECORD MIRROR

# Melody Maker

● Penetration have been banned from playing two main London pub and club venues after violence from disappointed fans unable to get into recent gigs by the band.

About 500 of the band's followers were left outside the Nashville on Friday last week after the house-full signs had gone up and the pub's manager was injured with a bottle when he tried to stop some under-age girls coming in. The doors were damaged and the police were called to disperse the crowd.

Penetration have now been told they are not a suitable group for the Nashville. They have had a similar reaction from the Marquee, where 400 fans damaged the doors a fortnight ago after being unable to get in to see the group.

# JUICY LUICY

While more realistic outrage has been caused in the metropolis as a result of the increasing popularity of beat combo **Penetration**. The aforementioned, whose audience I'm assured by a spokesman is of the punk revival kind, have now been banned by the "internationally famous Marquee and the Nashville after incidents of an explosive nature. Why only last week hundreds of punks were locked out of the Nashville while the band played, provoking crowd scenes not witnessed since the Costello 9 were arrested last year! What will this new craze lead to, I wonder?

**VIOLENCE TWO:** **Penetration** *do* have trouble with their fans. First, the other week at the Marquee, so many fans came along that a whole crowd had to be locked out and a lot of shoving and pushing ensued, resulting in the Marquee doors being kicked in. Then, last Friday at the Nashville, there was the same kind of embarrassment of riches. This time, approximately five hundred fans where shut out. One of these fans was a clearly underage girl fan who decided to her revenge by bottling the Nashville manager which resulted in a *lot* of blood. Now, the band finds itself, thanks to some of its fans, in a position where it is unable to play those gigs. Which is a pity because they were planning to do a night at the Marquee as a warm-up for their date at this year's Reading Festival.

# CHAPTER FIVE
# SHOUT ABOVE THE NOISE

**We were snowed in at the flat as 1979 dawned, but at least we had a few weeks off to relax, have a few lie-ins and spend quality time with our families.**
Nana Murray was in St Margaret's Hospital and I had time to visit her. My mother was working as a shop assistant in the local painting and decorating store and would come to the flat during her lunch break. We were able to visit my parents' house and enjoy the treat of a traditional Sunday dinner. Neale and Susan got married at a registry office during this short break and the band attended the wedding reception. Some semblance of normality had returned, but it was to be temporary and short-lived: the band soon returned to the forefront of our minds as we were all aware that we needed to start writing new material. In the music business, you were only as good as your last record and it was a highly competitive and well-subscribed game – like snakes and ladders. You rolled the dice, climbed a few steps, but each roll was a gamble where you could easily slide down the snake and end up back where you started.

We had gained a good live following but our recordings had failed to produce hits and we had never appeared on *Top of the Pops* or *The Old Grey Whistle Test*. There were plenty of other bands trying to gain the public's fickle attention and I was a shy person who recoiled from self-promotion and blowing my own trumpet. I still held on to the punk ideals of hating the establishment, an attitude seemingly at odds with a successful career in music. We had started the band as a fun hobby, never once imagining that we would take things this far, and we hadn't been realistic about making a sustainable living. Before the band, I had managed to acquire my first secure job and would have had financial independence by now, but then again, I wouldn't have had this unique experience or any knowledge of my singing, performing or creative abilities. This was something that money couldn't buy.

Quarry had failed to send the band any wages over the Christmas period, and we had to borrow money from our parents to go to the pub. Nothing arrived until the third week of January, and attached were conditions to sign a production contract. 'Please browse through it and sign!' I thought we'd already signed our lives away but apparently there was more to be had. John Arnison was working for Quarry, not the band, and we had no one to turn to for advice or guidance. John ended up coming to Ferryhill with the contract, piling on the pressure, and we just signed it. As I reflected in my diary at the time, 'we didn't have much choice but to sign the bloody thing and get it over and done with'. Not a good feeling.

Robert was heading to London to play bass for punk poet Patrik Fitzgerald's first LP *Grubby Stories*, which also featured Buzzcocks' John Maher on drums. I also made the trip to London, but this time it was for an initial meeting regarding an acting audition for an American version of the 1970s series *Rock Follies*, which told the fictional story of the trials and tribulations of an all-female rock band called Little Ladies, with music by Andy McKay from Roxy Music. I'd watched this series before I was even in a band. Could I act? Well, as I reflected in my journal. 'I'd never sung before and I'd managed that!' They must have been suitably impressed with my interview as I was asked back for a 'readout' and would be expected to adopt a Cockney accent.

We returned home and booked into a small, primitive studio called Bullseye in Spennymoor, just down the road from where we lived, where we were expected to record demos of new songs for Virgin. We managed to get musical backing tracks recorded but I still needed to write the lyrics and tunes. As usual, the flat hosted a steady stream of visitors and I had no private, quiet time to get my thoughts and lyrics together. Young fans would arrive at our door unannounced and we would let them in but would be too polite to ask them to leave. I would usually have to wait until everyone had gone and Peter had gone to bed and wrote most of my lyrics through the night.

Then came the news: 'Sid Vicious is dead'. I felt sick to the stomach and recalled the lift we'd given to Sid

Opposite page: Onstage at The Rainbow, 9 April 1979. Photograph by Paul Slattery.

99

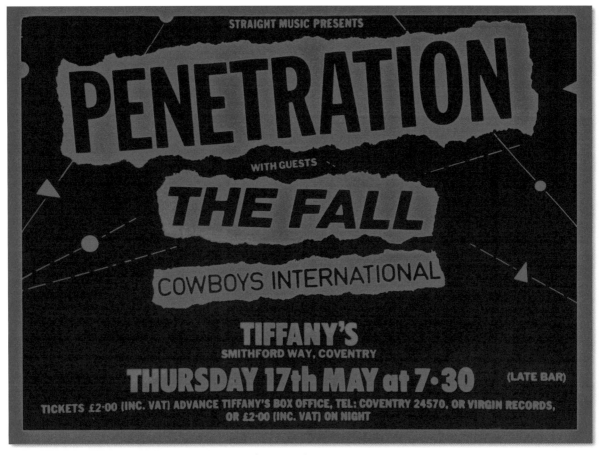

Tiffany's Coventry poster, 17 May 1979. Courtesy of Kevin Mckimmie.

and Nancy in our van. Now they were both dead, both of them around the same age as myself. The Sex Pistols had split up just over a year ago and Sid had been on a downward spiral of drug abuse ever since. He'd been accused of murdering Nancy and the tabloid press had dined out on the whole sordid affair. His death of a drug overdose came as no surprise but it was still a shock when it happened. Punk had turned into a self-destructive caricature; it was becoming embarrassing and a bit of a bad joke. We returned to Bullseye to work on the demos but I 'Felt really depressed about it all... Feel like packing it all up,' I wrote in my diary. I was reluctant to make the trip to London the following day to deliver the demos to Virgin and attend the acting audition but I didn't want to let anyone down.

Handing the recordings over to Simon Draper, I made some excuse about how rough and half-finished they were and made a hasty exit before making my way to United Artist Films. I was given part of the script to read, and was then invited into another room to read it aloud in front of the casting team. At the end of the text, I was expected to improvise in character for another ten minutes, leave the room, learn the script by heart and go back in. I was totally out of my depth, self-conscious and embarrassed. My acting skills were painfully inadequate and the character, with the punk cliché name of 'Vomit', just wasn't for me. I never heard another word about the project, which was just as well as I was busy with the band and that acting game was a whole other world.

Come mid-February, Penetration were due to visit Ireland for the first time, with shows in Belfast, Dublin and Cork. This was during the Troubles in Northern Ireland, which I'd seen on the news sporadically throughout my life. I perceived it to be a warzone with civilians and soldiers fighting on the streets, and didn't really understand the political situation. Many bands had bypassed it on tour schedules and The Clash had pulled out of a gig in Belfast, causing disruption amongst disgruntled fans. We set off with a sense of trepidation for our first gig the following night on 14 February, Valentine's Day. The weather was bitingly cold and the sea rough as we boarded the ferry from Stranraer to Larne, then on to Belfast.

The streets were deserted, shop windows boarded up and we followed an army vehicle with young soldiers in the back with guns pointed in our direction. There was a gloomy atmosphere and a general look of dilapidation. We spotted posters for our gig, which said, 'Penetration, St Valentine's Massacre' which we thought was someone's idea of a sick joke. This only added to the tension. At the hotel that night, we finally had the opportunity to speak to John and express our concerns regarding Quarry; we told him that we wanted to leave the company. His reaction was guarded as he played his cards close to his chest.

On the day of the gig, more stress was added to the mix as the PA we'd hired from Dublin had broken down so we had to use a borrowed patch-up job. John must have spoken to David Oddie at Quarry about the conversation we'd had the previous evening and his response was to cancel the proposed American tour. (Virgin stepped in at a later date and reinstated the tour.) Our spirits were low and I kept feeling that I wanted to leave the group altogether. According to my diary at the time, 'I just feel like getting the ferry home and calling it a day. Never moved from the hotel room all day – just sat – thinking'. But once the gig rolled around, our spirits were lifted again: the 500 or so people who turned up were really enthusiastic, and the audience in Dublin were equally appreciative. This made it all worthwhile and reminded us of why we were doing this in the first place. Their warmth

made up for the hardship of having no heating or hot water in our hotel. I sometimes wonder whether the fledgling band U2 were in the audience that night, picking up a few performance tips on their road to international stardom.

Cork was a very late gig as we took to the stage at the ungodly hour of one in the morning and played to a fairly disinterested crowd that was mostly made up of after-hours drinkers. We headed back to Dublin to catch the ferry to Holyhead but, as it was an overnight crossing, we went to the cinema to fill in time. We watched *Capricorn One*, an American thriller where the astronauts on a mission to Mars are removed from the rocket before take-off. Unbeknown to the public, they have to fake their trip from a makeshift film studio in an aircraft hanger in a remote desert location. Things get dangerous as the conspiracy unfolds and a suspicious journalist attempts to reveal the cover-up. I enjoyed this low-budget movie as the two fictional narratives played out at the same time, blurring the line between truth and lies.

The day after we got back, Mike Howlett and Mick Glossop were driving up to Newcastle to work on the arrangement of our next single, 'Danger Signs', one of the new songs from the recent demo. I only had the title and we were booked into Wessex Studio in Highbury, London, in three days' time. The lyrics were percolating in my subconscious but had yet to reveal themselves in full, and I was taking the art of brinkmanship to an uncomfortable and stressful level. 'Have faith, oh ye of little faith…'

Before our trip to London, we had to record a live TV performance at Tyne Tees Television Studios in Newcastle for a show called *Alright Now*, presented by former Darts singer Den Hegarty. (This show was a forerunner to *The Tube*, a hip music programme produced by Tyne Tees and broadcast live by Channel 4 during the 1980s.) We'd already recorded it once but the studio engineers had messed it up so we had to go back and do it again. We performed 'Future Daze' and 'Lovers of Outrage' live. I was wearing a green painted shirt and this time round, they had amassed an audience of young aspiring actors known as 'The Coffee Bar Kids' whose job it was to jump around enthusiastically as if they were having the time of their lives.

We were back in the ABC guest house ('one egg or two') for the duration of the recording of 'Danger Signs'. On the first day, the backing track was completed and the whole time, I was in a state of anxiety. Finally, by around ten o'clock in the evening, I was inspired and wrote the full set of lyrics in one go. My words were always oblique and this song was no exception. The lyrics refer to a fictional female who based her life decisions on the advice of daily horoscopes – a bit like the Luke Rhinehart novel *The Dice Man*, where the main character acts on random instructions from the roll of a dice to see where his life will go. An interesting and dangerous concept.

**Danger Signs**

The voice of fate is calling her
Protecting her from fear
The special words control her thoughts
Locked firmly in her memory
She let the stranger change her life
She can't resist the danger signs

The guardian of her destiny
Delivers her from sin
Which course to take
Which ties to break
She knows she'll always win

The messages that tell the truth to her
There's nothing can go wrong between the lines
The danger signs are urging her
Go on, go on, go on, go on, go on...

The vocals and Fred's quirky guitar solo were completed the next day, then we were off to Red Bus Studios for the mixing. We met up with Russell Mills who'd once again been commissioned to design the sleeve. We had no visual ideas of our own and gave Russell full artistic freedom as he'd done a good job with *Moving Targets*. His style was unmistakable: the sleeve was classy and incorporated silver printing

ink into the design. The single was to be in 12″ and 7″ vinyl format with two songs from the live recording at Thames Polytechnic, so we trusted that the sound quality would be good.

We went to Virgin's offices and played it to Jumbo, the head of A&R for Virgin's Front Line reggae label and Simon Draper. Both agreed that there was something not quite right with the arrangement of the song. We were a bit deflated after all that hard work, but I actually agreed – there was something jarring about the flow of the song. We had another John Peel session booked in two days' time so we rented a rehearsal studio to go through the songs. We only had three new songs and usually you record four, but we weren't superhuman; we had been so busy that we hadn't had time to work on the new song ideas that were still really works in progress.

We took advantage of the cheap food in the BBC canteen and then set to work. The new arrangement of 'Danger Signs' was executed and was a definite improvement. We recorded 'Last Saving Grace' and a song entitled 'Coming Up For Air' whose title was later changed to 'She Is the Slave'. Mike Howlett arrived during the process and seemed a bit subdued regarding the changes to the arrangement of 'Danger Signs' and the fact that we were talking about possibly re-recording it. The creative process is organic and my interest was in the music, so we had to be happy with it ourselves before it was released to the general public. It was agreed at Virgin that the John Peel arrangement was much better than the original but we would have to re-record the single through the night, taking advantage of the cheaper rates because we had already spent/wasted our allocated budget. Nothing was ever straightforward.

The Town House recording studio on Goldhawk Road, Shepherds Bush, was owned by Richard Branson and was a top-class, state-of-the-art studio. We began recording 'Danger Signs' all over again at midnight until eight in the morning over a two day period; this was tiring and could have been all-out soul-destroying, but we wanted to get it right. Mike's approach to the mixing was to listen back on small

Afternoon before Rainbow Theatre gig, 8 May 1979. Photograph by Jack James.

speakers in mono. The guitars sounded weedy but would apparently lose their sharpness in the cut. We set off home with the final mix and everyone listened on their own hi-fis. The verdict was a resounding thumbs-down and Mike himself admitted that it needed remixing. Three mixes later and everyone was finally happy.

The stakes seemed to get higher and higher the further we progressed on our musical journey. I was feeling really exhausted most of the time but I was young and resilient. John Peel played the new session on his radio show on the eve of my 21st birthday and it sounded great. Virgin sent a big box of flowers on the day – pink carnations, coral red freesias and big chrysanthemums. Peter was off to Newcastle to

buy new records but I preferred to stay in the flat on my own all day, relishing the peace and quiet and catching up on things. My parents called in, then in the evening we went to the pub to celebrate with friends and band members. It was good to have time out to relax and socialise.

We had about three weeks off which was to be spent writing songs. During this time, the seed was planted to write my most personal song yet. I'd always sent postcards whenever I could to Nana Murray, as she was always interested in the activities of the band. She was now permanently confined to St Margaret's Hospital in Durham, next to the church hall where the band had first practised. Her health had deteriorated and she looked sad as we waved goodbye for the last time. I later wrote the song 'Judgement Day' that reflected on that final visit.

**Judgement Day**

You have no possessions
You have no illusions
No arrangements
And no future plans
A day of memories with absent friends
I hold on tightly to your hand.

A photograph's the only proof
But what's the use, they don't exist
I touch your head
Your eyes are dead
And still you hide the fear inside

Judgement day has come your way
I hold on tightly to your hand.

There's no breathing space inside this place
There's no escaping
I search your face
I see no trace
And still you hide the fear inside

Judgement Day has come your way
I hold on tightly to your hand.

Our time for writing songs and dealing with personal family loss was over and a 22-date tour of the UK was announced to promote 'Danger Signs', which was to be released at the start of the tour. The capacity of the venues we were playing had stepped up considerably and we were now booked to play the Rainbow Theatre in Finsbury Park; a huge and iconic London venue where most of my heroes from the 1970s had played. Support bands for the tour were Radio Stars and Cowboys International. We were still banned from both the City Hall and Mayfair in our hometown, and played two nights at Middlesbrough's Rock Garden instead. Everything was lined up for our highest profile tour to date.

We had a couple of new songs for the tour – 'Come Into the Open' and 'Too Many Friends' – and were in conversation with Virgin about what the next single would be and who would produce it. It was decided that 'Come Into the Open' would be a double A-side with 'Coming Up For Air' (aka 'She Is the Slave'). Steve Lillywhite, then a young, up-and-coming producer, arrived at the flat to exchange ideas; this visit was also for us to determine whether or not he would produce our next record.

Within the week, we were back in London at Phonogram Studios recording 'Come Into the Open' with Steve. His approach was very different to Mike Howlett's: he had the guitars blasting and didn't seem too concerned about any mistakes, 'Which could be a good thing or a bad thing. We'll wait and see', I observed in my diary. Phil Sutcliffe called in to the studio on the second day as he was writing a massive feature on the band for *Sounds*, which would coincide with the tour. On the third day, we did a photo session in Covent Garden then I returned to the studio on my own to do the vocals while everyone else went off to the pub. When it was all finished and mixed, we set off back home in the van, following Robert in his car, having had about three hours sleep. Just outside London, Rob's car broke down, and we selfishly left him there at the side of the road. It was a Bank Holiday, everything was closed and it took him another day before he eventually got home. The real hero of the band, he took on more of the practical burdens yet never complained.

The tour kicked off in Middlesbrough and in the morning we went to Listen Ear in Newcastle to do an in-store signing of autographs, which was wild and chaotic. There were three journalists reviewing the gig that night and we were back in at the deep end. Phil Sutcliffe wanted to interview each member of the band separately, writing everything down in his little notebook, and was around for the whole weekend, perhaps hoping to discover some new insights or hidden depths to the five individuals that made up the band Penetration. By now, I had very little to say in interviews and couldn't even rationalise what was going on myself at this point. We did a photo session around the environs

'Danger Signs' record sleeve. Design by Russell Mills.

of Ferryhill with Jill Furmanovsky for Phil's *Sounds* article, then an interview for his Bedrock radio show.

'Danger Signs' was *NME*'s single of the week, reviewed by Charles Shaar Murray who wrote that Penetration were 'sounding like Blue Öyster Cult back when they were good. Quietly unsettling in a thunderous sort of way. [This is] some kind of masterpiece.' Chris Westwood for *Record Mirror*'s opinion was that 'it slowly assembles itself into a logical, uplifting number which will reap dividends if granted a fair deal by the radio station powers that be'. Simon Frith, writing for *Melody Maker*, admitted that 'I don't know what this song is about but I find myself moved by it.' It sold 26,000 over the first weekend but only went into the chart at number 83, which was really disappointing. The following week it had sold another 10,000 copies and dropped to 94. We couldn't understand how it hadn't reached the Top 50. Only John Peel had played the record – no mainstream BBC shows had given it airplay and it was game over for 'Danger Signs' within the first week.

We put the lack of chart success behind us as we had a big tour ahead. We were well supported by the music press and Phil Sutcliffe's feature appeared in *Sounds*,

although his infatuation with our family backgrounds and our pit village location was starting to wear thin. I thought it made us look soft. The shows were well attended and sometimes wild, with certain factions of the audience stirring up a violent atmosphere. In Liverpool, our white hire-van was covered in black tar, which someone had poured from a bucket on the hotel roof where repairs were in progress. At Essex University, the audience got overexcited and managed to get up on the stage. They meant no harm but the bouncers got heavy-handed and I tried to intervene. Afterwards, the enraged bouncers were looking for me, growling that 'no woman talks to them like that'. I had to lock myself in the dressing room and we were ordered off the premises by the Student Union social secretary, who insisted that we had incited a riot. We were travelling with a hired PA and lighting rig and that was the extent of our stage production. Still on a wing and a prayer, still on £30 per week.

During the tour, we went back into Phonogram Studios with Steve Lillywhite to record the B-side 'On Reflection' for the next single. Virgin had arranged for Paul Morley to visit us at the studio to do an interview for *NME*. At first, he seemed to be trying to provoke us and we could do without the confrontation – we were dealing with enough pressure at the time. I was beginning to feel numb to it all and was trying to stay positive. Some of the band and road crew were feeling ill with colds and tonsillitis and some dates had to be rescheduled. Stan Tippins, legendary tour manager for Mott the Hoople, had been appointed by Quarry to make the tour run as smoothly as possible. We were playing to crowds of 800-900 per night. When we arrived at the Norbreck Castle in Blackpool, we thought we were playing the larger hall but we had actually been booked into the Norbreck Nite Spot, a tiny venue tagged onto the end of the hotel. We wanted to cancel the gig but the promoter went mad, threw us out of the venue, locked the door and impounded our equipment until we agreed to play. Four hundred people turned up and it was like a steam bath – almost as hot as the Marquee the previous year. After the gig, according to my diary, 'everyone went back to the bar, got pissed and made arseholes of

take a trip to lourdes
for a miracle cure
spend your last
ounce of hope
on a wooden madonna
kiss
the feet of the statue
count
the rosary beads
watching
the candle burn bright
disappear
in wax tears

*Deviation Street* fanzine. Courtesy of Kev Anderson.

themselves (especially Arnison)'. I felt utterly drained and 'couldn't be bothered to watch them all'. Every day was filled with drama and some sort of stress.

We had an interview with Steve Taylor from the *Melody Maker*, the same guy who had slagged us off at the Nashville with the headline 'PENETRATION SHOW PROVES DEAFENINGLY AWFUL', and I was in no mood for this encounter. I was sick of having to be nice to people and putting up with all of the crap, and I confronted him as soon as he walked in. He was trying to apologise and make excuses, dangling the carrot of a possible front page but I just didn't care anymore.

We had the Rainbow Theatre gig the next day and I just couldn't get excited about it. The morning of the gig, I felt really ill with period pains. We called in at Quarry then went to Mr Chow's, an expensive restaurant in Knightsbridge, with Steve Lewis, PR from Virgin, then on to the Rainbow. The venue was huge and cavernous and our tiny amps looked ridiculous on the massive stage, the onstage sound was really empty and only the downstairs was open. The venue was just too big; the support bands went down terribly and the overall atmosphere was cold. My nerves kicked in as we went onstage and my throat closed up, but we went down well towards the end and the audience seemed to enjoy it. I was relieved when it was all over. There were plenty of liggers in the dressing room after the show but I didn't know who these people were.

We met up with Steve Lillywhite the following day to discuss the album, then on to Guildford Civic Hall for the gig that night. We went down well with the audience; I was utterly exhausted but managed to get through the show. I wrote in my diary, 'I feel so tired. I just couldn't get my legs to move'. I told John afterwards that I couldn't carry on physically but it just didn't seem to matter to him. I asked him to cancel a few shows but it was like talking to a brick wall. The show must go on, despite the personal cost. We played Northampton Cricket Club which was hot and sweaty and the audience were good, but after the show, fans invaded the dressing room and it felt like I was fair game for anyone to take another piece of me. We were all feeling tired but I was reaching breaking point: after the show at Chelmsford Chancellor Hall, I just came off stage and cried. We had a row with John about how we'd been pushed too far and he had to agree that we would go home to rest after the gig in Norwich the following night; this meant pulling out of Cleethorpes Winter Gardens, Coventry Locarno and the Manchester Apollo show which was to be the last date of the tour.

Gary was in an increasingly strange mood: we were all feeling the pressure and had to deal with it in our own way. The promoter from Cleethorpes got back in touch and threatened to sue the band if we cancelled for the following night. Gary was adamant that he was going home after the Norwich gig (as agreed with John) and sure enough, after the gig, he got the 11.30 p.m. train back to the north-east. He had made his point and we were all sick of being messed about.

Outside the Rainbow Theatre, 9 May 1979. Photograph by Jack James.

Of course, the fans don't see any of the trials and tribulations involved in delivering a show. They buy a ticket, turn up for a night out, see the final outcome, the performance, then go home and do it all again when the next band comes to town. It's like a travelling circus moving from one city to the next and as a way of life, bears no resemblance to most people's everyday existence. Life may be made easier for a highly successful band but we were operating on a shoestring budget and in the middle of it all, it became difficult to rationalise why we were putting ourselves through this. At first it was fun and different but now things were serious and everyone involved wanted a piece of the action. Spending most days travelling with the same eight people in a

cramped van soon became tedious and claustrophobic as it would with anyone.

Gary didn't get home until 9.30 a.m., by which time John was on the phone trying to persuade him to do the gig in Cleethorpes that night. When he finally agreed, John had to drive to Ferryhill to pick him up, Terry Chimes (ex-Clash drummer), now playing with support band Cowboys International, played drums for our soundcheck as Gary and John didn't arrive until 8 p.m., just in time for the show. We went straight home after the gig. Back at the flat, family and friends were keen to see us, so there was no peace or recovery time to be had. I cried and told Peter that I didn't want to do this anymore but he said nothing. I realised I was on my own

*In the City* fanzine, 1979. Courtesy of Kevin Mckimmie.

with this and had zero emotional support; there was absolutely no one I could turn to. We had four days off in which to sort out our personal lives, wash our clothes and pack our bags, because next up was a five-week tour of America; an exciting prospect under normal circumstances but we were so exhausted from being on the road that the idea of it seemed daunting.

*Moving Targets* was being promoted Stateside by Virgin Records, and the tour was organised by Frontier Booking International (FBI), headed by another of the Copeland brothers, Ian. It was set up as a circuit to bring the British punk/new wave bands like The Police and Squeeze on Miles Copeland's Step Forward Records to the USA. As one band finished the circuit, another was being picked up at the airport to start the tour. The bands all used the same equipment, so all we had to take were our guitars, a snare and cymbals and our own

personal luggage. The entourage included the five band members, the two Peters, John and our tour manager Stan Tippins. On the day of the flight, we took all of our baggage to Heathrow Airport, but our visas still hadn't been processed. The flight was at 6 p.m., so we were cutting it fine. Just in the nick of time, John arrived at 5.30 p.m. with the visas and we boarded the plane for the seven-hour journey to John F. Kennedy Airport, New York. Now *this* was exciting!

We arrived at 1 a.m. New York time, five hours behind the UK, and were met at the airport by two impressive chauffeur-driven stretch limousines, supplied by Virgin. The New York skyline was an amazing sight at night as we drove to the Empire Hotel, 63rd on Broadway. My initial impressions of the city was that it was very run down, and I described it in my diary as 'dropping to pieces'. There were bulletproof doors on our hotel rooms, something I'd never encountered before. After checking in, we went straight around the corner to Hurrah's, the small club where we would be playing for the next three nights. After only a few hours' sleep, we were woken up at 7.30 a.m. with the sound of pneumatic drills and bulldozers as construction works were in progress just outside of the hotel, a pattern which repeated itself and intensified over the next three days. The weather was scorching hot and because our visas had arrived so late, we hadn't been able to allow ourselves a day or two to combat the jet lag. Our first show was that night.

We didn't go on until 12.30 a.m., which was akin to doing a gig at 5.30 a.m. as far as our body clocks were concerned. The PA system was primitive and there were, at the most, 200 people in the audience, which included a lot of posers who just stood there, unmoved, applauding politely at the end of each song. Patti Smith was playing down the road and I was thrilled to hear that she had apparently given Penetration a shout-out.

Ian Hunter from Mott the Hoople came to the venue the next night to see Stan, and he stayed for our set. I'd been a fairweather fan of Mott in the glory days of 1972-73 when Bowie resurrected their career with 'All the Young Dudes', and I'd enjoyed their subsequent hits 'All the Way from Memphis' and 'Honaloochie Boogie'.

I'd even seen them play live at the City Hall. But that seemed like a long time ago and things had changed. He was like the elder statesman of rock'n'roll at 40 years of age, and we were young contenders with an average age of 20. We listened to his sage advice about the music industry but afterwards, we were irreverent punks who couldn't help finding something amusing about the encounter. It became a running joke in the early part of the tour as Gary would periodically don John's glasses and say ''Allo, 'unter 'ere' and we would all fall about laughing. Virgin flew in *Record Mirror*'s Chris Westwood for our third night at Hurrah's and the following date at Philadelphia Hot Club. His feature gave us our first front page for the paper.

From Philadelphia onwards, we were expected to play two shows a night, but by the following morning both Peter and I had developed sore, scratchy throats and my voice was cutting out. Peter couldn't eat, Fred had a bad chest and Gary had lumps on his forehead. It was possibly due to jet lag, tiredness or a virus but we were worried enough to go to a nearby hospital. I was the only one who was examined as it was so busy, and I remember sitting in a room with a drug addict who was moaning and being sick all over the place – I wished I hadn't gone there. The doctor just said it was tiredness, so off we went to the next gig, which was at the 4th Street Saloon, Bethlehem. There were about 20 people there for the first show at 10.15 p.m., but it filled up slightly for the second show at 1.30 a.m. My throat throbbed the whole time and I was starting to feel bad-tempered – I knew I shouldn't have been doing this.

It was a long drive to the Heartbreak Hotel in Providence, Rhode Island, not least because there was a petrol shortage – and it was Memorial Day – so we had to make several detours to fill up our tank. Once we'd finally arrived at the venue, Peter was feeling decidedly ill and had to lie down after he'd helped to set up our gear. I croaked my way through the soundcheck and still John wouldn't cancel the gig, despite my pleas. We went on at 12.30 a.m. and my voice was cutting out, making me feel and look like a fool. I wrote in my diary, 'I've had enough. I'm not going back onstage until I'm better'. To cap it all, at the hotel after the gig, Gary played

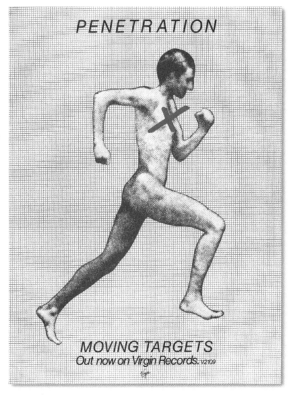

Poster for *Moving Targets*. Photography by Brian Cooke.

a trick on John and told him that Peter and I had left for the airport. He recorded the whole conversation on his ghetto blaster as John made angry and disparaging comments about the pair of us. Gary then brought it to our room and re-played the recording to us. My sense of humour was non-existent at this point and the joke turned sour, causing more bad feeling in what was already a potentially explosive environment. 'They can get a new singer. I'm not a machine,' I ranted in my diary after the episode. I woke up in a terrible mood and didn't speak to anybody all day – mainly because I was angry but also because I had now lost my voice completely. I confided in my diary that 'I may leave the group after this tour if I don't start to feel more enthusiastic. I don't feel as if we are all united – pulling together. Everyone seems to go off in different directions. I should never have gone onstage last night and made a fool of myself. I blame Arnison for that.' The diary was the only place

Penetration in New York, May 1979. Photograph by Ebet Roberts.

where I could vent my true feelings. It had become my best friend and confidante as the neatly written pages bore witness to what was happening on a daily basis. We cancelled that night's gig in Newhaven and set off for Boston. I was living on McDonald's Hot Fudge Sundaes, the occasional hot meal if the hotel had a restaurant and I was clearly running out of steam. In Boston, Stan took me to the local hospital where the doctor used an anaesthetic spray to numb my throat before examining me. There was no infection but I was told to rest my voice for four days and to quit smoking. This meant that we would have to cancel the next four nights, so our next gig would be Toronto in Canada. We drove all day, 500 miles to Buffalo on the border, and as we tried to cross the following day, we were stopped as we didn't have the correct visas and had to drive all the way back to Buffalo. Eventually, we had the documentation and crossed the border into Canada, just about mustering the energy to take in the sight of the Niagara Falls on the way.

We were booked to play Toronto's Edge Club for two consecutive nights, two shows per night: one at 10 p.m. and one at midnight. I wondered how my voice would hold up but there was no problem, and we played two great shows; most of the audience stayed for both and were dancing and leaping about by the end. The second day in Toronto, I had time to look around the shops and bought a red military style vintage jacket. Some of the others decided to go to the hairdressers: Fred came back looking like a Bee Gee and Gary had a curly perm. The first show went well but Gary's hair went into even tighter curls with all of the sweating and he started to mess up the set, I thought, on purpose – the start of a Gary sulk.

We drove back to Buffalo for a gig at the Stage One Club, which was a dump. We had to borrow the jazz-rock support band's PA – they thought we were supporting them – and the dressing room was essentially a small cupboard. Of the 80 people there, about 20 had actually come to see us. I wasn't speaking to Gary and he was being funny with me. Next up was Detroit Bookies. I remember driving into Detroit and being struck by how run down the city looked. The hotel was filthy, so the morning after the gig, we got

up early and had a quick look around a few shops in the immediate vicinity. I bought a large American flag before setting off on the long drive to Chicago. The weather was hot and humid and we arrived at 8 p.m. We settled into our hotel rooms and I was in the middle of cutting Peter's hair when Gary knocked on the door and apologised for his behaviour. I was pleased about this as we were a long way from home, into our third week and I could do without the drama. It was a unique situation we were in, all going through this together, each with our own thoughts, in a bubble from which there was no escape. We were living out of suitcases and there was plenty of dirty laundry. Gary was only 18 and I was 21. It was a pretty mad experience for people of our age to be caught up in and we were still only half way through the tour. We played two nights in Casper's, Chicago, and all I can remember is that after one of the shows, a man entered the bar, brandishing a gun, demanding to be served. This was pretty scary. We beat a hasty retreat after that.

We drove to Minneapolis, Minnesota, played at Jay's Longhorn Saloon and that was the first leg of our tour completed. The minibus, our home for the past three weeks, was cut loose without any sentiment as we made our way to the airport for an internal flight to San Francisco on the West Coast.

On 25 May 1979, one of the deadliest aviation accidents occurred in the United States. A McDonnell Douglas DC-10 aircraft crashed whilst taking off due to a design fault wherein the left engine detached. All 258 passengers, 13 crew and two ground staff were killed in the terrible incident. Just days later, we boarded a DC-10 before they were all grounded later that month. Of course, all of the passengers were nervous, so we were plied with free champagne for the duration of the four-hour afternoon flight. We took full advantage of the courtesy refreshments and by mid-flight things were starting to get out of hand. John told me that the studio was booked to start the recording of our second album three weeks after we got back. I was overwhelmed with this information – the free drinks had taken hold and I started to cry. He then ripped open one of the cushions used as a head-rest and threw the contents, white feathers, which swirled around the pressurised cabin like a snowstorm. The other passengers were disgusted with these antics and we were warned that we would be arrested when the plane landed.

We weren't arrested, but there was no one to pick us up on arrival, so we had to cram nine people into two taxis with all of the guitars and luggage. As we pulled up to the hotel in San Francisco, the door to the taxi behind opened and Robert and Pete Dewhirst (who were usually good friends) rolled out fighting with each other, tumbling onto the pavement and into a landscaped garden shrubbery, where a startled Chinese man was pruning the bushes. One of the freshly cut wooden plant stems pierced Robert's neck like a stake and tore a five-inch gash into his flesh which began bleeding heavily and took several months to heal. I couldn't believe what was happening, but was even more startled when I saw John running away in the distance, disappearing over the top of a hill.

Everything eventually calmed down and we had a couple of days off in San Francisco before our gig at the Old Waldorf. The weather was sunny but windy and chilly at the same time and the place was unique, with its steep rolling hills, cable cars and the Golden Gate Bridge. We explored Fisherman's Wharf and John and Stan got up early to visit Alcatraz Prison on a boat trip. We decided to track down cult band The Residents, an avant-garde music and multimedia operation, formed in the early 1970s. The band members were anonymous – they famously wore giant eyeball masks over their heads and we knew that their headquarters, the Cryptic Corporation, was at 444 Grove Street, Hayes Valley. A gang of us turned up and were welcomed by Jay Clem, the spokesperson for the group and also the only one in the building at that time. We walked through a narrow, black, plastic-lined corridor and into a bright open space with a large plastic palm tree housed in a pot of empty drinks cans. There was a mezzanine floor above which was divided into offices where the artwork for the band was created, stock rooms and this industrial-type building contained everything required for the Resident's creative activities, including a small

recording studio and an area for filming videos. I'd never seen anywhere like it: a self-contained set-up where artistic creativity was the prime factor, and the means of production and distribution were all done in-house. Jay was friendly and we left with armfuls of records and t-shirts, and the promise that he would attend our show the following evening.

We did a radio interview on a college campus on the other side of the Golden Gate Bridge, then on to the gig, our support act being female-fronted local band the Avengers. My voice was playing up again but we were getting near to the end of the tour now and I hoped it would hold out till the end. We received a letter from Jay to say that he'd really enjoyed the show and what a pleasure it had been to meet us.

After a bumpy internal flight from San Francisco, we landed in Los Angeles, the largest city in California. I don't know what I was expecting but it was totally different to San Francisco and what I'd imagined; an endless metropolitan sprawl with no discernible centre. Sunset Strip was as disappointing as the Kings Road had been on my first visit: it was a long, wide road with no concentration of shops, and seemed to be made up of restaurants and night clubs. The most interesting place was the Whisky a Go Go, the club we were due to play over the next two nights. We checked out the venue the night we arrived and watched The Roches, a trio of sisters from New Jersey. It was a treat to see them performing their quirky, humorous songs, singing in unison with occasional harmonies.

We were booked to do the usual two shows per night and as we went on for the first show, I was surprised to see Paul Morley, the photographer Pennie Smith and Al Clark, the press officer from Virgin, standing in the audience. No one had told us that they were coming. It was good to see a few familiar faces but we just weren't expecting it. Between sets, our dressing room was full of strangers and liggers, drinking our beer and posing about. It was a strange dynamic and hadn't occurred at our other gigs; it was also slightly disconcerting, as we had to prepare ourselves for the second set.

Virgin had assigned a very bossy and upfront lady to look after our press interviews and she was on my case

Opposite page: Unreturned keys. North American tour. Photograph by Robert Blamire.

4407A
BOX 402
STATION
TORONTO,
CHARTER
HOUSE
MOTOR INN
6643 TRANSIT ROAD
BUFFALO, NEW YORK
14221
158
DROP IN ANY MAIL BOX
WE
GUARANTEE
POSTAGE
ACRES
MOTEL
LINCOLN AVE.
IL 60659
19
ANY MAIL BOX
WE
GUARANTEE
POSTAGE
P.O.
ANSONIA STATION
NEW YORK, NY 10023
BEVERLY
TERRACE
MOTOR HOTEL
469 N DOHENY DR.
BEVERLY HILLS, CA. 90210
241
DROP IN ANY MAIL BOX
WE
GUARANTEE
POSTAGE
IF CARRIED AWAY
INADVERTENTLY
DROP IN ANY MAIL BOX
708
P.O. BOX 308
MINNESOTA 55402

for the duration. The weather was hot and sunny which was nice, but I was consigned to doing interviews all day in the hotel room, missing out on the glorious weather while the others relaxed in the swimming pool. There were people lined up to interview me and this press officer was making them wait as if I was a star – a tactic which backfired: the people from *Slash*, a respected and widely distributed punk zine, left in disgust as they felt they were being disrespected.

LA punks seemed to be inspired by the British bands whereas the East Coasters were more arty and introspective. On the second night, Joan Jett, guitarist from the all-female teenage band The Runaways, turned up to our show. I'd heard their album *The Runaways* in 1976 and the band had garnered plenty of attention at the time but had already split up by now. She stood at the front of the stage with some of her friends during our first set, which was well attended. Between sets, the dressing room filled up again and Joan slouched in a chair and was so out of it that she was oblivious to the fact that someone was repeatedly bouncing a football off her head.

During the second set, one of Jett's friends, whom I suspect was Darby Crash from LA punk band the Germs, was hooking the handle of his walking stick around my ankle and trying to pull me over. As I recalled in my diary, '(Jett's) friends caused trouble, shouted abuse and grabbed me with a stick and finally Stan threw them out'. When it was all over, the lady from Virgin was still in my face so I locked myself in a toilet and wouldn't come out until she'd gone.

We hired a small minibus and drove south to our next destination: Costa Mesa on the coastal suburbs of LA. Looking back at Los Angeles from a distance, you could see a yellow toxic smog that hung over the whole city. Our hotel was at Laguna Beach about 20 minutes from Costa Mesa, and was located on the beach. The Pacific Ocean waves were fierce, ideal for experienced surfers but Fred nearly drowned as he was caught up in a massive breaker. We went to the Cuckoo's Nest in Costa Mesa for the soundcheck then returned to the hotel, as we weren't onstage until midnight. I found a great outdoor pottery shop and bought tea sets to take home as presents, Mexican pots, a large ceramic ice cream sundae with salt and pepper ice cream cones and a plastic pink flamingo, giving no thought as to how I would get these bulky and fragile items on the plane home.

We gave our all as usual at the gig and the audience gave us very little in return. We didn't get back to the hotel until 2.30 a.m. and we would be returning to LA the next day. Fred and I drove to KROQ radio station and the interviewer asked dumb questions like 'Which one of you used to be in Buzzcocks?' These interviews were becoming more of a pain than a promotional exercise. Mick Ralphs, the ex-guitarist with Mott the Hoople and Bad Company, whom I assumed was now living in LA, came to visit Stan; they obviously had a shared rock'n'roll history. We played at Madame Wong's, a hip Chinese restaurant that had gained a reputation for hosting and supporting up-and-coming punk rock bands and musicians. The old lady herself, Esther Wong, affectionately known as the 'Godmother of Punk' was in attendance but not many people turned up that night. The gig hadn't been advertised due to the fact that we'd just played two nights at the Whisky a Go Go. The gig at Riverside the following night was cancelled after health inspectors had closed it down due to an infestation of rats, so at least we got a day off. Peter went looking for record shops, there was nowhere nearby to get anything decent to eat and there were no cinemas in the vicinity. Hollywood!

The final date of our tour was mercifully upon us. We drove about a hundred miles south along the Pacific Coast to San Diego, not far from the Mexican border. The venue, the Roxy Theatre, was the best of the whole tour: a small theatre, 650 capacity, good stage, PA and lights. It's a pity that only about 50 people turned up but we played a good set and those 50 people enjoyed it, which was all that mattered. As a treat to ourselves we went to Disneyland, the prototype for all of the Disneylands to follow. It was an amazing experience as we'd never seen anything like it. We sampled 'Pirates of the Caribbean', 'Haunted Mansion', 'Submarine Voyage', 'Bobsled' and the most nerve-shattering of all, 'Space Mountain', an indoor, space-themed rollercoaster ride which hurtled through the darkness at high speed.

Opposite page: Band on the road.

'Come Into the Open' record sleeve. Binocular Images.

I managed to get the bags of pottery and the pink flamingo onto the plane as we made the thirteen-hour journey back to the UK. When we got home, my mother thought I'd been taking drugs as I had lost so much weight, 'seven-and-a-half stone wet through'.

John was true to his word. We were indeed due to start the recording of our second album in three weeks' time, with Steve Lillywhite producing and Ian Taylor engineering. First we had to record a live show for the BBC at the Paris Theatre, London, on 7 July with The Ruts, but, as I recall, the event was marred by skinheads and troublemakers in the audience. This now seemed to be a regular occurrence in the UK.

Three days later, we were on our way to Ridge Farm, a residential recording studio located in the village of Rusper, near the Surrey and Sussex border. At the time, I had no idea where we were. I just remember driving through the countryside and arriving at a location in the middle of nowhere. There was a large farmhouse, a barn that had been converted into a top-class recording studio, a building used as sleeping quarters and an old stone outbuilding next to the studio, painted white, with a small living room and kitchen on the ground floor and one bedroom

upstairs. This dwelling was to be mine and Peter's home/prison for the duration of the album recording. (The Slits followed us into Ridge Farm to record their iconic debut album *Cut*, and the album cover photo of the band, topless and mud-smeared, was taken by Pennie Smith outside this very building.)

On the first night we were all invited into the farmhouse, which seemed to be run by hippy types, for a meal – which we later found out was a magic mushroom stew. I didn't have any, so I felt fine when we crossed the dark lawn back to the cottage. Some were feeling the effects and Fred almost fell into the swimming pool, which was located near to the house. Work began on the musical backing tracks. Four days into the recording, we had to interrupt the sessions and return to the north-east for a show that had been booked at Peterlee Leisure Centre on 14 July. This was both a relief and a distraction. We had to do an afternoon show for under 18s and another show in the evening. Around 1,300 people turned up from all over the area, and all the local press could focus on was negative incidents, such as police collecting weapons from punk rockers and the amount of spitting which was, in truth, disgusting. It was disappointing that people still thought that this activity was acceptable.

We returned to Ridge Farm and continued recording live backing tracks. Songs like 'She Is the Slave', 'Last Saving Grace', 'Come Into the Open', 'On Reflection' and the music for 'Shout Above the Noise' were already written but we were having to pull ideas together and put them into some kind of arrangement as we went along. The amount of pressure I felt was like having a heavy weight around my neck and being thrown into a deep dark lake. We were on a tight recording schedule as there was a lengthy UK tour booked to promote the album. The machine had everything in place. The band were recording backing tracks and sending them over to me in the dark stone cottage to come up with titles, lyrics and tunes. I would play each track over and over again on the ghetto blaster until I could get something to fit and at times, felt like I was crawling up the walls in my solitary confinement. The situation I found myself in was a far cry from the joy, innocence, punk ideals and

UK Tour dates, Autumn 1979.

musical creativity that I had started out with and I now felt like a prisoner in a nightmare from which there was no escape. I was serving the band, the management, record company, the entertainment machine and the whims of the public. My own resources were massively depleted and to say that I was disillusioned would be a vast understatement. I managed to get some vocals done but I was clearly on the edge of a nervous breakdown. The following lyrics reflect my state of mind at the time.

### Challenge

I was standing at the border
Didn't know which road to take
Seems like obstacles blocked every pathway
Preventing me from escaping
And I turned around
And stood face to face
With a stranger staring straight at me
He said…

They'll suck you in and spit you out
Without a thought or feeling
Then vanish without trace
Into oblivion
But they leave their poison.

Watch the good Samaritan
Stand fearless by the path
He lost his nerve and ran away
And I never saw him again
I'm moving forward cautiously
My knife down by my side
He said…

Think once
Think twice
Won't you listen to my advice
You're outnumbered
It's a loser's game
So go back where you came from

Challenge me now
Don't be afraid

We left Ridge Farm and I still hadn't finished all the lyrics and vocals. When we got home, we had to go to Newcastle to file documents for the Pete Brent court case, which was still following us around. I was back in London early August to finish the vocals and the album was completed on 3 August, just hours before Steve Lillywhite went on holiday. It was a miracle that the record was finished but the experience for me had been traumatic. The album artwork had been executed while we were recording and we had no time to get involved with it. My heart sank when I saw the sleeve: the illustrations of the band members on the back were poor. The one of Gary made him look like Clarence the Cross-Eyed Lion.[1] We were out of the loop in decisions over our creativity and how the band would be perceived. Not a good feeling.

'Come Into the Open' was to be the single released on 17 August and the album, *Coming Up For Air*, had a release date of 14 September. The title, a reference to the George Orwell book of the same name, was also a reflection of how I was feeling at the time; drowning and surfacing for a gasp of air. A 26-date tour was scheduled to start on the release date and it was a pretty overwhelming prospect. There were decent reviews for 'Come Into the Open' and it reached no 63 in the official charts, but received virtually no airplay. The reviews for the album were less than favourable with disappointment all round. It was clearly a rush job and left some of our fans dissatisfied, although those who were just discovering the band thought that this album was better than *Moving Targets*. Music is subjective, and tracks like 'Shout Above the Noise', 'She Is the Slave' and 'Come Into the Open' were certainly up to standard. I believe that if we'd had more time for writing and recording instead of constantly being on tour, it may have been a different story.

Before the tour was due to start, Neale told us he was leaving the band. I don't remember him giving any particular reason but his demeanour was always sullen and miserable. I'd had enough of the band myself at this point and almost felt relieved. I couldn't contemplate carrying on, finding new members and beginning another phase. It had all become too

---

1. From the 1965 film of the same name.

Backstage at The Nashville, 5 November 1979. Photograph by Paul Slattery.

much of a burden. I couldn't see any way forward and didn't have the energy or the will to pull things back together. It was understood that the band would split up after the tour and no one tried to persuade us otherwise. We were young and had no counsel. We'd had a good run, taken things as far as we could and at least now the end was in sight. I had dedicated my life to Penetration 24/7 for the past three years, which seemed like a lifetime. I'd never had a break, I'd pushed myself to the limits and met many tough challenges, but our efforts to break the band had literally broken the band.

The tour was our most ambitious to date, taking in large ballrooms, universities and civic halls, concluding with a show at the Lyceum in London. We were travelling with trucks for the PA and lighting – it really was resembling a travelling circus. The bigger it got, the

more pressure was felt. We should have been pleased that we had reached this level but I had a strange, punk outlook and felt that there was no security or solid foundation involved. Knowing that it was to be our last tour made things even more uncertain.

For most of the gigs, Neale stood behind the PA speakers so no one could see him which I thought was ignorant and unnecessary. From my own personal point of view, I have never gone onto a stage and given less 100 per cent, even if I felt ill or under the weather. We hadn't said anything about our plans for the future and this added more pressure to the situation. Newcastle City Hall had finally relented and allowed Penetration to play what was a hometown gig. A mobile recording studio was set up outside of the venue to record the performance. Word had seeped out to the music press that we were splitting up and they sent journalists to review the gig. We played the main set and I was sick of the charade and said something like 'This is the last gig that this line-up is going to do here. Everything has got to change sometimes' (subconscious echoes of Bowie's last performance at Hammersmith Odeon in 1974). It just came out – I wasn't really thinking but something had to be said.

It was a shock and blow to the fans but it was our own personal lives involved. In the few interviews that followed, only Neale seemed to have an idea of what he wanted to do next, which was make his own music in small studios. No one else had any plans and all I wanted to do at that point was get off the rollercoaster and have some time to myself. I felt angry, sad, exhausted, confused, relieved, frightened, disappointed, betrayed, exploited, financially broke, jaded and old at 21 years of age. We managed to get through the tour and when everyone was dropped off at their respective homes, I didn't see Neale or Fred again for at least another twelve to fifteen years. Peter signed on the dole, Robert was still calling in at the flat and Gary was looking for a job. Wow! What was that all about?! Were we really that stupid? Apparently so.

Next came the financial tsunami. We were still signed to Quarry and from accounts prepared by our own accountant from 18 February 1978 – 5 November 1979, which included advances from Virgin for both albums, tours, radio sessions and merchandise, the total income was listed as £93,058. Management fees were £26,602, tour costs – £23,277, recording costs (some of which were for Virgin's own studios) – £21,246, and the list went on. Band members and Peter had received a mere £3,231 each as wages over the two years and the final outcome was that we owed Quarry £19,871 and we still owed Virgin £35-40,000 in un-recouped royalties. (Many years later, I would spend a whole week analysing the accounts from Virgin and eventually discovered that our royalty rate was 8 per cent. The debt never seemed to go down.)

Naturally we would be leaving Virgin, and I thought that the original demos, recorded at Virtual Earth, should be released as soon as possible as they were an important part of the band's history; I didn't want them to disappear without trace. John hastily set up an off-the-shelf company called Cliffdayn to release the album *Race Against Time* as it was not part of our Virgin contract. With just a plain white cover with a live photo of Robert and I on the front, it resembled a bootleg album and wasn't an official release, but Virgin agreed to put it out. I don't know how many were pressed but the sales would go towards repaying some of the debt.

Next came the question of our publishing, which was signed to Quarry. David Oddie had apparently 'done a runner' to Australia, taking all of the publishing money with him, and I didn't receive a penny for any of the songs I'd co-written during the whole period. Eaton Music had collected publishing royalties on Quarry's behalf and continued to account to me in subsequent years, but this was breadcrumbs as the main income from our three years of activity was gone and I was in no position to challenge this criminal manoeuvre.

I had joined the band as an optimistic, naive 18-year-old, fired by punk ideals and a desire to change the world. For me, it was never about money but we had got ourselves into a financial, physical and psychological mess; we should have received treatment for post-traumatic stress disorder after going into battle in the 'Punk Rock War of 1977-79'. Most of the original bands had been beaten down or absorbed into the industry, split up or become household names whilst others transitioned into the newly labelled 'post-punk' with bands such as Public Image Ltd (PiL) and Joy Division redefining its parameters both musically and visually. The many aspects of punk had such an impact that this Black Swan event informed everything that followed.

At the end of 1979, a seismic shift was taking place, mainly due to the British Conservative Party's first female leader and the UK's first female prime minister, Margaret Thatcher. Her cruel policies of deregulation, privatisation, the crushing of workers' trade unions and the 'loadsamoney' culture was just the start of an ongoing power grab from the British people. The music business had sucked up the energy and creativity of punk and had regenerated itself for the next phase: the 1980s.

"PENETRATION", 116 RABY ROAD, FERRYHILL, CO. DURHAM

PROFIT AND LOSS ACCOUNT FOR THE PERIOD

18 FEBRUARY 1978 TO 5 NOVEMBER 1979

| | | |
|---|---|---|
| Receipts | | |
| Sundry Tours | | 40049 |
| BBC | | 1201 |
| Virgin Records | | 50714 |
| Merchandise | | 1094 |
| | | 93058 |
| | | |
| Less Expenses | | |
| Agency Commission | 79 | |
| Equipmentand Van Hire | 4197 | |
| Travelling and Subsistence | 8941 | |
| Motor Expenses | 1942 | |
| Equipment Repairs and Consumables | 576 | |
| Room Hire | 62 | |
| Postage, Stationery and Telephone | 147 | |
| Insurance | 432 | |
| Bank Charges | 74 | |
| Accountancy Charges | 605 | |
| Road Management | 3030 | |
| Studio Recording Costs | 21246 | |
| Tour Costs | 23277 | |
| Management Fees | 26602 | |
| Stage Clothes | 1046 | |
| Merchandise Publicity Costs | 1794 | |
| Legal Expenses | 1313 | |
| Subscriptions and Sundries | 394 | 95757 |
| | | |
| Less Financial Expenses | | |
| Hire Purchase Charges | 65 | |
| Depreciation | 3440 | 3505 |
| | | |
| Net Loss for the Period | £ | (6204) |

Final band accounts, November 1979.

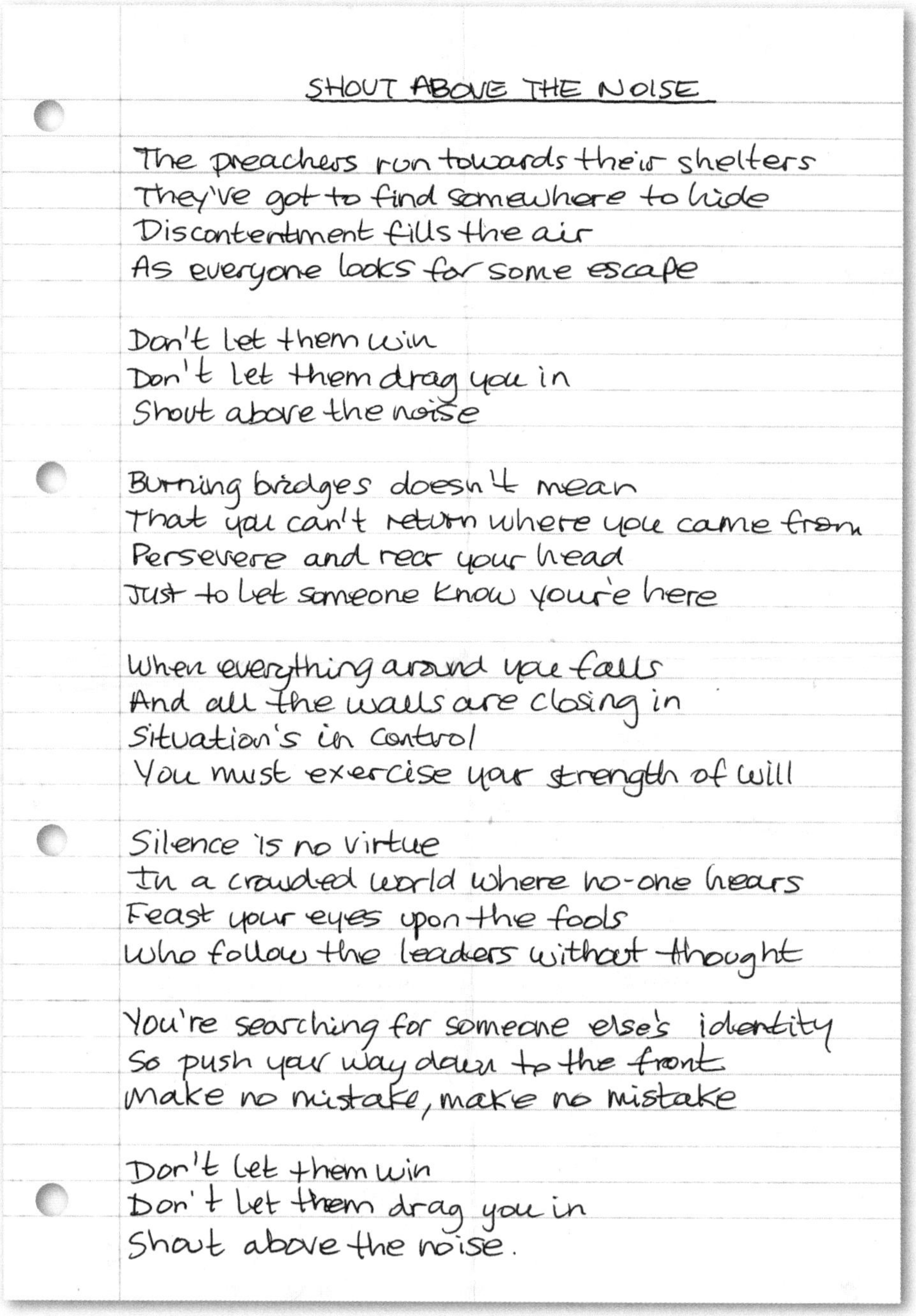

## SHOUT ABOVE THE NOISE

The preachers run towards their shelters
They've got to find somewhere to hide
Discontentment fills the air
As everyone looks for some escape

Don't let them win
Don't let them drag you in
Shout above the noise

Burning bridges doesn't mean
That you can't return where you came from
Persevere and rear your head
Just to let someone know you're here

When everything around you falls
And all the walls are closing in
Situation's in control
You must exercise your strength of will

Silence is no virtue
In a crowded world where no-one hears
Feast your eyes upon the fools
Who follow the leaders without thought

You're searching for someone else's identity
So push your way down to the front
Make no mistake, make no mistake

Don't let them win
Don't let them drag you in
Shout above the noise.

Opposite page: The Nashville, 5 November 1979.
Photograph by Paul Slattery.

# CHAPTER SIX

# THE VISITOR

In 1980, Thatcher's government had created a steep rise in inflation with their free market economy and brutal cuts in public spending, and a recession was the inevitable result. Factories and heavy industry were closing down, while unemployment figures climbed to more than three million. These developments hit the North of England especially hard. The fear, uncertainty, tension and anxiety permeating the national psyche was palpable.

On a personal level, with the demise of the band, I felt that a heavy weight had been lifted from my shoulders. The endless cycle of writing, recording and touring was something that I couldn't see myself doing for the rest of my life. But at the same time, I couldn't give up on music and didn't even contemplate a change of career. I needed time out to recover both physically and mentally and disentangle myself from the dodgy business deals we'd entered into with such a *laissez faire* attitude. It was all still too raw to process, so I turned my back on the past in order to move forward. John was still in touch but the one condition for his continued involvement was that he would leave Quarry, which he did. I was hoping to do things differently and give myself time and space to work on new ideas. From the remnants of the band, it was only Robert with whom I continued to work in a creative capacity. I was still living in the flat with Peter and didn't really take the proper time out to recover.

Not having to comply with a merciless band schedule was a relief in itself. As the year began, Robert and I borrowed money to buy a Teac four-track tape-recorder and set up a recording space in an extension of his parents' house known as 'the Big Room'. The room was split in half with home-made floor-to-ceiling panels and wooden frames padded with rock wool and covered in hessian, which served as a soundproofed wall. We met there weekday afternoons to write and record new song ideas with a Dr Rhythm drum machine, a basic mixing desk and various instruments that we played ourselves. It was a peaceful environment and we had time to experiment as there was no overbearing pressure to meet external deadlines. Robert was originating musical ideas that we would work on together ('When Will We Learn', 'Shoot You Down', 'Thundertunes'). I would write the lyrics and melodies and for the first time, I was coming up with complete songs of my own which we both played on ('Dream Sequence', 'Sympathy'). All of the songs that would become the *Pauline Murray and the Invisible Girls* album were written in 'the Big Room'. We had no overall plan at the time and just took each day as it came.

One day, a message arrived from The Only Ones via John: they were recording their third album *Baby's Got a Gun* and asked if I would contribute backing vocals, along with Koulla Kakoulli from Lonesome No More, who'd sang on their previous two albums. I agreed without hesitation: backing vocals were the fun part of the recording process and I'd never sang on someone else's record before. I didn't want John to discuss fees for my singing as I was a fan of the band and wanted to do it anyway. I admired the dark, sardonic lyrics, meandering, melodic songs and the understated singing style of Peter Perrett, the band's frontman, songwriter and rhythm guitarist. He was older than me and had a reputation for being a heavy drug user but we'd met the band before and had visited Peter and his wife Zena's house; he was down to earth, modest, intelligent and quite shy. The Only Ones were signed to CBS and while their music was too sophisticated to be perceived as punk, they had built up a good following and were highly respected in the music press. However, like Penetration, they hadn't had a hit single or managed to break into the mainstream. Their first single for CBS, 'Another Girl, Another Planet' was their most well-known song but it wasn't a hit at the time.

When I arrived at Red Bus recording studio in London, most of the musical backing tracks had been completed with producer Colin Thurston and only the band's bass player, Alan Mair, was there for most of the session. The other members would call in separately

Opposite page: Southwark, London 1980. Photograph by Paul Slattery.

Pauline and Robert, London, 20 March 1980. Photograph by Virginia Turbett.

throughout the day. I was asked to sing on 'Fools', a country song written by Johnny Duncan, which was to become a duet with Peter Perrett, though we didn't sing it together in the studio. Peter had already completed his vocal and I originally sang the whole song, adding harmonies on the choruses, then when it was mixed, we sang separate verses. All of the backing vocals were sung with Koulla and myself around one microphone. I joined the band for a sold-out gig at the Lyceum in London on 24 February with Simple Minds supporting and it seemed like second nature for me to be back on that stage again. 'Fools' was released as a single on 2 May but failed to chart and *Baby's Got a Gun* would be The Only Ones' final album with CBS.

In early March, I was asked to do a John Peel session. Initially, it filled me with panic as I didn't have a band and Robert and I were still immersed in our creative songwriting endeavours, but this was too good an opportunity to miss. We hadn't developed our sound as we were concentrating on the songwriting, so we brought in Pete Howells (Drones) on drums and Alan Rawlings (Cowboys International) on guitar and we played the keyboards ourselves. I have no recollection of how we put this together but on 19 March we were once again at Maida Vale recording a Peel session.

We didn't have a band name so it was broadcast as Pauline Murray (which made me feel very exposed, a reluctant star) on 31 March. Songs included 'Sympathy', 'When Will We Learn', 'Dream Sequence' and 'Shoot You Down', which had all the components of later versions but some included lyrics in progress. At this point, there was no recording contract in sight but the session gave John some ammunition to approach various record companies while we could return to the sanctuary of 'the Big Room' and continue writing songs. We were making good progress and had 'Screaming In the Darkness', 'European Eyes', 'Mr X' and 'Judgement Day' in the pipeline.

John was approached by Ashley Newton, a young A&R manager who'd recently been appointed by RSO Records to develop a more contemporary side to their roster. He liked our new material, our situation was flexible as we weren't tied to a band and it was a new, fresh project for us. We were still signed to Quarry and would have to pay off Penetration's debt before they would release us from the contract. I remained wary of the music business and didn't want to sign with a major record label so it was agreed that John, Robert and I would set up our own label and license our music to RSO Records. We called our label 'Illusive'. The name just came to me – it was suitably ethereal and not grounded in harsh reality. RSO would pay us an advance, we would pay off the outstanding debt to Quarry and be responsible for our own recording costs. At this point, RSO Records were one of the most financially viable record companies, having just had multi-million successes with the soundtracks *Saturday Night Fever* and *Grease*. It was a fortuitous turn of events and happened quicker than we were expecting. I was happy, optimistic and felt elevated within myself, floating rather than drowning. It was exciting to be working with a new record label, with people who professed their belief in me as an artist.

The song 'Dream Sequence' was chosen to be the first single and we needed to decide upon a producer. Peter, who always had his finger on the pulse of music's latest developments, suggested Martin (Zero) Hannett, whose unorthodox recording methods and distinctive sound was gaining attention through his work with Joy Division on *Unknown Pleasures*, the Factory Records roster and amongst others, *The Correct Use of Soap* by Magazine for Virgin Records. I was interested in Martin's other projects like the Jilted John album *True Love Stories* and John Cooper Clarke's *Disguise In Love* where he worked with his own in house studio band known as The Invisible Girls, with pianist and musical director, Steve Hopkins. I didn't have a permanent band, nor did I want one, so this seemed like the ideal set-up. Ashley Newton

was in agreement, so I nervously rang Martin and explained the situation. He was a man of few words but in his dry Mancunian manner, he asked me to send copies of the John Peel session and our four-track versions of 'Dream Sequence' and the other songs we were working on. Both Robert and I were big fans of Martin's production and were delighted when he agreed to get involved with our music.

Martin enlisted Karl Burns from The Fall on drums, Steve Hopkins on keyboards, Robert on bass and we persuaded him to keep Alan Rawlings on guitar. The music was keyboard-led and Martin took it into Phil Spector territory with the drums, but kept it light and airy. He even resembled Phil Spector with his curly hair and aviator shades, but wore shirts and woolly jumpers rather than a suit and tie. Martin was obsessive about the drum track being in time. For the album, everything was played to a click-track, but on 'Dream Sequence' the backing track was played live without a metronome. It irritated him that the drums slowed down in a certain passage, so later he erased the original drum track and hired Trevor Spencer, a session drummer who played for Cliff Richard, to re-do the drums. I'd never seen such a professional in action before. His drum kit sounded great immediately, he listened to the song once and replaced the drum track in one take, pulling the faulty section back into time. For the B-side, Martin took our original four-track version of the song, I re-did the vocal through the night at Strawberry Studios in Manchester and as the cleaner arrived in the morning, he sampled the hoover with a vocoder on my vocal, mixing the track in his own unique way.

Peter Saville, graphic designer and part of the Factory Records team, was commissioned to produce the artwork and he arranged for the photographer Trevor Key, best known for the cover of Mike Oldfield's *Tubular Bells*, to do a photo session with me. Without the punk and band restrictions, I was able to get closer to how I wanted to look and allow my femininity to re-balance itself, away from the male-dominated environment that I'd been part of. I had my hair cut in the style of French singer and artist Lizzy Mercier Descloux: short at the back and sides, long on the top.

I wanted to find my own style again outside of the confines of punk, which had become predictable in its music and fashion. The black-and-white portraits that came out of this session were reminiscent of Man Ray's abstract photographs, the satin gloves and bare neck and shoulders were more in-keeping with a 1920s silent movie star.

When the single 'Dream Sequence' was released on 11 July, it was described by the press as 'superb', 'sensuous', 'mysterious', 'intriguing', 'surreal', 'floating', 'light', 'airy', 'dreamlike', 'eerie' and 'mystical', but despite this cascade of compliments, it received very little airplay and failed to reach the Top 50 (67) in its first week of release. This meant no *Top of the Pops*, and no mass exposure. Still, there was support from *Sounds* journalist Jon Savage, who was now working for Granada TV in Manchester as a researcher. Jon arranged for us to do a mimed performance of 'Dream Sequence' on a Saturday morning kids TV show *Fun Factory* – which was fun (as the name suggests) and certainly not punk. It was also the first time we'd presented our new music in a live setting. At this point, the band presented as John Maher on drums, Alan Rawlings, guitar, Steve Hopkins, keyboards and Robert on bass.

Work was due to start on the album at Strawberry Studios and Robert and I (and sometimes Peter) would be staying at Martin's first-floor flat in Didsbury, which he shared with his partner Susanne, for the duration. Joy Division singer Ian Curtis had committed suicide only a few months earlier and Martin was clearly still grieving. He had just finished mixing their song 'Atmosphere' and played it to us on his state of the art sound system; it sounded beautiful, otherwordly. A sense of sadness and melancholy hung in the air and this was a feeling that I found difficult to shake off in the coming weeks.

We would go to the studio in Martin's Volvo with the BBC's World Service on the radio and work until the early hours of the morning, or sometimes all through the night. John Maher, who'd joined Buzzcocks as a 16-year-old drummer and had experienced their tumultuous success, was now at the top of his game. He was a realist and didn't suffer fools. He'd played with Robert before and together they made a great rhythm section, tight and inventive. Steve Hopkins was older than us, gentle and intelligent and played piano in a sensitive, flowery style that had more in common with a cocktail pianist than a vamping hammer-fist rocker. During the first week, we recorded nine backing tracks, played to a click track with the core band: John on drums, Robert on bass, Steve on piano and I sang guide vocals. Steve, as musical director, kept the ball rolling and sound engineer Chris Nagle was responsible for the actual recording. Martin, who didn't really talk much, was in a world of his own, playing with new studio gadgets, smoking dope and sometimes falling asleep. Martin had also recently produced the album *The Return of the Durutti Column* for Factory Records and he invited Durutti Column guitarist Vini Reilly to add his delicate and distinctive guitar playing to some of the songs. Dave Rowbotham from Manchester band The Mothmen was also asked to contribute rhythm guitar to add more contrast to the sound. Vini was diminutive, reserved and painfully thin. It was difficult to guess his age, although I suspected that he was older than he looked. It was great to hear his precise, glacial guitar tones picking their way through the songs but I was beginning to feel a little intimidated by the calibre of musicians working on the album.

During the second week, I began to feel depressed and anxious and retreated into myself, unable to speak or communicate with anyone. I felt very alone, out of control and that familiar impulse to run away and disappear was building up inside. After one of the recording sessions, in the middle of the night, we were followed back to Martin's flat by a police car. I was totally paranoid and panic-stricken and locked myself in the bedroom. Martin was unfazed and invited the police into his flat for a cup of tea and they happily left without incident. Being in a recording studio for days on end, sleeping on a mattress on the floor of Martin's spartan spare bedroom and the uncertainty of how this album would turn out were all starting to get to me. We needed a couple of new songs for the album and Martin presented me with a backing track that he and Steve had been working on.

ROBERT BLAMIRE & PAULINE MURRAY

Robert and Pauline promotional photograph, Illusive/RSO Records 1980.

I went home for a week to try and pull myself together. Back at the flat, I re-arranged Martin and Steve's backing track and wrote lyrics and a melody for it ('Time Slipping') and wrote another set of lyrics with a simple tune ('Drummer Boy'). I returned for the third week and didn't know what musical parts had gone onto the tracks but progress had been made in my absence. I'd reconciled myself to the fact that the music was almost complete and that it was sounding good, and now it was time for me to add my vocals. In the past, producers had given guidance and encouragement to get the best take but this time around, I found that the process was a deeply distressing experience: the track would come through the headphones and I would sing it all the way through. Then it would start again and I would sing it again. There was no communication from the control room to advise me on where I was going wrong or what could be improved.

After what felt like the tenth time through, I was exhausted, demoralised and felt like crying as my confidence had evaporated. When I went into the control room, Martin was asleep under the mixing desk and the track was set to repeat. He would spend hours tapping a guitar lead connector through some studio toy, laughing and stoned out of his mind. I don't know

129

Larking about with John Cooper Clarke, September 1980. Photograph by Fin Costello.

how that album finally came together, I didn't even know what was on there but, to his credit, Martin came into his own in the mixing process, stripping everything out, creating space and performing his magic tricks with the overall soundscape giving the album a strange and unique signature.

Peter Saville and Trevor Key were again in charge of the artwork, which consisted of colour photograph headshots and body parts with thin lines of white light projected across them, arranged into 25 squares. Originally, the border was white but I thought it looked too surgical so it was changed to black.

The album was completed and an eight-date UK tour of large venues was announced under the moniker 'Girls Night Out', which was to be a double headline bill with John Cooper Clarke; we would take

turns to close the show. We'd seen and played on the same bill as John Cooper Clarke in the early days of Penetration. He would stand alone on stage, looking like a skinny beatnik Bob Dylan in shades, and deliver his wry and hilarious poems in a Mancunian accent, sometimes at breakneck speed. John's recorded output had been tempered by the musical backing of The Invisible Girls – Martin Hannett, Steve Hopkins and additional musicians of their choosing. The six-piece band would back each artist, the only difference being that Robert would play bass for my set and Martin would join JCC. Vini played a solo opening set. The line-up was Paul Burgess (10cc) drums, Steve Hopkins, piano, Pete Barrett, keyboards, Vini Reilly was on guitar, Dave Hassell percussion and Martin and Robert were on bass.

Opposite page: 'Dream Sequence' photo session.

When the album *Pauline Murray and the Invisible Girls* was released in early October, coinciding with the tour, the reviews were positive and favourable, although nobody seemed to quite know what to make of the music. It sounded like nothing else and stood out on its own. Paul Morley writing for NME described the music as 'eclectic – yet very distinctive' while John Gill for *Sounds* praised its 'strong lyricism, technique and locomotion'. Chris Westwood for *Record Mirror* observed 'not only its distance from Penetration, but its distance from almost anything else.' Journalist Steve Sutherland hailed it as 'a musical highpoint of this or any other year.'

We were delighted when the album entered the national charts at number 25. It was, for me, an artistic highpoint. All of the creative elements had fused together to produce a unique piece of work that in some ways preceded the producer-albums of the early 1980s. With the advent of the new studio technology: Fairlight CMI, Jupiter 8 synthesisers, Linn LM-1, Roland TR-808, Simmons drum machines and sequencers – producers like Trevor Horn (Frankie Goes To Hollywood) and Martin Rushent (Human League) were in full control of the artist's musical arrangements and sound.

The tour was an uplifting experience and another learning curve. The band was unusual in that it included two drummers, two keyboard players, bass and guitar, and as a result it produced a totally different musical dynamic. I was used to singing against loud, riffing guitars with Penetration and this set up was much more controlled, like a big band, with me out front singing. For our intro music, we chose the instrumental album *Katzenmusik* by Michael Rother, an experimental musician from the German band NEU!. The hypnotic multi-layered guitars and electronic instrumentation set up the musical atmosphere for the evening perfectly.

My confidence was a little shaky as I felt quite exposed and out of my comfort zone. I had to concentrate more on singing than performing but things improved as the tour progressed. After one of the earlier shows, when my nerves were still getting the better of me, I was running to the toilet to be sick when

Glamorous image, 1980. Photograph by Fin Costello.

I saw our A&R man, Ashley, approaching with two of his RSO bosses, both wearing flashy white suits and gold medallions. As one of them reached out to shake my hand and introduce himself, I threw up on the floor, splattering his white shoes in the process. Not a great first impression, or a good omen.

The extreme change in musical direction was a brave artistic gamble and I'd put myself on the line. Some Penetration fans didn't like the transformation but it caught the attention of a more open-minded audience during a new phase that the music press called 'post-punk' but I would describe it as 'the flowering of punk'. The original authentic punk artists had started out with limited musical ability, pushed their own creative envelopes, gained so much more experience in their craft and were now able to express themselves in a more sophisticated way. The new, emerging bands had the

Opposite page: Polaroid tests for Invisible Girls album sleeve.

Promotional shoot, late 1980. Photograph by Fin Costello.

advantage of learning from the triumphs and mistakes of the punk pioneers and were able to enter on a different timeline.

'Mr X' was to be the second single taken from the album, a bubbling, euro-disco type track whose lyrics described a game show where the contestants would do anything to become rich and famous. Martin had used an aerosol can on this track, spraying in synch with the bass drum beat. The B-side, 'Two Shots' was recorded in 'the Big Room' on the Teac and mixed by Martin. Of course, it was way off the mark for mainstream success or chart positioning. This wasn't '9 to 5' by Sheena Easton; it was a more twisted form of pop by someone who'd been radicalised by punk at

a young age and had emerged from this subterranean world and its nihilistic doctrines.

After the release of The Invisible Girls album, Robert was asked to produce an album for Edinburgh band The Scars, who'd just signed to Pre Records, a subsidiary of Charisma Records. The Scars were a few years younger than us and we'd first met them in the early days of punk. They'd released a single 'Horrorshow' b/w 'Adult/ery' in 1979 on Fast Product, an independent label responsible for initial singles by The Mekons, Human League and Gang of Four. Robert's time in the studio with Martin Hannett had sparked a growing interest in studio production and he was confident that he could do a good job. The album

*Author! Author!* got great reviews and the single 'All About You' was catchy and fresh but didn't get the exposure required to make it a hit.

A tour of Europe and Scandinavia had been booked for the spring of 1981 and we decided to scale down the live band to a five-piece, including myself. Steve was busy and Vini had his own thing going on and always seemed to be ill – he was frail and seemed to survive on baked beans. We advertised in *Melody Maker* for a guitarist and only received one reply from a musician in Liverpool called Wayne Hussey. We invited him to Ferryhill, paid his train fare and auditioned him by getting him to play on the new material we were working on. His appearance was preppy: short hair, spectacles and a long tweed overcoat. He was from a Mormon background and didn't smoke or drink. His experience was confined to local bands in Liverpool, but he was a good guitarist so we took him onboard. Wayne quickly started contributing to the creative process too, coming up with the chord progression for what was to be our next single 'Searching For Heaven'.

Around this time, Robert and I signed a publishing agreement with Chrysalis Music. All of the songs up to this point (including the Invisible Girls album) were still tied up contractually with Quarry Music. Even though the company had collapsed and defaulted on their obligations, we hadn't managed to get our songs back. We received a small advance from Chrysalis and bought a Prophet-5 synthesiser, quite a costly item at the time. In our everyday life, we were still surviving on a retainer of £40 per week.

New Year dawned and we welcomed 1981 by working on yet more new songs in 'the Big Room'. Wayne visited a couple of times in early January and we demoed the basic structures of what would become 'The Visitor' and 'Animal Crazy' which we then recorded at Strawberry Studios over a four-day period later that month with Steve Hopkins, John Maher, and now Wayne Hussey on guitar, with Robert on bass with Martin producing. The backing tracks were sounding good; they showed a subtle stylistic shift from the album but were still in the same vein. By the end of February, we were picking up the master tapes from Martin in

'Mr X' record sleeve.

Manchester for the two new songs – things were moving quickly. We went to London to do a photo session with Sheila Rock for the single sleeve, and I was booked in at the Sound Suite Studio with engineer Laurence Diana to record the vocals for 'Animal Crazy' and 'The Visitor'.

Over the past year since Penetration had split, I had been spending more time with Robert, writing, recording and working together, than I had with my husband. Peter didn't seem interested in anything other than buying records, listening to music and keeping track of the latest musical trends, which changed on a monthly basis. He had worked as part of the road crew with Penetration and the Invisible Girls' *Girls Night Out* tour but it was a role he didn't particularly enjoy. He didn't even seem interested in me or my music at this point. Meanwhile, an unspoken mutual attraction had been building up between myself and Robert for the past five years that neither of us had realised or acknowledged.

The night before I was due to record my vocals at Sound Suite, Robert and I were staying at the Lindsey Hotel, opposite Hyde Park in separate rooms. Robert was in my room and as he was about to leave, I said that he could stay if he wanted to. The next minute we were locked in a romantic embrace, as if drawn together by some invisible force which, on physical contact, struck like a bolt of lightning, sending shockwaves through our bodies and causing both of us to shake uncontrollably. When we had calmed down, he returned to his room and I wondered how things would be the next day after this dramatic turn of events. When he put his arm around me and we got into the taxi to go to the studio, we were both on cloud nine, and oblivious to the world around us.

**The Visitor**

Can't find an explanation
There's magic in the air
I'm reaching out to touch you
But I find there's no-one there
I'm calling your name
Please come back again

If this is an illusion
Then my life has been a dream
Your presence is surrounding me just like reality
I'm calling your name
Please come back again

Two lives – it's a strange affair
Two worlds – is the message clear
Calling – breaking down the walls
Meeting – when the darkness falls
And I call your name

Voices loud in the air
Sense the danger everywhere
They're on the trail
So run for your life
They smell the fear of the innocents

You're frightened now
It's only natural

In the studio we carried on as if nothing had happened, completed the vocals and returned to Ferryhill, Robert to his parents' house and me back

*Smokin'. Photograph by Jill Furmanovsky.*

to my husband in the flat. I was really confused and didn't know what to think. My emotions were all over the place. I couldn't say anything to Peter and only saw Robert in a working capacity, rehearsing with the band for the forthcoming tour in March. We did some of the rehearsals in a local church hall but figured it would be better to do them in Liverpool, as all of the band members lived in the north-west.

In mid-March, we were back at Strawberry Studios with Martin recording the lead track for the single 'Searching For Heaven' with the same line-up as the previous session. Wayne had completed his guitar parts and returned to Liverpool, and we were over-running on our allocated studio time. Upstairs, the remaining members of Joy Division, who'd now changed their name to New Order, were waiting to begin their session.

Polaroid test for the 'Searching For Heaven' record sleeve.

Martin suddenly decided he wanted a simple guitar solo on the song, and asked a bewildered Bernard Sumner to play on the track, which he did, without a word being spoken by any of the parties. The solo sounded good and enhanced the song but it was such a last-minute and hasty addition that we forgot to credit him for his contribution.

The tour was imminent and arrangements had been made for everyone to meet at Felixstowe to catch the overnight ferry to Gothenburg, Sweden. For the first time, Peter wasn't coming and as we hugged and said goodbye as I was leaving, I didn't know at the time that I would never be returning to Peter, the flat or indeed life as I'd known it.

We either missed the ferry or the rest of the band did but only Robert, Gary Townsend (our sound engineer and tour manager), the monitor engineer and myself boarded the large ship. Luckily we all managed to get to Gothenburg and drove to Oslo in a minibus the following day; John Arnison was to join us later in the tour. We'd never toured Scandinavia before so it was new and exciting and this was a different live band, with John Maher, Wayne Hussey and Pete Barrett onboard. I was able to spend more time with Robert as we were in the very early stages of a clandestine romantic relationship, and, for a change, I was feeling happy.

We drove back to Stockholm and performed on a TV show with Randy VanWarmer, an American singer-songwriter whose big hit was 'Just When I Needed You Most' and then played the following night at the Underworld, a 1,000-capacity venue. The following morning we discovered that Robert's white Rickenbacker bass guitar had been stolen from the hotel reception's lock-up, but we didn't have time to do anything about it as we had a 14-hour journey ahead of us. As we drove through the Scandinavian forests listening to ABBA at full volume in their native environment, all was good with the world. When we reached Arnhem in the Netherlands, The Scars joined us there as support band for the rest of the tour and John Arnison may also have arrived at this point. Rotterdam, Den Haag, Eindhoven then on to Amsterdam. This is where the shit really hit the fan.

John Arnison came to my room in the afternoon and Robert was there, sat on the bed. John asked if there was something going on between myself and Robert. At first I denied it. I thought we were being discreet in our loved-up state, but either the people around us or John himself had noticed something different about us. John then proclaimed *his* love for me – a total curveball that threw me into confusion. My hand had been forced and I knew the game was up. I felt that I had to tell Peter immediately about my infidelity before he found out from someone else. I rang him from the hotel lobby and told him that I wasn't coming home. He asked if there was anyone else involved and I didn't have the guts to tell him. I rang my parents straight after and told my mother the same thing, but she pressed me for more details and I told her about Robert. She said 'I'll never accept him'. I'm assuming that his family went to the flat to rally around Peter in the light of his shocking news. I, meanwhile, had to go onstage that night at the Paradiso and perform on autopilot to a heaving and enthusiastic sold-out show.

My brain was battered and I felt numb. Both Robert and I were in a state of confusion. There were three more dates in the next six days. We drove to Hamburg and made our way to Berlin via the East German transit route, which was more like a dirt track as neither East or West Germany took responsibility for it. You were timed at the beginning of the journey and only allowed to stop at designated places. Armed guards in watchtowers were positioned at regular intervals along the route. The villages we drove through all had bunting along the main street and the factories were painted with Communist insignia, hammer and sickle and clenched fists. The cars were all the same – dull brown Trabants – and the workers in the fields were still using scythes. When we got to Checkpoint Charlie to enter Berlin, it was a whole different world. Coca Cola signs, neon lights, bars and cafes open all night and the speed of the traffic was manic.

John Maher somehow managed to steal a large East German flag and would probably have been arrested if he'd been caught. He would sometimes re-arrange hotel rooms – upturn the wardrobe and put the mattress in it, hang his clothes on the upturned bed base and turn the pictures on the wall upside down. It was a creative pursuit that had probably been developed to stave off the boredom and monotony of hotel rooms whilst on tour.

We received another piece of bad news on the tour when our A&R manager Ashley turned up to tell us that RSO were in financial trouble. The label had taken a chance on backing the musical comedy film *Sgt. Pepper's Lonely Hearts Club Band*. It had a cast led by Peter Frampton and The Bee Gees and had been an artistic and commercial flop. Additionally, The Bee Gees would bring out a lawsuit against Robert Stigwood, their long-time manager and owner of RSO Records. Although the claim for mismanagement was settled out of court, it damaged the company, which would be absorbed into PolyGram later that year. Our single 'Searching For Heaven', which had been released during our absence, failed to turn around the company's fortunes.

As for my own fortunes? When we returned to London from Brussels, I had nowhere to live, no recording contract, no money, a new relationship, a broken marriage and a suitcase full of dirty laundry. Of the most stressful events one can experience in life, I had at least five all playing out at the same time, and it was so overwhelming that I had no idea what was going to happen next.

'Searching For Heaven' record sleeve. Design by Martyn Atkins.

Newcastle Quayside. Photograph by Kev Anderson.

# CHAPTER SEVEN
# SOUL POWER

**The bombshell I'd dropped at home was still reverberating.** My parents lived directly opposite to Peter's mum and dad, and were caught up in the scandal and condemnation as gossip spread through the (small) town. We couldn't return home while emotions were running so high. John Arnison was sharing an office with Rory Gallagher's brother in Fulham and there was a flat on the upper floor where we were able to stay for a week.

My father, in his wisdom, advised my mother that if they didn't board the next train to London to see me, 'you will lose your daughter', such was the gravity of the situation. It was important to them and to me that they were showing their love and support at this crucial time. We met them off the train at King's Cross, my mother almost crying at the incongruous sight of us both: Robert towering tall, and me, a slip of a thing. I was so pleased to see them and it was reassuring to know they had accepted the situation and would stand by me no matter what. They stayed overnight and headed back north the next day.

The following week Robert and I headed up to the north-west to prepare for the ten-date UK tour to promote 'Searching For Heaven'; we were rehearsing at Liverpool's Ministry Rehearsal Studios with the same live band, but I just wanted to get it out of the way. The tour passed by in a blur as I went through the motions. There was so much going on in the background, like trying to find somewhere to live. I was filled with overwhelming feelings of shame and guilt about what I'd done to Peter and when I visited him after the tour, even though he was upset and started to cry, I was emotionless, numb and still in a state of shock. All the same, I knew deep down that there was no going back.

Our past was catching up with us as we received a summons to attend Bow Street Magistrates' Court to defend the claim that Pete Brent had lyrical input into the song 'Don't Dictate'. There we all were – Gary Chaplin, Gary Smallman, Peter Lloyd, Robert Blamire, Kev Anderson, Pete Brent, myself and

'Don't Dictate', transported from the band practice at the Miners' Institute four years earlier, to a wood-panelled courtroom with a judge. John Arnison and representatives from Virgin Publishing were also in attendance. The chugging introduction of 'Don't Dictate' emerged from the silence, through loudspeakers set up for the occasion, the song, now in full swing, filled up the room and played itself out. It was comical if not for the seriousness of the matter. Brent had no knowledge of the chords and his suggested changes to the arrangement didn't constitute writing lyrics that already existed. The case was resolved on the first day with a £900 settlement, £300 of which I had already paid into court. Punk rock? Don't make me laugh.

The day after the court case, Robert and I began our new life together as we moved into the downstairs flat at 134 Princes Road, Toxteth, Liverpool 8; a three-storey Victorian house on a wide tree-lined avenue. It was furnished with a bed, wardrobe and two bedside tables, one of which was home to a gang of fleas who instantly greeted me by jumping onto my bare foot as I opened the door. The two-bedroom flat upstairs was vacant and being painted out, so we rented that instead, unfurnished. At least it was clean and the landlord had fitted new, cheap black carpet throughout. We had nothing, so visited Swainbanks, the closed down Rialto Cinema at the end of the street which was now full of second-hand furniture. We bought an old wooden wardrobe with ladies' profiles painted in coloured woodstain on two of the panels. We ordered two light-pink, two-seater sofas and a black coffee table with chrome legs from the Reject Shop, a cut-price furniture outlet where you could pay for items in monthly instalments. We opened an account at the UK's first drive-through bank, NatWest, which was next to the Rialto. Finally life was starting to make sense again.

Wayne was the only person we knew in Liverpool. We'd played there many times in the past, seen Deaf School and shared a bill with Big In Japan but we'd never met any of the musicians. Liverpool had recently emerged from the shadow of The Beatles and was enjoying a musical renaissance, with the likes of Echo and the Bunnymen, The Teardrop Explodes, Wah! Heat and many other Scouse pop bands. By the time we moved there, these local bands were operating on a national level and busy doing their own thing. Wayne once brought Pete Burns from Dead Or Alive to our flat: he threw talcum powder all over the bathroom.

We were still settling in and didn't venture out much. Wayne lived within walking distance from our flat and we would visit him at the house where he rented a room from Kris and Nina Guidio (better known these days as rock biographer Nina Antonia). They had a young daughter called Severina, and the terraced house was a quiet family home but the curtains were always closed and the couple embraced all things Gothic. Kris was mysterious, with black hair, dark eyes and an ageless countenance, dressed in black with skull earrings and the odd crucifix. He was well spoken and gentle and could have been of Italian or Romani descent. He was an illustrator working on a series of black ink drawings of the American horror-rockabilly band The Cramps. Nina, who was younger than Kris, had black backcombed hair, black eye make-up, dressed in black and was making her first tentative steps towards writing a biography about her friend and hero Johnny Thunders, the guitarist from the New York Dolls.[1] Our visits usually involved conversations about art, books, music and films over endless cups of tea.

We'd been in the flat for about a month when my parents came to visit. As they were leaving in the late afternoon, we saw about fifty policemen run up the avenue and thought it was a strange sight. Half an hour later, Kris called at the flat to tell us that Lodge Lane was on fire and the shops were being looted. The now infamous Toxteth riots had kicked off, just minutes from our door. We jumped into the car and the bottom of Lodge Lane was inaccessible as fires raged and black smoke billowed into the air. We drove up Smithdown Road to the junction with Upper Parliament Street, parked up and saw that the dairy was on fire. Young children were driving milk floats and throwing milk crates and stones at the lines of policeman who were

trying to protect themselves with plastic shields. It was utter chaos, a surreal sight – we stood and watched in disbelief. There had been no prior indication that civil unrest was about to break out but the word on the street suggested that the local police had harassed an innocent young black youth using the Sus Law. This draconian law was the Vagrancy Act from 1824 where the police were given powers to stop, search and potentially arrest anyone on the street that they thought was loitering with criminal intent. The bystanders who witnessed this incident confronted the police and anger spread through the community like a forest fire.

Night fell and the violence was still raging. We returned to the flat and watched the scene all night from a safe vantage point; my parents got home and watched it on the news. Helicopters flew overhead all night and in the street below, we saw people trying to steal cars or empty their car boots of looted goods such as fridges and clothes. Who could have predicted that we had just set up home in a war zone? The Specials' 'Ghost Town' reached number one in the singles chart where it stayed for the next three weeks, an ominous commentary echoing what was happening for real in Thatcher's Britain: recession, mass unemployment (mainly youth and ethnic minorities), industrial decline and deprivation.

As dawn broke, we ventured out to view the scene and were horrified to find that the Rialto had been burned to the ground, along with many other buildings. The NatWest bank was damaged and had been looted. For the next three nights as dusk rolled in, the unrest would escalate again, although not as intensely as it did on that first night. Extra policemen had been requisitioned from other parts of the country for the following two weeks and were stationed at regular intervals along both sides of the avenue, one being outside of our front gate. All seemed quiet on the Western Front until the eve of the Royal Wedding between Charles and Diana on 29 July 1981. The national and local media had been building up to this event for months, and the general public as usual had bought into it. The lavish expenditure and glittering details were in stark contrast to the inner-city

1. The book was eventually completed and released through Jungle Records in 1987, titled *Johnny Thunders... In Cold Blood.*

Tussling with Lil. Photograph by Kev Anderson.

degradation and poverty, and these two extremes would play out simultaneously.

As darkness fell, a mob gathered at a fork in the road that led onto the aptly named Princes Avenue. Lines of policemen in full riot gear set up a blockade to prevent them from moving forward. Rocks and stones flew through the air, fires raged and the noise of the crowd can only be described as the primal baying of wild animals. We were frightened and packed our suitcases in readiness to flee if they advanced onto our street. The police held them back all night and as it began to get light, they dispersed and we went out to survey the damage. Paving stones had been ripped up for ammunition, concrete cased lamp posts were reduced to short stumps with electrical wires sprouting from them, about five cars were overturned and burned out and, incongruously, in an adjacent street, a PA system,

bunting and tables were being set up in preparation for the Royal Wedding street party celebrations. Nothing was reported on the news about the riots.

Robert travelled to London for a recording session with Scars and I accompanied him, but stayed in the hotel most of the time. I was beginning to feel depressed, lonely, confused, disorientated and disconnected, trying to make sense of all of the life changes that had occurred as a result of the commitment we'd made to our love for each other. I was supposed to be writing songs for a demo session that we had booked at Pink Studio in Liverpool with Wayne, Pete Barrett and John Maher, but found it difficult to concentrate. My brain felt like a block of cement and there was an undercurrent of panic and anxiety building up within me as I struggled to write lyrics for the sketchy musical ideas that we were due to record. I was too sensitive to meet the demands

Chinatown, Newcastle upon Tyne. Photograph by Kev Anderson.

of the music industry, recent events had undermined my stability and confidence and this pattern of unease was becoming more frequent whenever I was under pressure. At that point in time, I would need to find a new record label, producer, re-invent myself, possibly use my sexuality as a marketing tool and lose myself in the process. This was something that I wasn't prepared to do.

The backing tracks with the band weren't particularly inspiring and as I began to sing a song called 'Breakdown Beat', which suitably reflected my frame of mind, I stopped mid-sentence and that was it. I had reached my breaking point – I just didn't want to do this anymore. I walked out of the studio, back to the flat and immediately rang John to tell him that I was quitting music.

Initially I felt relief but, over the next few weeks, overwhelming waves of emotional sadness would rise up and come crashing down as I cried uncontrollably for no apparent reason, my whole body trembling and shaking involuntarily. I had no motivation, was unable to function, wasn't sleeping and felt paralysed, tired, lost and afraid. This was a nervous breakdown or severe depression, but at the time, I couldn't rationalise what was happening to me. It was as if I was grieving the death of my former self, former life and my lost youth. Robert was my source of strength and support in a situation that neither of us had experienced before. We were due to play Rock On The Tyne Festival on 29 August with Elvis Costello, Ian Dury, U2 and others, but the thought of going onstage filled me with dread, so we pulled out of the event.

And so we joined the growing ranks of the three million unemployed and signed on the dole to gain some form of financial stability. In all of our time in music, we had struggled to make a living but were willing to endure such hardships for the sake of our original music, beliefs, integrity and artistic freedom. In the early Eighties, the music industry was gearing up for maximum profit. With the advent of the Compact Disc format, record labels were able to sell the whole of their back catalogues like money for old rope. Major record companies were clearing out their rosters and dropping artists and musicians who were deemed commercially and financially unsuccessful. Even bands who'd had chart success like Buzzcocks, The Jam and Blondie were disintegrating and splitting up, with The Police and The Clash heading in the same direction. Songwriters Paul Weller and Sting managed to carve out solo careers from the wreckage, bands like The Damned, Siouxsie and the Banshees and The Cure resonated with the emerging Goth scene and individuals from punk like Boy George, Steve Strange and Adam Ant fronted up the New Romantics with their colourful make-up, costumes and innocuous chart friendly pop. When the American music channel MTV launched in August 1981 with the music video for 'Video Killed the Radio Star' by Buggles, the doors were opened for a whole host of bands like Duran Duran, Spandau Ballet, Eurythmics and Wham! to gain worldwide mass exposure and portray affluent lifestyles to the aspiring middle classes. It was a whole new world.

Punk was now a dog on a string of dirty words, words like: mohicans, tattoos, fishnets, hardcore, studded jackets, tartan and Doc Martens boots. It was left up to bands like the UK Subs, Crass, The Exploited, Discharge and Vice Squad in the UK and their American counterparts Black Flag, Dead Kennedys and Minor Threat to continue punk's legacy as an underground and independent movement.

Scars had split up, but their singer Robert King had been retained as a solo artist on Charisma (Pre Records). He was staying at our flat, working on new material with Robert; the single 'Paper Heart' was released in 1982 but failed to chart. Liverpool band Send No Flowers recorded a single with Robert, 'Wall of Convention', on the independent Praxis label, and he

recorded some demos with Dead Or Alive (who Wayne had now joined due to my own inactivity) at Cargo Studios in Rochdale.

I was still feeling depressed and visited the local GP. I didn't know how to get myself out of this desperate situation and was hoping to receive some guidance. Mental health issues at the time were marginalised and the support system and medication weren't widely available, so I received no help. As winter approached, I was staying in bed until the early afternoon and it was getting dark again at around 4 p.m., so we were living in perpetual gloom. I could feel myself sinking deeper into a black hole but felt powerless to do anything about it. I was 23, in the grown-up world, seeking a divorce, feeling old and burned out, like a broken vase in pieces, with a past and no future. Meanwhile, John was now managing prog-rock band Marillion who were on an upward trajectory and had signed to EMI. He was using the same formula he'd used with Penetration – work them till they drop.

Thatcher's government had entered into a conflict with Argentina over the disputed sovereignty of the Falkland Islands in the South Atlantic Ocean. Closer to home, secret discussions were taking place about whether to let Liverpool go into 'managed decline' (sounds familiar). After the riots, it was a depressing place to live. We knew we couldn't stay there, so packed up our belongings in the spring when the lease expired and moved in with Robert's parents who had a spare bedroom and a 'Big Room' to store our furniture. I felt like a failure in the new aspirational climate and would wake up crying every morning, my musical past becoming a distant memory.

We would go to stay with Kev (Anderson) in Newcastle for several days at a time. He was one of the few people other than our families who'd kept in touch and visited us in Liverpool. We slept on a mattress on his floor and, under the criteria of being homeless, applied for a flat through a local housing association. Eventually, we were offered a one bedroom upstairs flat in Simonside Terrace, Heaton, which we decorated and moved into with our black-and-white cat from Liverpool. We were close enough yet far enough away from our families and hoped to find some stability after what we'd been through in the past year and a half. Kev was the only person we knew in Newcastle and he would come to our flat or we would go to his. We immersed ourselves in watching movies from the video rental shop that had opened next door to his flat. We would go on day trips to the coast or interesting locations in the area, and Kev would take photographs. My life felt pretty aimless but I was keeping on top of everyday chores – my home was always clean and tidy. Robert was still making trips to London to complete the Robert King album (although it would never be released) and we maintained tenuous links with John.

I tried to pull myself together and began writing again; the songs that came were simple, with sparse lyrics. We recorded them on the Teac with the drum machine and played the instruments ourselves. 'Body Music', 'Soul Power', 'Don't Give Up' and 'All I Want' were almost like re-affirmations of belief in myself. We got in touch with Chrysalis Publishing whom we'd signed to after The Invisible Girls, but had yet to deliver any new songs. They agreed to pay for some demos at Rooster Studios in the basement of 117 Sinclair Road, London, to record our new compositions. In December 1982 we recorded three of our own songs with the exception of 'Don't Give Up' and two cover versions, Alex Chilton's 'Holocaust', whose lyrics expressed perfectly the depressive experience I'd just been through, and John Cale's 'Close Watch', a beautiful, melancholic song. Robert created the music for 'Holocaust' with drum machine and arpeggiated synthesisers. We asked Steve Hopkins to play piano on 'Close Watch' and keyboards where required.

I'd gained enough confidence to approach some record companies and had managed to arrange a meeting with RCA. John said he would accompany us, but as we waited outside of the London offices, he failed to show up, so we went into the meeting on our own. We played the A&R man the new demos and he was less than enthusiastic, saying that if we'd taken him the Invisible Girls album, or 'Every Breath You Take' by The Police, he might have been interested.

I had a depressive relapse. Robert started to work at his family's printers for a few days a week and I was in the flat on my own feeling useless and hopeless. Tears would roll down my face as I walked to the shops and my voice was so quiet and introverted that the shop assistant would ask me to repeat what I'd said. When my mother rang up, my voice would start to quiver and I would start to cry. I began to think that they would all be better off without me and entertained suicidal thoughts, and how to go about it. These thoughts were intensifying and reached a peak one afternoon when I looked in the bathroom mirror and gave myself the ultimatum: was I going to kill myself or not? The answer turned out to be 'no'. From that moment onwards, I only looked at what my next meal would be and made it healthy, which in itself created incremental positivity and took attention away from the bigger picture of what to do with my life.

I was building myself back up, but each time we approached anyone in the music business, it would knock back my progress and confidence. I finally got the message and stopped looking in that direction. I even felt that we'd been blacklisted. The only way forward was to release a record ourselves. Tony K at Red Rhino Records in York was a key member of the Cartel, an independent distribution network set up with Rough Trade to supply independent records on independent labels to independent record shops, as well as to some of the bigger chains like Our Price. We approached Red Rhino and they agreed to release 'Holocaust' b/w 'Don't Give Up'/'Aversion' on our own label, Polestar Records. We were offered a pressing and distribution deal. We supplied the master tapes and artwork (a black ink drawing by Kris Guidio of myself and Robert with Kev's layout) and Red Rhino organised everything else, although it was up to us to promote it. It was an achievement and something we'd never done before.

Released in November 1984, it reached number ten in the *Music Week* independent singles chart, number six in *NME*, five in *Sounds* and nine in *Record Mirror*, and it stayed around those positions for the next three weeks, with Depeche Mode and This Mortal Coil heading up

On the beach. Photograph by Kev Anderson.

the singles chart and *Hatful of Hollow* by The Smiths at number one in the independent album chart. This is a reflection of what was going on at the time and I almost felt like an imposter, although it was a great victory that we'd got it there ourselves.

In the real world, my father, who was due to retire, had been on strike for nine months. Arthur Scargill, leader of the National Union of Mineworkers, had confronted the NCB[2] and Thatcher's government over more proposed pit closures. My father didn't agree with the strike as Scargill hadn't obtained a national mandate from all of the mineworkers and other trade unions via a national ballot, but he was on strike nonetheless. Many miners in the streamlined 'super pits' continued to work and had to be protected by mobile police riot units from 'flying pickets' (miners bussed in from other areas to prevent 'the

scabs' from going into work). Militant miners fought pitched battles with the police and the strike caused irreparable damage within communities – there was so much bad feeling. The general public was unsupportive and disinterested. Some people thought Thatcher was doing a great job in smashing the miners' union. The strike lasted a year. Deliveries of tinned goods as handouts was scant recompense for my proud parents who'd spent their life savings in that year just to stay afloat.

I had written another batch of songs which were more guitar orientated: 'New Age', 'This Thing Called Love', 'Another World' and 'Pressure Zone'. I asked Chrysalis if we could demo them in their basement studio below their offices. The person we'd previously dealt with was no longer with the company and a younger person was now in charge. We asked if he

2. National Coal Board

knew any guitarists that we could try out at the session and he suggested Paul Harvey. A thin young lad with dyed blonde hair turned up with a Squier Stratocaster and nervously played through the songs along with bass, drum machine and guitar, played by me. We were happy with the results at the time but it was definitely a demo, a work in progress and not something we were looking to release.

Returning from London, we decided to put a live band together again. It always speeds up the process of making music when other people are involved – the momentum increases. We didn't have the resources to spend time programming machines and playing everything ourselves in a recording studio so began searching for a guitarist and drummer. There were few rehearsal facilities in Newcastle at the time so we booked Desert Sounds in Felling, Gateshead, which was a dilapidated upstairs room in an almost derelict building. A couple of drummers turned up and Paul Harvey travelled on the coach from London. Kev Anderson, guitarist Mick Mason and, strangely enough, Gary Chaplin were in attendance and cast their critical eyes over the proceedings. Paul was on the same page but the drummers were unsuitable.

We heard that a music collective had formed to pressurise Newcastle City Council into making provision for the city's youth, and a four-storey former printing factory had been earmarked to become a live venue, cafe, rehearsal rooms and offices. We were shown around the place when the building still housed the printing machinery and it was like a deserted ship. Before work began on the building, we asked if we could shoot a video on one of the empty floors, and Robert and I were filmed by Kev miming to 'Don't Give Up'. A strobe light flashed continually in the dark room throughout the performance which made the visuals look stark, primitive, and intense and worked organically with the music. We were doing it for our own amusement and it cost only our time and effort.

We were still looking for a drummer and eventually found Tim Johnston, a capable musician who was possibly still in his late teens. In the meantime, Paul,

Young love. Me and Robert Blamire. Photograph by Mick Mercer.

who had a job at the comic shop Forbidden Planet in London, decided of his own accord to move to Newcastle. He was showing his commitment to working with the band but at this point we didn't have much to offer. He said he wanted to get out of London anyway and executed the big move. Paul stayed with us for a few weeks then managed to get a flat across the road from us, from the same housing association.

Work was underway on the council building which was to be called 'Riverside', and the basic rehearsal rooms were in place. We painted one out ourselves and started rehearsing with the band at least three times a week. Both new members were inexperienced compared to ourselves and I was also playing electric guitar, which I hadn't done before; it was like starting from scratch. I became a musical dictator and wanted every note and drum beat in its proper place. This was possibly a reaction to having felt so out of control in past situations, but the band went along with it and seemed to understand and accept the strict guidelines that I was imposing. It was all about the songs and I wanted the playing to be confident and tight so I put them through their paces. We eventually had a live set together and started to ring venues ourselves as we were so disconnected from the music business.

Our first two gigs were at Edinburgh's Hoochie Coochie and the recently opened Riverside, Newcastle, in December 1985. We were playing a set of new songs with a couple from the Invisible Girls album; the music was medium-paced, simple and melodic which didn't fit with anything else going on at the time. It was around this time that Wayne Hussey reconnected with us. He and bass player Craig Adams had just left The Sisters of Mercy and formed a new band, The Mission, who were about to embark on their first tour. We were invited to support them, along with Rose of Avalanche. The dates were all big venues with large crowds of Goths. Since we'd last seen Wayne, he'd transformed into a long-haired, shade-wearing Goth frontman and had fully embraced the rock'n'roll lifestyle. I wasn't particularly into their music but the band treated us well. As for our own music, with jangly guitars and polite songs, we were totally unsuited to such an environment and more often than not it was like playing to planks of wood – no reaction at all. It made us feel even more isolated from the current musical trends. After the tour, we recorded the single 'New Age' b/w 'Body Music' and 'Archangel' at the newly opened Slaughterhouse Studio in Driffield. It was released on Polestar and, again, pressed and distributed through Red Rhino and the Cartel. The single disappeared without trace as usual. That year, 1986, we played 25 shows all over the country, under our own steam, without help from anybody and there was a lot of work involved with very little reward or outside interest.

Robert and I were invited to the London headquarters of Granada TV for the showing of *The Way They Were*, a 90-minute compilation of punk archive footage from 76-77's *So It Goes* and *What's*

Pauline Murray live at Riverside, Newcastle upon Tyne, 21 December 1985. Design by Kev Anderson.

*On*. In attendance were Pete Shelley, Howard Devoto, Mark E. Smith, Jimmy Pursey and Jordan. Those exciting punk days of our youth were now ten years ago and the 1980s had not been kind to any of us – we were mocked in the press for looking older and our achievements disparaged. Now it was up to The Smiths and The Jesus and Mary Chain to motivate Britain's disaffected youth. Both of these bands were inspired by punk and its rebellious attitude, and although there was nothing I could learn from it, they no doubt eased the passage of many a misfit teenager from their bedroom to full-blown adulthood.

The Storm at Tiffany's, Newcastle Upon Tyne 1986. Photograph by David Ord.

Our drummer Tim's brother and sister, Peter and Sophie Johnston, had just been signed by Sony Records after being championed by John Peel on his radio show. Peter was a studio whiz kid and spent their advance on the latest recording equipment, so we asked him to remix four songs from the Rooster demos. The tracks were released on Polestar as a four-track EP under the title *Hong Kong* by Pauline Murray and the Saint, with a drawing of mine on the cover. This was the last record we released via the Cartel and Red Rhino, who were heading towards voluntary liquidation a couple of years later. It was getting too difficult to keep things going and I was again wondering what the purpose of all this effort was.

We still had a few gigs in early 1987 and one was at the Fiesta in Plymouth. Paul had booked the gig and the fee was reasonable, but on the day of the show I woke up with a terrible cold and had to take Sudafed to ease my symptoms during the seven-hour journey. When we finally arrived, we discovered that it was a private birthday party for a fan who'd booked us into this large venue and only a handful of people had turned up. It was embarrassing and I had to make the best of it but

my spirit was at a low ebb. After the gig, he offered for us to stay at his parents' house who were away at the time (he stayed elsewhere). I found myself in his bed, with pictures of myself and Siouxsie all over the walls. I didn't dare move lest I should leave a stray hair or fragments of myself in his bed. We got up early and beat a hasty retreat. This was perhaps the lowest point in what had once looked like a promising career.

Polestar had been set up as an independent record label to release our own recordings. We had no money and limited resources and operated on the basis of 'where there's a will, there's a way'. Robert and I attended an independent music seminar under the banner 'Umbrella' in Manchester. It was a boring event and the only person we spoke to was Rhys from the Welsh band Anhrefn, who later asked me to write lyrics for one of their songs. We were just about to leave when a chap called Abbo (previously in a band called UK Decay) introduced himself to us and said that he had a record label called Cat and Mouse, which operated out of Southern Studios in the Wood Green area of London. It looked like a residential house from the outside but inside it was a hive of activity. A recording studio,

Taking a break at Madhouse studio, Luton.

Poster for the Marquee, London, 27 April 1989.
Design by Paul Harvey.

record labels, offices and a music distribution company (SRD) operated from the premises, co-owned by sound engineer and producer John Loder. John was a friend of Penny Rimbaud, co-founder of the Anarcho-punk band Crass. I'd never listened to Crass as I perceived them to be punk hippies but they had recorded at Southern Studios and had sold a substantial amount of records on their own label, Crass Records, through SRD. Abbo expressed an interest in us recording an album for his own label and so we agreed.

We were struggling and needed some help. We were also due to release an album on our own personal band timeline. Abbo booked us into a Luton recording studio called Madhouse, where we recorded eight new backing tracks for 'This Thing Called Love', 'Another World', 'Pressure Zone', 'Time', 'Mr Money' for a B-side,

the Fred Neil song, 'Everybody's Talkin'' which we had been playing in our live set, and we re-recorded 'Don't Give Up' and 'No One Like You' with the live band. We then moved on to Southern Studios to do overdubs and vocals with John Loder, who tried to pressure me into signing my songs over to his publishing company. He used the leverage of threatening not to finish the album – a move I strongly resisted. There's a notion that independent record labels are somehow more virtuous than their major counterparts but this isn't always the case. Both operate in the same way. The only difference is that the former had less money to gamble; both have taken advantage of plenty of artists.

Around this time, Robert was pulled in by the dole who had noticed that he hadn't had a job for seven years. They immediately sent him for job interviews, but his

Heaton Park, Newcastle upon Tyne. Photograph by Kev Anderson.

family intervened and offered him a full-time job. It was now up to myself and Paul Harvey to return to Southern and we were determined to oversee the final mixes and completion of the album, which I'd named *Storm Clouds*. We'd organised some live dates to promote the album and added a keyboard player, a bespectacled eccentric known as L.J. ('Loud John', because he was so quiet). Dressed in his customary old man's suit, he played on the tour and we were supported by Carter USM, a duo who used a drum machine with tape loops, guitars and rap-style vocals over the top. They were working with Abbo and there was nothing happening for them at the time. The following year, they were championed by the music press and went on to have a successful career. Our final gig was at the new Marquee which had moved to Charing Cross Road. Before we went on, a water pipe

burst, flooding the dressing rooms in the basement but as far as I can remember, the gig went well. (Though Paul Harvey recently told me that we got absolutely slated in a review at that time.)

Just as the album was released, Abbo left Southern Studios to set up a management company with Linda Obadiah, wife of Nick Mander, an A&R man at EMI. Within a year, they had a worldwide hit on their hands with the single 'Unbelievable' by EMF. Our album, on the other hand, received very little promotion and was totally overlooked. I was 31 years old and the majority of the 1980s had, without doubt, been the most personally challenging and worst decade of my life. We were back to square one again and it was time for me to admit defeat, face the future, forget about making music and concentrate on making money.

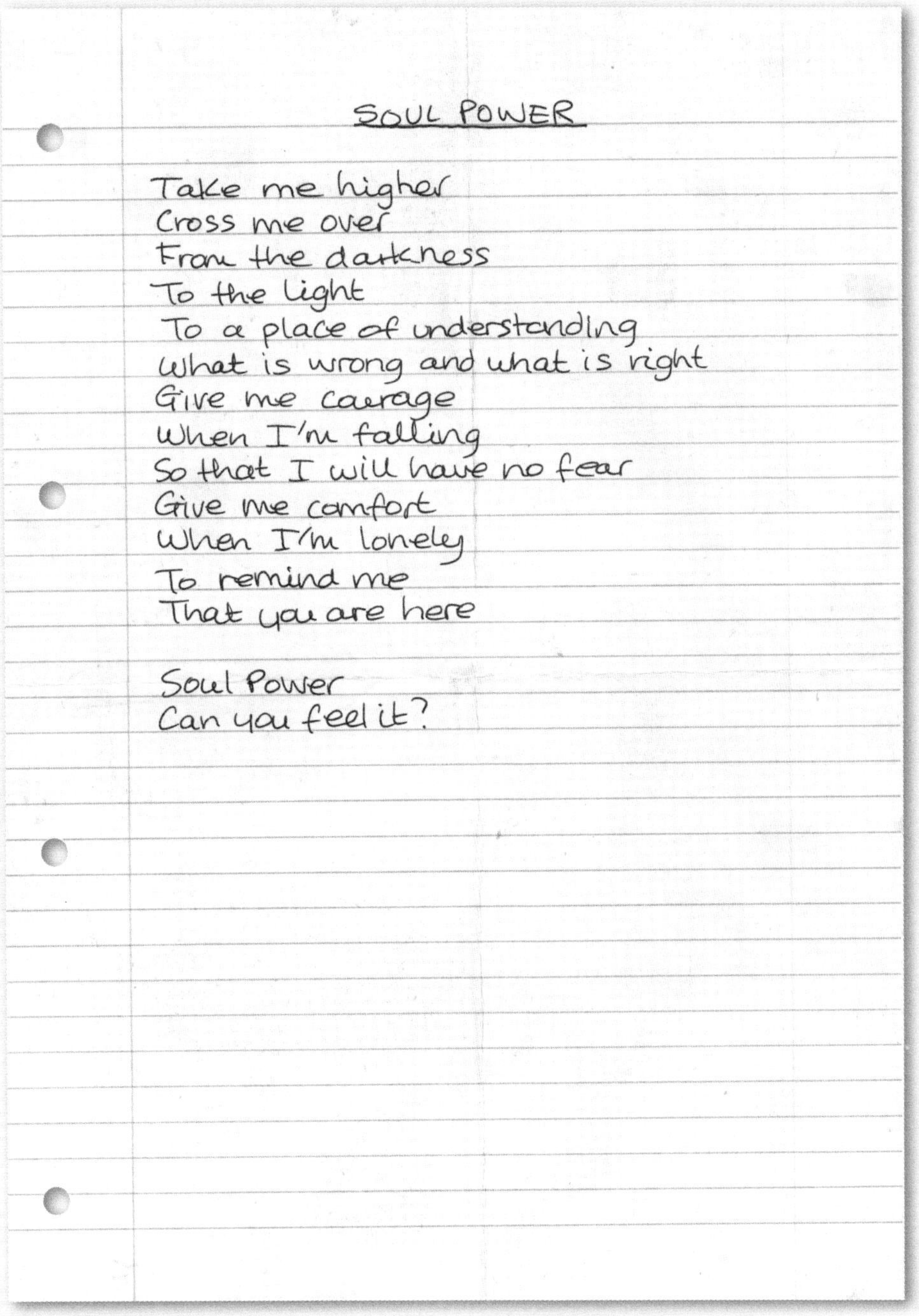

# SOUL POWER

Take me higher
Cross me over
From the darkness
To the light
To a place of understanding
What is wrong and what is right
Give me courage
When I'm falling
So that I will have no fear
Give me comfort
When I'm lonely
To remind me
That you are here

Soul Power
Can you feel it?

Tying the knot. Tapestry by Kate Thompson.

# CHAPTER EIGHT

# POLESTAR

**Now that Robert was working full time at the printers, we were in a position to apply for a mortgage and we bought a three bedroom upstairs Tyneside flat[1] near to where we already lived.** As we were signing the documents, I felt overwhelmed, as this was a big commitment and I'd signed papers in the past that had got me into trouble. I realised I would have to find a job to contribute to the mortgage payments, but my activities over the past twelve years had rendered me useless in the employment market. I aimed low and eventually got a job washing dishes three evenings a week in a local family-run Italian restaurant. Each five-hour shift was a continual onslaught of dirty crockery, glasses, cutlery and pans, which I loaded into a dishwasher or washed by hand. At the end of the shift, a mountain of dirty pans would arrive to be cleared before I could leave. It was both soul-destroying and character-building, and put me right back into the real world. None of the staff had a clue who I was or what I'd done in the past. I thought I'd been rumbled when the chef asked if I got out on the road much these days. I answered 'no' then realised he was referring to the pubs on Shields Road. It was better for me to remain anonymous, and they just took me as I was, without any preconceived ideas.

Since moving to Newcastle, I'd harboured a pipe dream of opening a music rehearsal studio. I was tired of fronting up bands and wanted something more tangible and solid in my life. I wanted to create a supportive space where bands could come together as more of a music community. The Ministry in Liverpool was a good example of a hub for local musicians and there was a lack of this type of dedicated facility in Newcastle. I would periodically check the council's commercial property listings even though I had no money. I enquired about a property on City Road near Newcastle's quayside; it had already been let but the private landlord directed me to another of his buildings, an old red-brick Victorian school on Stepney Road, Shieldfield. It had closed as a school prior to World War Two and had been used to house prisoners of war; an underground warren of bricked-up air raid shelters ran along the length of the back of the building. After the war, it was used as laboratories for Berger Paints and now, a car body repair shop, Uptin Motors, occupied the middle section, with the North and South Wings empty and derelict.

I was shown around the South Wing; there was a tower, a creepy basement with toilets, a ground floor with one room, a first floor with two rooms and a second floor with one room, all around a central pillar with stone steps in a spiral from top to bottom. The landlord offered a three-year lease with a rent-free period if I supplied an alarm system, roller shutters, doors and generally did the place up. Security grants were available at the time and I applied for a new business start-up grant, submitting a comprehensive business plan; I was awarded £2,500. I attempted to join the Enterprise Allowance Scheme, which guaranteed £40 per week for a year, but was turned down because I was living with Robert and they wouldn't acknowledge that I was a separate person. I appealed the decision and took it to a tribunal where I was cross-examined by three people about my personal living arrangements; I eventually swung it in my favour.

Everything was set up and I was due to sign the three-year lease. Robert was panicking as this was a high-risk gamble that would leave us in deep financial trouble if the enterprise failed. I was determined to make it work, so I hung up my rubber gloves at the restaurant, and, in February 1990, took a massive leap of faith to establish and run my own business, Polestar Rehearsal Studios. Polestar had been the name of our record label, a monicker I'd come up with that referred to the bright North Star, Polaris, and our northern location.

The building had been unoccupied for years and was filthy and in a poor condition but, with the help of family and friends, it was cleaned, painted, and the security systems and telephone line installed. The ground floor room was the reception and the two first

1. A Tyneside flat is a form of single-storey domestic housing within a two-storey terrace which first appeared in the 1860s.

How I spent my 31st birthday.

floor rooms were rehearsal studios. The top room was unusable for rehearsals as there was no fire escape. It wasn't long before the landlord wanted his first month's rent so I had to open there and then. We'd equipped the rooms with second-hand drum kits, amplifiers and PA systems, but we couldn't afford carpets. The grant money had all been spent and I asked to borrow £500 from my parents to pay the legal fees for the lease. Serendipitously, they'd just had a life insurance policy come to fruition and were going to give me that amount anyway. At last, things seemed to be falling into place and moving in the right direction.

Robert printed up leaflets which I distributed around the local music shops, record shops, venues and pubs, and I took out small ads in the local newspaper. Another rehearsal studio had opened about three months earlier, so I would have to compete for customers. Before the days of mobile phones, computers or the internet, I went to Polestar every day and willed the phone to ring.

The first band arrived, a group called Long Tall Shortie who'd discovered us through word of mouth. A steady trickle of bands followed: established bands, new bands just forming, young and old. Behind the reception desk, I took the bookings, supplied them with equipment and made cups of tea. Some knew about my past, others didn't, but I didn't care and was happy to be in the background. I was on a learning curve and determined to make a success of this new venture. We were still rehearsing with our own band but didn't have any major plans. Then came the break-ins.

A gang of kids was patrolling the area and would frequently steal cars and burn them out on the back field. This type of activity was synonymous with the

Opposite page: Original Polestar entrance.

Polestar ★

Polestar
REHEARSAL STUDIOS

For Details and Booking
Telephone:
130 1831 or 265 2531

Polestar, Uplin House, Stepney Road, Shieldfield,
Newcastle upon Tyne. NE1 2PZ.

times as the UK was once again in recession, with rising (youth) unemployment. They entered the building through a high side window, wrecked the alarm system, kicked in every door and stole equipment from the studio rooms. They also took Robert's Music Man bass guitar, my Fender Telecaster, Paul's guitar and pedal boards and my Webley air pistol, all of which were locked in a cupboard in reception. It was a real blow but we were insured. We needed a new alarm system, replaced damaged doors and my father, being a blacksmith and welder, installed iron bars to the window. They broke in again a few weeks later, hacksawed through the bars, wrecked another alarm system, spray painted the walls in every room and stole all of the confectionary from reception. This was all during the first three months of opening. We changed the alarm system again, upgrading it with a new company, bricked up the side window and my father installed three barred gates at intervals down the stairs and bars on the reception window. It now resembled a prison but was finally secure. The ringleader of the gang was identified, separated from his followers, and we didn't experience any more trouble.

New bands were forming as the city emerged from eleven years of Thatcher's tyrannical rule, and the studios got busier. For the third time in eleven years, Robert asked me to marry him. I had been traumatised by my previous experience but realised that this was his final proposal and agreed, on the condition that I would retain my own name. The week before the wedding, Martin Stephenson (The Daintees) asked me to sing on *The Boy's Heart*, an album he was recording at Fred Purser's studio Trinity Heights with Lenny Kaye of the Patti Smith Group producing. I was a big fan of the band and it was amazing to meet him, especially in the guise of working with him as a fellow artist. Lenny knew all about my musical past and Penetration's cover of the song 'Free Money', and he sometimes gave us shout-outs at Patti Smith gigs. The timing was perfect as Lenny was still in town when Robert and I exchanged wedding vows at the Civic Centre on 7 March 1992. He attended our evening reception at Polestar before returning to the USA.

Within a year I was pregnant. At 34, this was a whole new world to me; I'd never had any close contact with babies or children. I carried on as normal, working at the studio, lugging drum kits and amps about as my belly grew bigger and bigger. It was only when I attended an antenatal class with other mums-to-be that the reality of the situation finally dawned. I had no idea what lay ahead but vowed that it wouldn't change my life! After nineteen hours of hard labour and diamorphine, the final push was like passing a bowling ball as our son entered the world. The midwife put him straight onto my stomach but he was lifeless, so they immediately took him away and began resuscitation. Robert was in a state of shock and I was oblivious to what was going on. Alex finally took his first breath. They said that he was lucky to have two knots in his umbilical cord, which I took to be a good omen. What they meant was that he was lucky to be alive!

I felt like I'd been hit by a bus, but there was no time for self-pity. Breasts were filling with milk and babies needed feeding. The other mothers on the ward talked me through my first nappy-change as I didn't have a clue. Baby would sleep and then wake up crying – rhythmic and unnerving, the hormones in my brain reacting on high alert. Robert was working all day so I was on my own with a new baby and found it difficult to leave the house. I'd stayed in touch with a few mothers from the class: they'd all had boys and were a great source of mutual support. I still had to work at the studio, so I took Alex with me and worked evenings when Robert got back. When Alex was only a few months old, Carlton Sandercock (Easy Action/Trident Records) got in touch with a view to releasing the Invisible Girls album on CD. We travelled to London with our young baby, and did a series of interviews to promote the release.

We met up with the members of Penetration for the first time in fifteen years when Carlton wanted to release the album *penetration* on CD. Whispers of getting the band back together floated through the air like stale cigarette smoke. I wasn't interested. I was concentrating on establishing my own business and looking after a young child.

Willing the phone to ring.

We spotted a three-bedroom Victorian terraced house for sale, still in the Heaton area of Newcastle. The property needed complete renovation, and the old lady living there was running the TV from a round Bakelite light switch, carpet samples covered the floor – everything needed replacing. We put in a low offer as there was so much work to be done and the offer was accepted. We sold our flat and rented somewhere for four months while the house was ripped apart by builders and put back together again. Alex was still a toddler when we moved in. We'd only been living there for a few months when I realised I was pregnant again. It took me about a week to come to terms with this, knowing the amount of work involved in looking after young children and keeping a business running. I was 37 years old when Grace was born on 29 December 1995.

The studios were busy – a reflection of the city's musical activity. Riverside was now on the national touring circuit with bands playing there every night. Local pubs such as the Broken Doll, Cumberland Arms, The Cooperage and the Bridge Hotel were regular venues. Bands such as Crane, Puppy Fat, Hug, The Songs and others had an authenticity about them, and were beginning to develop a Newcastle 'sound', abrasive and tough. Local listings mag *Paint It Red* promoted the burgeoning scene. A&R scouts would visit our studios, sniffing out potential talent, but that was as far as it got. You would have to show your face in London before you could be taken seriously (or not) and bands were finding it difficult to get out of the local area.

The studios were a hub of musical activity, but any profits we made were reinvested in better equipment, carpets and advertising. I discovered that we could extend into a room at the front of the building on the ground floor, so this became our reception and there was a small room into which we installed our eight-track recording equipment. The old reception was used as a third rehearsal room and was themed in green, further enlivening our brightly colour-coded music facility.

I was busy looking after two young children and running the studios and wasn't particularly interested in the general state of music. I could see trends coming and going, but it seemed to be business as usual as far as the industry was concerned. During 1997, a band called Giro were one of a steady stream of bands rehearsing at Polestar. Their music incorporated elements of The Stone Roses, Radiohead, Oasis, psychedelia, chav and rave culture. Out of the blue, I received a phone call from a friend of Abbo, an Irish chap called Pete McCarthy who'd bumped into members of the band as they touted their demo around the London record companies. He enthusiastically proclaimed that this band were going to be 'bigger than The Beatles!' They were a fairly dodgy bunch but he insisted that there was music business interest in them, and he specifically wanted me to manage them. I'd never managed a band before and it wasn't something on my bucket list. I knew how the whole thing worked but hadn't been on the other side of the fence. Perhaps I could learn something from it and gain some insight into what had gone on with my own band. Perhaps there was money to be made with this malarkey after all. Pete was very persuasive and against my better judgement I agreed to take on the challenge.

As usual, I went about the task in my own way, learning as I went along and using common sense as guidance. I thought the band should change their name, as Giro referred to dole cheques, which didn't exactly give off a successful vibe, plus there was a prog-rock band who already had the name, so they changed it to Solavox, referencing 1970s hi-fi speakers. Their songs were well-written, melodic and accessible with dark undertones. I organised a show at Riverside and Pete attended with Kate Thompson from PolyGram/ Island Publishing, who immediately offered the band a publishing deal and they proved to be extremely supportive of both myself and the band. The advance was used to buy new clothes and instruments and a photo session was conducted. Robert recorded demos

With Alex, London 1994. Photograph by Glenn Miles.

with them and a deposit was paid on a rented flat, as some of the band members were homeless. I would be working into the early hours preparing press packages and then doing the school run. I had signed a contract with the band, taken management commission and was committed to doing the job to the best of my ability.

Abbo, who was now working for Richard Branson's new V2 label, got in touch to say that he wanted to sign local techno trio Elastik Trickery, who sometimes played with Solavox. Their lengthy techno instrumentals contained elements of dub and were creative, interesting and artful. Pete McCarthy had played Abbo a recording of their material and he wanted me to manage them. I knew nothing about the techno scene and told him so, but he was adamant and arrived in Newcastle by the end of the week to meet up with the band, offering them a recording contract on the spot. It was an unexpected turn of events and the band were as surprised as I was. I agreed to get involved as I understood that this would initially be a studio-based project. Their advance would be used to buy new equipment and set up a recording space to record an album. That seemed fairly straightforward. I rented a room for them in the Off Quay building. The night before they were due to move in, all of the new equipment was stolen from their flat. Luckily I was doing my job and had already had it insured, but it was a big blow for the band.

Word must have been circulating that I was managing bands, as a call came through from Mark Hobrough at Jealous Records in London, who asked me to manage South Shields band January Blue. Their music was in the vein of the Verve and Spiritualised but had more mainstream appeal thanks to their singer's soulful voice. The band were great musicians, full of potential and had been driven enough to get this far; they also had a record label who believed in them and a booking agent for live shows. I was starting to look at things through a mercenary's eyes – it wasn't about whether I liked the music or not. I would do my best for the band and believed at the time that it would benefit all of the bands by creating more contacts and opportunities in the bigger scheme of things. Initially, I thought that their name was sad and negative so they changed it to New Rising. They had recorded and were about to release a 7″ single called 'Drowning Reason', and Mark had put together a team to promote the record. It was favourably received by the radio stations and press. They'd filmed a video in the air raid shelter at the back of Polestar and I'd managed to get them a Firkin Tour – a chain of pub venues around the country. It was all going well.

I was managing three bands, running rehearsal studios, had rented an office at the Off Quay building for the management and was helping out our guitarist Paul Harvey's band, Nancy Bone. Alex was now at school and Grace was with a childminder for two days a week. As if I didn't have enough on my plate, I'd also teamed up with another local management company called Bright Orange Biscuit to promote a monthly club night called 'Twang' at the Bridge Hotel.

Ouseburn, late 1990s. Photograph by Leanne Holcroft.

This gave us a platform to promote our own bands, showcase up-and-coming bands and raise the profile of the rehearsal studios. There was quite a lot of work involved: three bands who complemented each other were chosen for the bill from the strength of their demos. Robert designed and printed the posters, which we distributed around the city, and adverts were placed in the monthly listings mags. On the day of the show, a good-quality PA system and lights were hired in and the entrance fee was £3. We as promoters received a cut of the bar takings, so any profits after expenses for the show were split fairly between the bands. It was important to me, on the other side of the fence, that the bands were treated well. Without them, there is no show. The profit we made as promoters was reinvested into extending the stage and buying a new lighting rig. It was all done in good faith and there was enough for

Sound City Twang poster. Design by Paul Harvey.

everybody. The events were always well attended and a good night had by all.

Regal Records came to Polestar to see Solavox with the view to releasing a single. The band managed to get the A&R man completely stoned before pouring him back on the train to London. I'd booked a gig at the Barfly in London so that his boss could see the band and make a decision. When we visited their offices the day before, they seemed keen but the band blew their chances at the show: singer Paul had his back to the audience the whole time and we didn't hear from Regal Records again. Luckily the band's publisher PolyGram/Island was willing to put up the money for them to record a 7" single to try and get the ball rolling. 'California Sunshine' was recorded at Trinity Heights (Fred's studio), and we released it on Polestar Records through the Cartel, with artwork by Paul Harvey.

Meanwhile, Elastik Trickery had finally replaced the stolen equipment, set up their studio and were working on new material. They delivered some new tracks to Abbo which weren't to his liking as he preferred the original demo tape. I thought they sounded great, but this negative response from the record company sent the band into a spiral of low confidence that eventually led to their split. The road to rock'n'roll stardom is littered with the broken bones of bands that might have been, their hopes and dreams shattered before they even get started.

My other management signing, New Rising, attempted to record new songs to follow up 'Drowning Reason' with a producer at the residential studio Monnow Valley in Wales. They ran into difficulty when they recorded backing tracks that were so fast the singer was unable to fit in his words. Mark Hobrough, from their label Jealous Records, was furious and headed up to Polestar for a meeting with the band and myself. He was demanding that they come up with a set of new songs by the following week, when he would return to hear the results. Their budget had been wasted on the scrapped Monnow Valley session and they would now have to go into a cheaper studio. Things were starting to unravel. The band had just signed to EMI Publishing and were due to record demos for them, so I sent them money to hire a van. They spent this money on repairing their own van, which duly broke down halfway to London. I was angry, it was all becoming too much.

Everything came to a head the week that Sound City arrived in Newcastle in late October 1998. Hosted by John Peel for the BBC, it was a week of gigs, events and seminars to publicise local promoters, music venues and talent. Riverside was central to the event, with live broadcasts on Radio 1 from a selection of national bands. The city was buzzing and the studio was a hive of activity as bands prepared for the programme of gigs; it was a rare opportunity, when the spotlight and attention was on Newcastle's music community.

'Twang' was hosting three bands each night at the Bridge Hotel. Only one local band had made it on to the main event at Riverside, and that was Solavox. The week before the gig, they ejected their singer and

London, 1994. Photograph by Glenn Miles.

replaced him with their young keyboard player and Paul Harvey on guitar. I couldn't tell anyone before the show and people in the audience were shocked when they saw the line-up change. The final straw came when I was expected to run around all day giving them lifts and sorting out their equipment. I left the venue in the middle of their set and went to Polestar as I was so pissed off and angry. The next day, I rang all three bands and terminated my involvement, prepared all of their accounts, dotting the i's and crossing the t's, delivered boxes of paperwork, tapes and press material to each band and was done with band management forever. I had taken on far too much and was feeling ill with stomach pains, headaches and insomnia. After Sound City, the city felt deflated as bands realised that the event was more about promoting the BBC, and once more there was nothing to work towards. As a result, the studios were quiet, but this suited me fine – I needed to recover.

We had a Halloween party arranged at Polestar and learned three Roky Erickson songs 'Stand For the Fire Demon', 'Creature With the Atom Brain' and 'Night Of the Vampire' to perform on the night, with Robert on bass, Paul Harvey on guitar and Jason Cox (Solavox) on drums. Afterwards, we recorded these songs on our newly upgraded 16-track recording equipment and released a CD on Polestar entitled 'Halloween 2000'. It felt good to be doing something for myself again – singing and being creative instead of running around after other people. I was even contemplating enrolling in a college course to study reflexology, as I felt the need to do something totally different that would lead to a more relaxing existence. I'd cleared the decks, wiped the slate clean, and the future was an open book. After all, we were now at the start of a new millennium.

# CHAPTER NINE
# BEAT GOES ON

Burning bridges doesn't mean that you can't return where you came from...[1]

**At the beginning of 2001, I was busy with my life and rarely thought about Penetration.** I was only ever reminded if a fan recalled seeing us in the past, or a retrospective article appeared in the music press during the days before social media. Punk had been analysed to death by fans, academics and journalists who'd picked at the flesh, and then the bones, to the point that all that remained was a pile of dust. I wasn't interested in the punk revival – I *lived* through those times and my own punk past had followed me around like a ghost.

I'd met Neale again whilst managing Solavox when they played at a small venue in Soho that he was running, and I started to receive letters from him suggesting we reform Penetration for a one-off London or Newcastle show. I wasn't interested and couldn't see the point of putting ourselves into the public realm with minimum rehearsals just for one show. But he wasn't deterred. Neale got in touch again during the same week that Gary Smallman also rang out of the blue – you guessed it – wanting to get the band back together. Was the Universe trying to tell me something, or were people just bored with their lives and craving some excitement? I opened the door and gave it some thought.

We got in touch with Fred and arranged a rehearsal at Polestar with the five members. I couldn't imagine singing those songs from my youth but was curious about how it would sound and feel after 21 years of not playing together. Either I would find it enjoyable, or close the door to it once and for all.

We struck up the first song, the musical parts appearing miraculously from the dark recesses of our memories where they had been stored for all those years. It was understandably rusty and I didn't have the stamina to sing a whole song, but as we worked through our old repertoire it was apparent that with more rehearsals, we could bring the set back together.

I saw it as a challenge to get the music back up to the standard we'd achieved before splitting up, which was quite a high bar.

Neale returned to London and Fred was gracious enough to tell us he didn't have time to commit. Gary, Robert and I got together once a week to rehearse drums, bass and vocals, and soon we were ready to add guitars. For someone so keen to reunite, Neale made no arrangements to attend another rehearsal even though he knew that we had been working on the music. I rang him to ask if we were doing this or not. He still talked about a one-off gig and was working full time, as we all were, but he didn't materialise, so we decided to move on without him.

We asked Paul Harvey to learn Neale's guitar parts and auditioned Steve Wallace from the band Automatic who was technically proficient, experienced and was able to reproduce Fred's unusual and complicated guitar work. Both players understood and respected the musical legacy of Penetration. We rehearsed once a week and eventually had a full live set in place. I was enjoying singing again, but the band had to fit in with our personal lives. Chasing carrots on sticks – a game much-beloved of the music industry – wasn't an option.

At the same time as reforming the band, I had enrolled onto a one-year diploma course in reflexology, anatomy and physiology at Newcastle College one day a week. Both kids were at school, the studios were well established and I wanted to do something completely different that would stretch my brain and teach me new skills. It was a fascinating subject, and my mind was blown on several occasions with the so-called alternative health therapy. I learned new Greek/Latin-based words that were difficult to remember, and the coursework enhanced my self-discipline. Even though I was now a trained reflexologist, enjoyed the practice and was good at it, I had no time to operate professionally and I only treated family and friends. I was overweight at the time from my pregnancy days and embarked on a healthy eating regime which shed

1. *'Shout Above the Noise'.*
Opposite page: Photograph by Angela Carrington.

Gary Smallman, Paul Harvey, me, Steve Wallace, Robert Blamire: the reformed Penetration. Photograph by Carol Lynn.

the extra pounds, making me feel more positive. At home, we were in the middle of a loft conversion and things were looking up. I'd invested in myself and was feeling happy and healthy.

Our first gig with the new line-up was booked in the upstairs room of the Chillingham Arms pub in Heaton on 1 December 2001. We didn't advertise and only told a few people that we were playing – it was more an exercise for ourselves to set up the equipment and play the songs in a public space. A small crowd attended and it felt like second nature to be singing and performing again; it was amazing that I was still able to do this at 43 years of age. What would my younger self have thought to see ourselves back with Penetration? We called people in their mid-20s 'old farts' and here we were now, *ancient* farts. I believe she would have said, 'Go lady! You've got balls – you are resolving unfinished business'.

And I was, although I had no idea where Penetration stood in the current scheme of things.

We booked another show in early January at a small pub venue called Sinatras in Sunderland. It was like going back to the early days, a return to the primitive conditions we'd all had to get used to during the 'punk rock wars', but we were still finding our feet, and the crowd was enthusiastic. Trillians, a 300-capacity venue in Newcastle, was the first properly publicised show that we played, and it sold out immediately with a great audience. This restored our confidence, reassuring us that there was still interest in the band after all these years.

The organisers of the Holidays In The Sun punk festival approached us to play the following summer at Blackpool Winter Gardens, an impressive late-1800s building with seven indoor venues including theatres, halls and the Empress Ballroom. We were reluctant as we were out of the loop and quite cynical, as original punks, to see that the bill was mostly made up of post-1980s hardcore bands, and the only woman on the bill was Beki Bondage from Vice Squad. We arrived there just in time to play our set which went down well but we didn't stick around and left straight after. Over the years, the annual four-day event, which we've played many times since, has become a great gathering for the punk community. It changed its name to Rebellion Festival, has expanded and grown, and is now the biggest punk/alternative music festival in the world, still run by the same people and without corporate involvement.

After our gig at the Victoria Inn in Derby, Robert received a phone call from a disgruntled Neale who'd found out that we'd gone ahead with the band, added other members and were doing gigs without him. The door had been open for Neale but we hadn't heard from him in months. He sent letters to our home to reiterate his feelings of anger, disappointment and bitterness calling us 'Penetraitors'. The opportunity for reconciliation had passed him by and he seemed to be blaming the band for his own failures and frustrations. Fantasy versus reality.

Our first London gig was at the Underworld in Camden. I was surprised to see my ex-husband Peter and his sister in the audience, but didn't get chance to speak to them afterwards as the aggressive security staff wanted us out of the building as quickly as possible, to make way for the club night that followed; there was a large queue of people waiting outside. As we loaded our gear into the van, we were horrified to learn that someone had set fire to a homeless person lying in a doorway. He was going up in flames and everyone just stood there laughing. Steve got involved and managed to put out the fire but was in a state of shock and disbelief, as we all were, at the callousness of the human race.

We played Newcastle University at the end of 2002 and the gig was filmed and edited by Carol Lynn, independent filmmaker, friend and partner of Paul Harvey. Robert recorded and mixed the soundtrack in our own studio. It was an achievement considering we had no budget and we released it as a DVD on Polestar with the title, *Penetration-Re-Animated: Celebrating 23 Years Out of the Music Business.*

The band took second place to our everyday lives, although we'd managed to play nine shows in 2003, the most memorable being Brixham Punk Aid Festival at Wall Park Holiday Centre (Pontins) in South Devon with The Damned, Dead Kennedys, and John Otway amongst others on the bill. When we were first approached by the promoter Tim Scargill, we said it was too far away, but he offered to provide a sleeper bus so we could turn it into an adventure and take our kids with us. At 10 and 7 years old, our children had very little knowledge of our history in music but were most impressed when a double-decker bus with beds pulled up outside of Polestar. During our set, they were standing at the side of the stage when the audience safety barrier broke. Health and safety didn't seem to be an issue, but in typical punk make-do-and-mend style, picnic tables from outside were passed above the heads of the crowd and installed as makeshift barriers and we carried on playing as though nothing had happened. The next day, we visited Brixham Harbour to see the Golden Hind – the sixteenth-century sailing ship captained by Sir Francis Drake – then we set off on the long journey home. At least we had beds and could sleep on the way back.

We were a heritage punk band now, playing for our own enjoyment rather than trying to re-establish any type of career comeback. We were mainly offered to play punk festivals, usually well-organised all-day events in large venues, professionally staged with decent dressing room facilities, a far cry from the usual toilets and broom cupboards. I wasn't particularly interested in the genre anymore and found it to be musically and visually predictable, not to mention still male-dominated. I was very much a woman alone in the band line-ups, although I did connect with and receive support from female fans in the audience. I always wondered how Penetration would fare alongside these hardcore punk bands, but we usually went down well, as our melodic style was in complete contrast to the shouty punk of most of the other bands. Robert would arrange small club dates leading up to these events where nothing much had changed in our time away. It followed the same routine: pick up the van, pack the van, get into the van, eat overpriced fast food at motorway services, drive for miles, arrive at some dark smelly venue, unpack gear, soundcheck, hang about in some tiny dressing room with no sink or mirror and sometimes no lights, perform our set, reload the van and stop at some soulless service station in the middle of the night, unpack gear and get to bed as dawn was breaking. If we were too far from home, we'd stay in budget hotels, Premier Inns or Travelodges. I didn't want to make a habit of this activity; the only part I enjoyed was the performance. We were hardly back in full-time action but whenever we played it was a special event, the audiences were appreciative and loved the band, and this made it all worthwhile.

I was 46 in 2004, standing in the middle of two generations; my young family and my elderly parents. On a weekly visit to my parents' house, I discovered that my father had lost the use of his right hand and we thought that he'd had a stroke. When the results of brain scans came back a few days later, we were devastated to learn that he had several inoperable brain tumours. Over the space of a month, he couldn't walk, speak or eat, just as the doctors had predicted. His last few days were spent in a hospice as my mother couldn't cope. On my last visit, he scanned every inch of my face as if committing all the details to memory. He took hold of my hand and squeezed it with an iron grip. I said, 'You've still got the grip,' referring to his days as a blacksmith. Hours later, he was gone.

I hold on tightly to your hand...[2]

As I took time out to grieve and adjust to the family's loss, the band was put on hold. When we did eventually reconvene, Gary Smallman decided to leave the band. He was involved in his own building project, was having dizzy spells in rehearsals and later developed tendonitis in his wrists which made drumming painful. Our sound engineer Graham Kay stepped into the breach. Paul left the band due to work commitments and was replaced by

Billy Gilbert, a local guitarist who'd played with Steve. His tenure was short-lived and when we received a text to say that he was 'knocking it on the uncle Ned (head)', he was replaced by Brian Atkinson, guitarist with the Coyote Men, Handsome Dicks, Country Irregulars and many other garage/rockabilly bands he has put together over the years.

We hadn't really applied ourselves to writing new material but made an effort in 2007 with this line-up and recorded a 7″ single, 'Our World'/'Sea Song' in our own upgraded 16-track recording studio at Polestar, releasing it on red and black vinyl through the independent label Damaged Goods in 2008. We only played about six gigs that year but the Shay pub in Halifax stands out for all the wrong reasons. We arrived to find that there was no stage and we had to set up on an old carpet with a Seventies stone fireplace behind us. Above was a three-globe domestic light fitting with only two bulbs working. The PA was supplied by the local butcher who hadn't finished work yet, and the kind of lightweight chrome frame you'd normally find in a restaurant carvery was set up as the safety barrier. I had to go into a room upstairs to get changed, then sat in the van until the band phoned me when they were about to start. I could hear the opening chug of 'Shout Above the Noise' and made my way from the van, pushed through the audience and arrived on cue for my singing. It was absolutely primal, raw and blistering and was probably the nearest you could get to an early punk rock gig. Next door was the football ground, The Shay Stadium, and this gig was forever to be known as our very own Shay Stadium, the antithesis of the New York Shea Stadium where The Beatles famously played. We laughed all the way home, my eye make-up smudged like a panda, at the absurdity of it all.

We managed to arrange and play ten shows in 2009, most notably Aylesbury Friars with Stiff Little Fingers. It was the final show at the iconic music venue before it was closed down and relocated. Promoter David Stopps greeted us in his customary white suit, just like the old days, and I was surprised and delighted to receive an award at the end of the night. The Friars Heroes Award was for the 40th Anniversary of the venue. It was a glass

2. 'Judgement Day'.

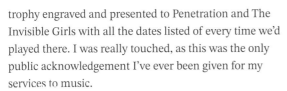

Damaged Goods 7" single sleeves.

trophy engraved and presented to Penetration and The Invisible Girls with all the dates listed of every time we'd played there. I was really touched, as this was the only public acknowledgement I've ever been given for my services to music.

Storm clouds were gathering in the world's financial markets, and the collapse of Lehman Brothers in the USA and the Newcastle-based Northern Rock had an immediate effect on my business. We had been facilitating 54 bands per week, had created a fourth rehearsal studio in the basement and I had only just taken on a full-time employee. The minute that the so-called credit crunch was announced, tumbleweeds appeared in the building instead of regular customers and I wondered if another rehearsal studio had opened up and ushered away all of the bands. It picked up slightly then plateaued for a full year as I worked to cover the rent, business rates, insurance, utility bills and sundry expenses. I thought that, after eighteen years, this was the end of Polestar Rehearsal Studios.

One Friday, Robert was driving along St Michael's Road in Byker, a working-class area in east Newcastle that was once home to workers in the shipbuilding industry. The terraced rows had been demolished

and replaced in the 1970s by the Byker Wall, a public housing estate designed by architect Ralph Erskine and sanctioned by disgraced council leader T. Dan Smith. He spotted a large council building for sale, so I made an appointment that afternoon and viewed the abandoned property. It had stood empty for eight years and had previously been a school dinner depot, where they made and supplied meals to the local schools. The vandals had been in and stripped out all of the wiring and anything that could be weighed in for scrap. The electricity, water, gas and phone lines had all been disconnected from the site. I only had four days to make an offer, write a full business plan and provide financial accountability as the sealed bids had to be in by 10.30 a.m. on Wednesday. We handed in the proposal at the last minute and waited...

Earlier that year, we'd recorded another 7" single – 'The Feeling'/ 'Guilty' – released on yellow-and-black vinyl through Damaged Goods, and we embarked on a twelve-date tour supporting Stiff Little Fingers. We'd played with them before and always got on well. The first date was in Oxford and Brian was to be arriving from Spain where he had been playing with one of his other bands. By soundcheck time there was still no

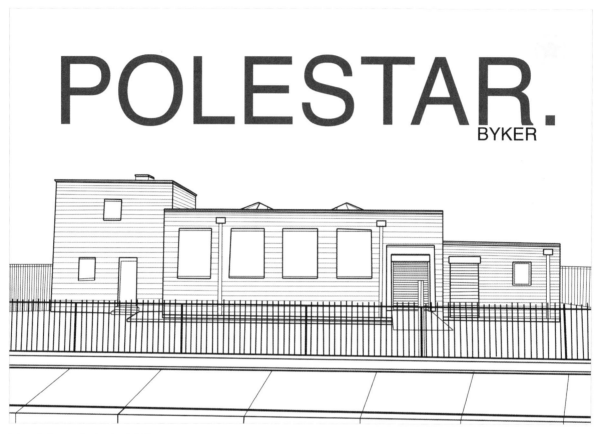

New Polestar. Art by Jack Tulley.

sign of him and we were beginning to panic, as our music relies on two integrated guitar parts. When he did arrive, he was in no fit state but we managed to get through the set. Not the most encouraging start to the tour. Another stop on the tour saw us playing at an unusual venue: the Leamington Spa Assembly Rooms. The old building had been decorated by Laurence Llewelyn-Bowen from the TV show *Changing Rooms*. The colour scheme was in various shades of rich blue and metallic silver; lavish blue drapes framed the stage and painted marble effect panels clashed with funky blue wallpaper. The backstage area was huge and housed what they said was Tammy Wynette's gypsy caravan, dodgem cars and other fairground memorabilia. We played fifteen live shows that year, which took a lot of effort from our point of view, but everything had gone well and we'd enjoyed it.

In my personal life, my mother had been diagnosed with bladder cancer eighteen months previously, and the doctors said that it was inoperable. She received radiotherapy treatment in the beginning but eventually, she was finding it difficult to walk and had to use a wheelchair. She came to see the band play at Sunderland's Split Festival in October 2009 and said, 'I don't know where you get the energy from.' We received confirmation that our bid for the commercial property had been successful and I took her along to see it. She could see the amount of work involved and simply said, 'You'll do it, Pauline,' knowing that once I put my mind to something, I'll see it through. Her health deteriorated in the months that followed, she passed away and didn't get to see us move in. I was pleased that at least she'd seen the building and had given me her blessing, but I missed her terribly.

Building work commenced at the depot in Byker. I had taken out a commercial mortgage with the bank and it was a leap of faith – a sink or swim situation. The property was huge and we enlisted local builder Neil Barton and his son Neil to oversee the project, with bricklayers, electricians and plumbers brought in when required. Windows were bricked up and four soundproofed rooms were built into the big empty space at the back of the building. It was a cold winter when work began, with no electricity on site, so a generator was used for power and cold water was accessed through one tap for the whole building. It was a big (and still ongoing) project. It took seven months to get the rehearsal rooms, reception, wiring, plumbing, alarm system and all utilities, ready for Polestar to move in.

We were still operating from Uptin House and the move was seamless as we finished the last booking at the old premises, commencing the next booking the following day at the Depot. Work began on the front of the building to create a studio to rent out and a large studio space for the band Maxïmo Park to lease. We ran out of money to renovate the rest of the building and were plagued with leaking roofs and collapsed ceilings, but at least we owned the property and had more control with regard to overheads for the rehearsal studios.

A new phase began. I was relieved and happy that we'd managed to get through all of the hurdles and that it had opened up new possibilities for our business. We tried to diversify and get into educational training but I didn't understand how it worked. Instead, I applied for and received a grant to set up and run Byker Community Choir which would operate from Polestar for two hours each week. Anyone could attend – there was no criteria for joining. I'd never been in a choir before but I believe that singing is one of the most therapeutic activities for stress, depression, self-confidence and social interaction. From my own point of view, when I'm singing, it's the only time that I can lose myself and my inhibitions, forget my worries and truly experience living in the moment. I applied my own ideas about how it should be done

and chose uplifting songs, working out three-part harmonies as we sang *a cappella*, which is a great discipline for timing and staying in tune. We performed at the Americana Festival at the Sage Gateshead, local care homes, parks and church halls. As time went by, membership dwindled as people had other commitments but a core of about eight remained. Unlike the punk scene, the choir was dominated by women and there was only one male member. He was shy and introverted when he first joined but by the end, he'd taught himself to play acoustic guitar and perform on his own. It was a joy to sing with the choir, human voices in harmony and unity, magical moments with no ulterior motive, and we all learned something from the experience.

Things started to get busy with Penetration again in 2012. Graham Kay had left the band to work full-time with the singer-songwriter Frank Turner, and he was replaced with Kev Hodgson on drums. We played eleven shows, including Rebellion Festival and Durham Punk Festival. Brian left the band and Paul Harvey re-joined.

I was approached by Martin Stephenson, who was organising an event in Gateshead with Viv Albertine (The Slits), Gina Birch (The Raincoats) and Helen McCookerybook (The Chefs), and he was asking me to perform a solo acoustic set. I didn't commit as this was something I'd never done before, but when I saw my name on the poster, I went into panic mode. I hadn't been onstage without a band and hadn't played guitar for years, and the date was fast approaching. I learned two of my own songs and 'Can't Get You Out Of My Head' by Kylie Minogue – a great song that would be totally unexpected. I'd never met any of these female punk contemporaries before, although they all knew each other and had already stepped out as solo performers. They were encouraging and supportive as I took to the stage with my acoustic guitar. I was so nervous and out of my comfort zone that I was trembling from head to foot as I began playing, but I found the experience strangely exhilarating and liberating, and later decided to expand my set and organise some more gigs. It was another learning

Solo acoustic gig poster. Design by Robert Blamire.

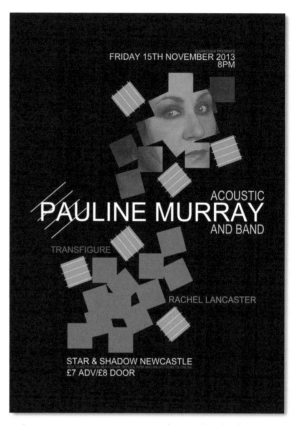

Solo acoustic gig poster. Design by Michael Robson.

curve and another string to my bow – a new avenue for artistic development. I kept in touch with Helen and Gina: both brave and independent ladies who had reinvented themselves after punk.

Many plates were being juggled at this time: family, studios and making a living, and still we managed to arrange and play sixteen shows in 2014 with the band. After the gig at the Garage in London, we were approached by James Nice of LTM Recordings; he had revived the Belgian labels Les Disques du Crépuscule and Factory Benelux, was releasing new material and curating reissues of Factory Records' back catalogue. James was interested in re-releasing the *Pauline Murray and the Invisible Girls* album, as most of the Factory Records creative team had been involved in it. His attention to detail was meticulous and the special-edition box set, numbered in invisible ink, contained

the remastered album, live recordings, John Peel session on vinyl and CD, a signed print and a t-shirt designed by Vaughan Oliver from 1981, reproduced to perfection. It was a beautiful package and extremely satisfying to me as an artist to see that whole project brought back together in one place.

Around this time, James also made enquiries with Southern Studios about re-releasing the *Storm Clouds* album, but they were uncooperative and hostile. John Loder had died nine years previously and a member of his staff was now running the company. They claimed that they had lost the master tapes and threatened us with legal action if we attempted to remaster the album from vinyl and release it. I was angry about this at the time as some of the tracks belonged to Polestar but there was nothing we could do about it, and we weren't prepared to get into a legal wrangle. It became my lost album. At least the *Invisible Girls* album was saved and available again.

Things went from the sublime to the ridiculous. The band was excited to be going to Ireland for the first time in 36 years, and we were picked up at the airport in Belfast after the short flight from Newcastle and taken straight to the venue (Voodoo Lounge) to check out the equipment supplied by the promoter, as we'd only taken guitars. Luckily, the hotel was within walking distance of the venue as by soundcheck time, our driver had already started drinking. The organisation seemed chaotic and the (late) gig was primitive and punky. We walked back to the hotel with guitars on a wild Thursday night in Belfast amid a group of naked young men running around the shopping centre.

The driver had at least sobered up sufficiently to drive us to Dublin the next day. We were staying in accommodation above the venue (Fibber McGees) and the sound engineer was a wizened old hippy whom we named Gandalf. While he may have looked like a hippy, there wasn't much peace or love in the room; he told Paul to 'get that guitar off my stage' like a miserable dictator. Again, the organisation seemed lax, with several entrances to the venue and no one taking money on the door. I was in our room on the top floor waiting to go on and it was now midnight – I was more ready to go to bed – and again asked myself what the hell I was doing here. We found the promoter lying on the floor inebriated and had to help ourselves to the money falling out of his pockets which served as our fee. The following day, we took an open-top bus trip to Kilmainham Gaol courtesy of Abbo's friend Terry, who owned the local Bureau de Change. It was a strange trip all round. Before we left for home the following day, Paul and I paid a visit to the venue downstairs and spat all over Gandalf's sound booth.

I started to get phone calls at the studio from an Australian called David Browne who'd found my number via Nick Logan, former *NME* editor and founder of *The Face*. Browne had apparently had a revelation whilst watching live footage of Penetration performing 'Free Money' at Rebellion, and subsequently talked non-stop to me about bringing the band to Australia. He'd promoted punk gigs in Canberra in the early 1980s, moved into the corporate business world and eventually worked for the Australian Government as their main press spin-doctor. He didn't have any recent track record in music promotion and the whole idea seemed fantastical, unrealistic and costly. But this stranger on the other side of the world was unrelentingly persistent, and announced that he had booked a flight to Newcastle to meet up with us and his partner George Howson, who would be travelling from London to discuss and sign a contract. I was suspicious and paranoid and thought that perhaps he was a spy from the Australian Government, or some nutcase stalker, and didn't even go to the airport to meet him when he arrived. After the long-haul journey, he was told to 'fuck off' by the local Byker residents at the Metro station when he asked for directions to the studio. All in all, it was not the warmest welcome he could have received.

David Browne was a large, overweight man, articulate and witty, but he didn't know when to stop talking. His partner arrived and it all seemed too bizarre, I didn't trust the situation – it was a long way to go for a few gigs. They left empty-handed but he continued to bombard me with phone calls. I suggested doing some solo acoustic shows which would be cheaper and easier to arrange, and would serve as a reconnaissance trip to check out the lie of the land. He agreed, I signed the contract, he booked flights and arranged visas for myself and Robert (who was still sceptical that this trip would even take place), and set up two shows in Sydney and two in Melbourne, interspersed with radio interviews over a two week period.

I'd only done a handful of solo shows and was being an absolute chancer, but I practised hard in the preceding weeks and we set off for Australia on a wing and a prayer. David was there to meet us at Sydney Airport after our 23-hour journey and took us to a lovely little house in Newtown, which he'd rented for the first week. I did interviews with Stuart Coupe at FBi Radio and Jonathan Green at ABC National over the first couple of days before my first acoustic show at the Camelot Lounge, a venue whose decor was dedicated to camels, the dromedary type, rather than King Arthur's castle. I was extremely nervous as I began my set and was heckled throughout by a drunken lady who was with the support band. I tried to ignore her as she shouted comments about my hair but it really got to me when she shouted 'where's your mother?' I got through the set but, as I left the stage, I started to cry uncontrollably. Perhaps it was jetlag, nerves or being verbally attacked by that silly bitch, who'd now been ejected from the building.

We had two days until my next show at the Basement, Sydney, so I did more promotional radio interviews. David was the perfect host and still never stopped talking, telling hilarious stories with his witty and intelligent use of language. We took a bus to Bondi Beach and he drove us to Newcastle, a few hours north of Sydney, past ancient forests and swamps, to see Radio Birdman, the Stooges/Detroit-influenced Australian band, at the Cambridge Hotel.

The audience at the Basement were seated at tables as was customary at these solo shows. I remember before I went on, David said to me, 'never mention the people behind the scenes – you are the star'. I followed support act Deborah Conway, whom I'd never heard of but was apparently a former model who'd had a top-five hit in the Eighties with her band Do-Ré-Mi; this must have been a comedown for her. As I sat on the stage in my white Eames chair that David had supplied, I felt nervous and exposed. The sound was dry and scratchy and my performance so tense and edgy that Robert couldn't bear to watch and returned to the dressing room. I thanked David Browne from the stage. So far, not so good.

We took an internal flight to Melbourne and David travelled for twelve hours on the train. It was clear he was not a well man: he struggled to walk and told us that he had suffered from cancer a few years earlier. George Howson met us in Melbourne and took us to a garden apartment at Williamstown Beach, which was our base for the second week. I was so ashamed of my performances so far that I spent several hours each day practising my set. David had arranged more interviews around the shows and we travelled to

Poster for Australian tour. Design by David Browne.

Frankston Beach where I was interviewed by Jon Faine for ABC Melbourne and played a couple of acoustic songs, broadcast live from an outdoor shopping centre. The next two shows were two consecutive nights at the Toff in the Town with supports from Deborah Conway and Lisa Miller, a singer-songwriter and lovely person. I played much better but the shows were poorly attended and my foray into the vast country of Australia had made very little impact. David must have lost money on this venture but he had succeeded in realising his dream of promoting music once again, and it was an experience that I will never forget. It was liberating to be thousands of miles away from the UK where nobody knew me and there were no expectations.

Back home, Robert was pushing for the band to record a new Penetration album. It had been 36 years since our last album *Coming Up For Air*, and I thought that it would be a tall order to make a record that would stand up to our past. Robert was enthusiastic and had a plan of action, which included asking John Maher to play drums, recording at Trinity Heights with Fred, and asking respected artist Vaughan Oliver, our old schoolfriend, to design the sleeve. We would set up an account with PledgeMusic, then a new online direct-to-fan music platform where we could pre-sell to fans and raise the finance for the project. Other items, such as signed coloured vinyl, CDs, t-shirts, a limited print of Paul Harvey's painting of me and some handwritten lyrics were exclusively available via the site. We were missing out the middleman and would have full control of every aspect.

Paul and Steve were keen to go ahead and when all of the elements were in place, we launched the album campaign in January 2015. It was exciting, overwhelming and also terrifying to see the orders roll in for an album we had yet to write and record, but it gave us the impetus to rise to the challenge and operate from a higher perspective in an act of faith. We decided to re-record 'The Feeling', 'Sea Song', 'Guilty' and 'Just Drifting', one of my solo songs, just to get the ball rolling. Steve and Paul were coming up with new ideas as John made his first trip from the Isle of Harris to begin recording the drum tracks at our own studio, which was now a 24-track. Robert wanted to involve Fred at an early stage to establish the overall sound so we decamped to his studio to work on guitars. On John's second visit, we worked on new songs, clarifying the arrangements and I had basic melodies but no lyrics. Throughout the session, Steve had been playing a little guitar phrase that was largely ignored and as we were about to pack away our equipment, John suggested that we put it into an arrangement. It was recorded in the final hour and became the track 'Aguila'.

The overall album was taking shape and I thought it would be good to start with an instrumental to ease into the album after all those years and I had a guitar phrase in mind which formed the basis of the track 'Instramantra'. We completed more guitar overdubs at Polestar and I arranged a house swap with Alex, who was now 22 and living in London, to focus and work

every day on lyrics and tunes for 'Betrayed', 'Beat Goes On', 'Makes No Sense', 'Calm Before the Storm' and 'Aguila'. I was allowing the music itself to inspire me for the lyrical themes.

We returned to Trinity Heights where Fred was to supervise the recording of the vocals as he had a good ear for the job and was patient and diplomatic. I sang every day for eight days with short breaks where final overdubs were added and Fred executed the guitar solo on 'Beat Goes On', which provided another link to the past. We had a piece of music that Robert had edited from the band messing about during the recording of the backing tracks – it sounded good but I wasn't sure what to do with it. I suddenly had the idea to recite the opening chapter of 'The Machine Stops', a short story by E.M. Forster which I've always loved. I found it on the Internet then proceeded to merge the futuristic narrative and dialogue with the music in a single take.

Fred was in charge of the mixing and had to get it completed before he went off on holiday. At the same time we were approached by Proper Music, a large independent music distribution company who wanted to get involved with the release of the album, which I'd decided to call *Resolution*. The crowd-funding campaign had gained momentum and anticipation was building up to its release. It had taken six months on and off to complete and we were happy with the results. Our faith, focus, creativity and commitment had paid off and it was a big achievement for the band. Robert was organising everything, from the artwork to the Pledge campaign, Proper Music, press, photo session, a video of lead track 'Beat Goes On' with Carol Lynn directing, organising a tour to promote the album and he was also in charge of the mail-out of the record and merchandise. It received great reviews when it was released on 9 October 2015 and reached number 88 in the mid-week National Chart. Not bad for a cottage industry!

We'd asked John Maher to play drums on the tour that we'd organised to promote the album. It was difficult logistically as he lived so far away and we only had two days to rehearse before the tour. His authentic drumming style was great on the new material but he didn't really know the old songs, which rely on specific

Video still for 'Beat Goes On'. Photograph by Davy Ellis.

parts to create the whole. Our first show at Stockton Georgian Theatre was sold out and we got by on sheer exuberance, but things unravelled in Wakefield Warehouse 23 on 19 September, as we played a terrible set that sent our confidence into a downward spiral. We'd committed to performing *Resolution* in its entirety at Whitley Bay Playhouse and some of the songs we had never played live. I was seriously considering running away and disappearing as the date loomed. Fortunately our morale was given a boost when we played a great, sold-out show at the Garage in London and we managed to bluff our way through *Resolution* at the Playhouse.

In early January 2016, I was shocked and deeply saddened when I heard the news that David Bowie, my all-time favourite artist, had died. It hit me in the same way as losing a family member. His music had changed my genetic make-up from a young age; he had influenced and inspired a generation to rise above the constraints of society, opening doors and minds and he was the catalyst who created the fertile ground from which punk emerged. He'd changed people's lives and now that his positive energy and presence were gone, it felt like the gates of hell had opened up. Celebrity deaths were announced on a regular basis: Prince, George Michael, Leonard Cohen, Pete Burns... it was like a psychological bombardment of doom and gloom.

This was also the year the Tory government had instigated a referendum, asking the British people to vote on the complex issue of whether to leave or remain in the European Union. The Leave campaign dubbed 'Brexit' emboldened attitudes of nationalism, fear and xenophobia; powered by lies and deceit, it left friends, families and communities bitterly divided

Opposite page: Vaughan Oliver's alternative artwork for the *Resolution* album sleeve. Courtesy of Lee Widdows.

RESOLUTION

1. Instramantra  2. Betrayed!
3. Just Drifting  4. Beat Goes On
5. Sea Song  6. Guilty
7. Dos Lugares
8. Calm Before The Storm
9. Aguila 10. The Feeling
11. Outromistra

Polestar
RECORDS

RESOLUTION

Instramantra (3.14) [Murray]
Betrayed! (3.00) [Murray/Wallace]
Just Drifting (4.45) [Murray] Guilty (4.45) [Murray]
Two Places (Dos Lugares) (4.54) [Murray/Wallace/Blamire/Smithson]
Aguila (3.58) [Murray/Wallace]
Beat Goes On (3.19) [Murray/Wallace]
Makes No Sense (3.24) [Murray/Wallace]
The Feeling (4.01) [Murray]
Sea Song (3.56) [Murray/Wallace]
Calm Before The Storm (3.41) [Murray/Murray]
Outromistra (4.23) [Blamire/Maher/Harvey/Wallace/F.M Forster]

Pauline Murray: Vocals, Guitar, Keyboards, Percussion.
Robert Blamire: Bass Guitar, Backing Vocals, Guitar, Piano
Steve Wallace: Guitars, Backing Vocals. Paul Harvey: Guitars. John Maher: Drums
Fred Purser: Guitar Solo, Beat Goes On. Backing Vocals Guilty
Mixed by: Fred Purser. Produced by: Robert Blamire
Recorded in: Newcastle upon Tyne at Polestar Studios and Trinity Heights. Mixed at: Trinity Heights
Studio Engineers: Neil Iceton, Alex Blamire, Robert Blamire at Polestar. Fred Purser at Trinity Heights
Sleeve Design: Vaughan Oliver at v23. Design Assistance: Brian Whitehead
Logo Typography: Aργyro Ouranou. Front Sleeve Image: Mark Atkins

Thanks to: Colin E Meredith, Mark Aerobins, Gwen McGhone
Davy Craig, Neal Burns, Paul Forbe, Judy Clayton, Ian Price
Beaton Cervera, Martin Mackburn, Deb Farrow, Tony Kerins

177

*Resolution* tour poster 2015-2016.

over the outcome. A dark cloud descended onto an uncertain future. Donald Trump became the 45th president of the United States and was running his office from a Twitter account. The whole world seemed to be turning upside down.

David Browne got back in touch and insisted on coming to Newcastle for my birthday and I worried about the state of his health. We saw him between bouts of sleeping at the hotel, he seemed to need constant rest. When he returned to Australia, he moved from Sydney into the countryside, then all went quiet. I received a call from one of his friends to say that he was very ill in hospital. I spoke to him that evening – it was so sad. Although we'd only known him for a relatively short time, he had made a big impact. He explained the gravity of his health condition and that he was facing imminent death. I thanked him for all he had done for

us and told him how much we loved him. We said our goodbyes and he died a few hours later.

We had a few live shows with Penetration and were still promoting *Resolution*. We'd also just drafted drummer Ken Goodinson into the band. He knew all of the songs, was a fan of our music, lived locally for rehearsals and was perfect for the live set. Paul was unable to play London's 100 Club and Brighton Patterns the following night so we rehearsed with Andrew Jennings who stood in on guitar for the two shows. I was taking part in discussion panels on punk at the British Library and Kings Place for an event organised by Abbo called Poet In the City with Penny Rimbaud (Crass), TV Smith (Adverts) and Steve Lamacq around the table. I'd met them all before and I'd done several punk discussions with Penny; he liked to play devil's advocate, which at first was annoying but I got to like the man. TV, Penny and myself had been allocated 15 minutes each to perform after the discussion. I didn't want to do acoustic songs so Abbo suggested that I just read out some of my lyrics. As the other two went ahead of me, I realised I had nothing prepared and would have to wing my way through. I recited the words to 'Silent Community' and began 'Shout Above the Noise' but when I got to the passage where there's usually a guitar solo, things unravelled. My mind went blank and I couldn't remember the rest of the words. It was a full house and they absolutely loved my downfall. I have no recollection of the content of my remaining time, but I got a huge cheer at the end of it. This was punk rock.

Later that month, I was playing live acoustic sets with Dead Men Walking: Jake Burns (SLF), Kirk Brandon (Theatre of Hate) and Segs and Ruffy (The Ruts), and I supported the legendary Ronnie Spector at Whitley Bay Playhouse. It was an honour to be on the same stage as Ronnie. I had grown up listening to The Ronettes and I was thrilled to meet her. She was lovely and down to earth. My solo set had definitely opened up more avenues and given me different opportunities as an artist. That year, as we played Rebellion with the band, I also performed a solo set.

I had quite a few new songs written on the acoustic guitar but hadn't had time or been focused enough

Onstage with John Maher, Whitley Bay Playhouse, 16 October 2015. Photograph by Davy Ellis.

to record them properly. That autumn, Robert and I decided to go to France for a month to stay at the house owned by my sister and brother-in-law, which they were in the process of selling after 15 years of happy family holidays. We left the studios in capable hands, packed our Volvo Estate car with musical instruments and recording equipment and set up in the stone-walled dining room at Chey. It was an idyllic setting – sunshine, morning markets and no pressure or distractions. We spent every day recording, tracking to a drum machine, using electronic and acoustic instrumentation and we also added vocals. I was hoping that the French vibe would filter into the music, and I saw this as a pastoral solo album. By the end of the month, we had the basic framework for the songs 'After All', 'Weeds', 'When We Were Young', 'Shadow In My Mind' and 'Secrets', a song written in the 1980s

that we'd discovered on an old cassette tape; it had such a good feel that we tried to reproduce it exactly how it was. As soon as we returned, I was opening for The Mission with my acoustic set at the Forum in London and Birmingham Institute, and Penetration had supports with The Damned in Leeds and Brixton Academy; all big shows. As usual, I was treated with great respect by The Mission but didn't really get to speak to The Damned as they were busy preparing for the show.

The year 2017 marked the 40th anniversary of the so-called 'punk rock explosion' of 1977 and I was invited to an event in Covent Garden to celebrate the unveiling of a heritage Blue Plaque to mark the spot where the legendary Roxy Club, now a fitness shop, had once stood. There was a great photo exhibition from the Roxy days and it was good to see Andy

Backstage at Brixton Academy, 26 November 2016. Photograph by Carol Lynn.

Czezowski and Susan Carrington looking colourful and dapper after all these years. I met up with Gaye Black and Peter Perrett, and spoke to Tessa from The Slits for the first time, along with Jordan who was friendly and not fearsome at all! I was already good friends with Gaye and had reconnected with her on many occasions since the band had reformed. I would usually stay at her house on solo trips to London and she is one of the few people with whom I've stayed in touch. The last time I'd seen Peter Perrett was when The Only Ones had reformed for a handful of gigs in 2007 with Penetration supporting, and I'd sang backing vocals on one of their songs for the encore. After the plaque-unveiling event, we all went to an Italian restaurant in Soho for a pizza and a catch-up.

I opened for The Mission once again with my acoustic set on six of the dates in May 2017 and could feel my performances improve each consecutive night. It was also good to have other women on the bill: Anne Marie (Skeletal Family) and Evie Vine, who was performing with The Mission. I supported Doctors of Madness, who had returned for a handful of shows, and their set was wonderful, Richard Strange as charming as ever, and it transported me back to the early punk rock chapter. I shared a discussion panel in Liverpool, 'From Eric's to Evol', with Don Letts, Steve Ignorant and Throbbing Gristle artist Cosey Fanni Tutti, who was promoting her new book *Art Sex Music*. It was good to be back in the city again. It still looked run down but I've always found the people there to be generous and friendly. I enjoyed

Steve Wallace and me, Georgian Theatre, Stockton, 18 November 2017. Photograph by Steve White.

these panels as it was good to meet fellow artists whom I'd never met back in the day, as we were all so busy doing our own things. We were being valued as elder statespeople as we had lived to tell the tale.

We decided to book a Penetration tour to commemorate the fact that we still existed. There had been 15 different members in the band over a 40-year period, all from the north-east with the exception of John Maher from Manchester and Paul Harvey, who was originally from Burton-On-Trent but had been living on Tyneside for over 30 years. Still holding on to our integrity, operating on our own terms and setting our own goals and high standards, we re-recorded two of our earliest songs from 1977, 'In the Future' and 'Duty Free Technology' b/w cover versions of 'I Don't

Mind' (Buzzcocks) and 'Shake Some Action' (Flamin' Groovies), a pre-punk song I've always loved. We released them as limited edition 7″ singles through PledgeMusic and sold the rest on tour. I painted some new stage shirts and we played a warm-up show for the tour at North Shields Customs House as part of the 'Punk In The Provinces' exhibition, where my old painted shirts were exhibited along with my acrylic painting of the QE2 entering the Tyne on its final voyage.

In September 2007, the QE2 ocean liner was due to sail into the Port of Tyne as part of its farewell tour. Thousands of people, myself included, lined the banks of the Tyne awaiting its arrival. We could see it sitting on the horizon but it was a foggy day so its entry was delayed until the weather cleared. After several hours, people started to drift away as they were cold and tired. We drove up the coast then noticed that things were starting to happen so dashed back to the riverbank where only a few people remained. It was dusk as we watched the massive vessel approach the river with a fanfare of fireworks and a fleet of tugboats accompanying its arrival. Specially commissioned music, which incorporated clanking chains and foghorns, played from loudspeakers set up for the occasion. It was a magnificent sight and I took photos on my crappy mobile phone. I vowed that one day I would do a painting of this event, a trilogy in fact. Several years later, I found the photos on the now defunct phone and completed the first painting just in time for the 'Punk In The Provinces' exhibition. I love painting but can never seem to find the time for it. The second painting has since been completed but the third has sat on my easel for several years, awaiting the final touches.

During 2018, things calmed down with the band and we were able to turn our attention once again to the solo project we'd started in France. When we listened back to what we'd recorded, Robert wanted to add real drums to some of the songs and plucked up the courage to ask original Roxy Music drummer Paul Thompson, who was rehearsing at Polestar with Lindisfarne, to play on the record. We were delighted when he agreed and it was a joy to hear him playing on the tracks. We'd asked Steve Hopkins from The Invisible Girls to contribute piano and keyboards, and he travelled from Manchester to add his own unique musical style. We were still working to the original French backing tracks, but the addition of other musicians was taking the music in a different direction.

Steve insisted that we record one of the songs live and it was a magical moment when the four of us – Paul on drums, Steve on piano, Robert on bass, me playing acoustic guitar and singing – recorded 'Dark Clouds' in the live room of our own studio, with our son Alex engineering the session. I was transported back in time, to my 14-year-old self, watching Roxy Music at the City Hall. How had life's twists and turns brought me to this point where we were playing one of my songs, and I was part of the band as an equal musician? We brought in other guest players for different tracks and the song 'Chains' was recorded from scratch three times by Robert and Alex before we were happy with it. Many of the French elements remained in the final mix and I couldn't improve on the original vocal for 'After All'.

My original title for the album was *Naturale*, which was still in-keeping with the French pastoral theme. I'd asked my friend, the illustrator Anne Yvonne Gilbert whom we'd originally met in Liverpool, to do a drawing for the sleeve. She was responsible for the artwork for Frankie Goes To Hollywood's 'Relax', and her work has been published in numerous books and publications. Yvonne presented a charming coloured pencil drawing of me with my acoustic guitar surrounded by elements of nature. PledgeMusic had just filed for bankruptcy so we approached Proper Music with the 'assets' but they were negative about the sleeve, saying that it didn't fit with the music, which was now admittedly more electronic and full-bodied.

It had been announced that Penetration were to play at the Royal Albert Hall with Buzzcocks the following summer, on 21 June 2019. This would be our most prestigious show to date and we were looking forward to it. There were still nine months to go and Robert began to organise live shows for the beginning of the year, leading up to this Summer Solstice event. It came as a complete shock when, on 6 December 2018, we heard that Pete Shelley, Buzzcocks' leading light, had died suddenly of a suspected heart attack at his home in Estonia, aged just 63. Everything was now up in the air as the band came to terms with their loss, but it was agreed that the Royal Albert Hall show would still go on as a celebration of Shelley's life. There were several other tribute gigs set up for Pete and I sang 'What Do I Get?' at the *Vive Le Rock* Awards, and presented the 'Rock In Peace' award to Buzzcocks guitarist Steve Diggle, in Shelley's honour. Afterwards the dressing room was crammed with people I'd never met before – Suzi Quatro, Rat Scabies, Jaz Coleman and Pauline Black.

We played small club gigs leading up to the RAH show and made our first trip to Europe to play a punk festival in Berlin. Again, I thought that musically our band was unsuited to these line-ups as we were more

Opposite page: Top. Original artwork for the *Naturale* album sleeve by Anne Yvonne Gilbert. Below. My paintings for the *Elemental* album sleeve.

Meeting Chris Packham.

Poster for solo acoustic gig, 20 June 2019.

melodic and not hardcore, but we went down well with the crowd. Undercover Festival was held at the Dome in Tufnell Park, London, and I was asked to do an interview in the afternoon with Chris Packham, naturalist TV presenter and punk aficionado. I knew he was a fan of the band as I'd read on several occasions that he wanted our song 'Shout Above the Noise' played at his funeral. As I sat in the basement of a pub opposite the venue, with a camera crew in situ, he was apparently nervous about meeting me. I, on the other hand, was relaxed, chilled out and wondered what all the fuss was about. Once we'd settled into the conversation, we discussed the early days of punk, how things had changed and he told me how that particular song of ours had always been a source of energy and inspiration to him whenever he was feeling down. I was humbled to think that our music could affect people on such a deep

level. I gave him a handwritten copy of the lyrics, which he framed and hung in his office. Chris and his crew stayed and filmed the whole evening, the footage later appearing in his BBC4 documentary *Forever Punk* and, as we left the venue, I could see him on the decks, in his element, DJ-ing till the end of the night.

The RAH show was now upon us, with Penetration opening, then The Skids, and finally Buzzcocks themselves, joined by guest vocalists Dave Vanian, Captain Sensible, Thurston Moore, Peter Perrett, Tim Burgess, Richard Jobson and myself on selected songs. Mine was 'Love You More'. We were informed by the promoter of the RAH that our set length was to be reduced from forty to thirty minutes while The Skids would play around seventy minutes. We weren't too happy about this but there wasn't much we could do. Our sound engineer/driver let us down three days before

Royal Albert Hall, 21 June 2019. Photograph by Steve White.

the gig, and this sent Robert's stress levels through the roof. We managed to find an engineer at short notice but Robert would have to do all of the driving to London, then to Portsmouth the following day and finally all the way back to Newcastle. He tried to cancel the extra hotel room, pressed the wrong button on the computer and cancelled all of the rooms, for which there was no refund. John Maher rang a few days before to ask if I was going to the rehearsals in King's Cross for the guest singers but none of the organisers had told me about it.

I had an acoustic show booked the night before at the Betsey Trotwood pub in London with Helen McCookerybook, a show Helen herself had organised. I insisted on taking my white Eames chair on the train: from early on, I'd adopted this chair as it looked good, was comfortable and would save me from having to find some random smelly chair in the venue. Grace and

I travelled on the train with the chair and were told by the guard that there was no furniture allowed. When we changed at York, I would have to be crafty – I didn't want to wave goodbye to my chair and abandon it on the platform. We waited until the train doors were about to close, then rushed onto the train with the chair. Mission accomplished. Arriving at King's Cross, I carried it to the rehearsal studio where Buzzcocks managed to fit me in for a couple of run-throughs of 'Love You More'. Everyone was busy so there wasn't time to socialise, but at least I'd sung the song with the band.

Friends and family were travelling to London to see the band play at the RAH and quite a few came a day early and attended the acoustic show, which was really good fun. I was told to arrive at the Royal Albert Hall the following day for 2 p.m., and our band were just arriving from Newcastle. Buzzcocks were finishing

Brudenell Social Club, 26 April 2019. Photograph by Steve White.

soundchecking with the vocalists and were starting to pack away their instruments. Apparently there was no time for me. I felt upset and rejected and seemed to have been excluded from the arrangements. Would they have done this to a man? (I was the only female on the bill.)

I'd never been to the Royal Albert Hall and it was a magnificent venue. I imagined that it would be formal and restrictive but the low stage curved into the audience and it felt close and intimate. As Paul Morley introduced us, the whole place erupted and we relished every minute of our short set. When all of the guest vocalists made their entrances with crib sheets, I realised I was the only one who had bothered to learn Pete's lyrics.

In complete contrast, we were back in London a month later to play the 100 Club. The majestic ambience of the RAH had been replaced by a small, overcrowded sweatbox. The organisation was shambolic with all of the bands using the same stinking dressing room, and although the gig was intimate and well-received, I was beginning to feel a bit long in the tooth for this type of caper.

We played Rebellion again to a packed Empress Ballroom and had put The Invisible Girls back together at relatively short notice with Steve Hopkins on piano, Tom English (Maxïmo Park) on drums, Paul Harvey on guitar, Robert on bass and our two kids on keyboards and backing vocals, performing the whole album at the Opera House. I was also doing an acoustic set, so it was a full weekend of all of my musical strands. We played a punk festival in Sheffield where I had a brief chat with the only other female on the bill, Beki Bondage. We played a sold-out Cluny in our hometown and Glasgow Audio on 19 October 2019 which was to be our last gig for the foreseeable future. It had been a busy, exciting

Great audience at the Royal Albert Hall, 21 June 2019. Photograph by Simon Balaam.

yet stressful year for the band, particularly Robert, and I was feeling that I needed time away from it again to work on my own projects.

The artwork for the solo album was holding things up. We reached out to several other designers but nothing seemed suitable. I changed the title to *Elemental* and decided to take matters into my own hands, creating a series of four small, colourful acrylic paintings with my own abstract theme of the four elements – fire, water, earth and air. Sections of each painting were laid out in vertical strips against a dark grey background and I was happy with the results. The contract from Proper arrived. We'd done everything ourselves up to this point and decided that financially we would be better off releasing it via our own website, taking pre-orders and enlisted the help of manager Martin Tibbetts to get us through the process.

The studios were busy, with about 34 bands passing through each week, and we were glad business was brisk as we had not yet fully recovered from the world's financial events of 2008. But an ill wind was blowing and as the month of March 2020 progressed, the colour-coded rooms of blue, red, yellow and green on the booking diary began to turn graphite grey as one band after another cancelled their session. To make matters worse, by the end of the month, Covid hysteria had gripped the world, everything closed down and we were told to stay at home, only leaving the house for essential food shopping.

It was quite exciting at first and a great excuse to do nothing. I'd always wondered what it would be like if everything stopped and it was playing out like a science fiction movie. The sun was shining, the birds were singing and everyone had time to tidy their gardens,

Stills from the 'Secrets' video. Carol Lynn.

make nice meals, do jigsaws, drink wine and there were no obligations to see anyone. People worked from home, schools were closed and all external activities were restricted. Robert's 93-year-old mother had gone into hospital the previous month for a gallstone operation and, at this point, we were still allowed to visit. This was soon to change. It was an eerie sight as we drove down the motorway with no other vehicles in sight. All of the cities had been cleared of people within a week and the homeless were nowhere to be seen. Where had they gone?

We received a grant from the local council's business rates department to compensate for loss of earnings, which covered about three months. The fear and euphoria began to wear off and was replaced by anxiety, worry, stagnation and uncertainty. We were getting confusing and mixed messages from the government, and there was no end in sight. We

were due to support The Psychedelic Furs with The Invisible Girls that spring but the dates were moved to the autumn when Steve and Tom weren't available, so we would have to find another drummer and piano player. The rehearsal studios were cleaned, re-decorated and opened in August but September brought new tiers of restrictions. There were still ways of reaching and connecting with others: I managed to do an acoustic Q&A set in Stockton on the eve of another full lockdown and Alex had applied for an Arts Council grant and ran a series of eight filmed live performance sessions from Polestar which were broadcast online. I didn't get involved in the project but Alex was showcasing new local performers who were trying to keep things going. The studios were closed again until the spring of 2021 by which time we'd had to rent out two of our rooms to bands on a permanent basis, as we'd received no further financial

Alex and Grace Blamire with me on the Psychedelic Furs tour, 2022. Photograph by Stuart McHugh.

support. After thirty years, my business had been destroyed through no fault of my own.

The album was being manufactured in the Czech Republic, and with all of the Covid disruptions, all we could do was wait for the orange and black vinyl copies to arrive. We had no idea when the world would open up again. There was no financial budget for promotion so we made videos for lead track 'Secrets' and 'Shadow In My Mind' ourselves. 'Secrets' was filmed in our attic during the early part of lockdown. I had the idea to paint my face with the same theme as the album cover and prepared my acrylics in a particular order as the room would be in darkness except for the light around a cosmetics mirror. Robert set a camera rolling and left the room as I began to paint my face with faith, courage and concentration. The camera had switched off half way through but luckily, Robert came to check and we

managed to capture the end of the painting. He edited the footage and interspersed it with home movie footage, recently discovered on a VHS tape from the early Eighties, featuring High Force Waterfall and me driving our white Volvo past our old school. I mimed to 'Shadow In My Mind' in the live recording room at Polestar, filmed by Alex and his friend Chunny, and Robert edited it.

The album was released in October 2020 and was sold out on the pre-orders. Reviews were good but we were limited in our promotional options. I'd originally envisioned visiting radio stations but this was out of the question and I don't think that any of the tracks even got played on the radio. We'd given up long ago in thinking that the mainstream media would have the slightest interest in our musical activities; we made music to satisfy our own creative urges and for anyone who was still willing to give it a listen.

Rotten scoundrels! With John Lydon in Glasgow, 2022. The circle is completed. Photograph by Robert Blamire.

We had found a drummer, Gary Binns, but struggled to find a piano/keyboard player for our upcoming Psychedelic Furs support and reached out to fifteen musicians. We rehearsed for ten weeks with one and eventually realised it wasn't working. Paul suggested Steve Daggett, a multi-instrumentalist currently playing with Lindisfarne. We worked hard to pull the set together and were almost ready when the live dates were moved again to April 2022. Covid had hit the entertainment sector hard, along with hospitality and travel, all things that give people pleasure and social interaction. Robert's mother began a cycle of hospital/care-home stays and now we weren't allowed to visit. We were reduced to standing in front of a window, writing onto a pad as she was hard of hearing. It was both inhumane and deeply distressing for all concerned. She died before the year was out.

During the lockdown, I was invited to contribute vocals to the song 'Ardour' on the new Maxïmo Park album, produced by Ben Allen in Atlanta, Georgia. The band had recorded their parts in isolation and my vocal was recorded at Polestar via a video link set up by Alex, connecting to Ben in America, who talked me through it. The wonders of technology! The album was heading to number one in the National Charts and was pipped at the post by a band called Architects, whom I'd never heard of. I joined Maxïmo Park onstage to sing the song in Newcastle, as a tiny window appeared in the lockdown restrictions.

The Psychedelic Furs dates went ahead and it was great to be performing and singing again. With my whole family involved, it was something special that may never happen again. Our own shows had to be cancelled as they had been moved to different dates, which put pressure on the band. It was difficult for musicians to just jump out of the box again to entertain people when we had been financially, physically and mentally battered by the events of the past two years.

In June 2022 Robert and I decided to go Glasgow to see PiL, whom we'd never seen before. Our sound engineer Walter Jaquiss was part of their crew, and he arranged a couple of guest tickets for us. The show was brilliant: the music challenging and unique. It was almost 46 years since I'd stood as an 18-year-old in the same Leeds hotel room as John Lydon on the ill-fated Anarchy tour. At the time, I had been far too shy and timid to speak to anyone, and now at 64, I had an after-show pass to meet the man himself. I was nervous but he shook my hand and made me feel welcome in an instant – kindred spirits travelling on the path of our generation – a dying breed with many of our contemporaries already gone. The banter in the dressing room was witty and funny and I hadn't laughed so much in a long time. It was his energy, attitude, courage and music that had inspired and emboldened me to join a punk band, find my own voice, express my creativity and set my life on an unusual trajectory for a northern, working-class lass, and I thanked him for that.

The world turns and the future is unwritten. What goes around comes around… and everything's connected.

## BEAT GOES ON

The past has gone and time is moving on
The present is a gift that won't last long
The ebb and flow will come and go
As things unfold without control
Yesterday is just a memory
Tomorrow is an unknown certainty

Your hopes and dreams like birds fly in the air
Where peace and happiness is all you wear
If fear is your foe, tell it to go
If fear is your guide, there's nowhere to hide
Moving through the cycles of the sun
For eternity and the beat goes on...

What's the point of keeping score
Nothing adds up anymore
Everything's been done before
Lose the battle - win the war

# ACKNOWLEDGEMENTS

**No man is an island and anything I've achieved in this life has been with the creative input, help and support of numerous individuals.** Special thanks go to Robert Blamire who has been with me every step of the way in my personal and musical life. His contributions as a great bass guitarist, co-writer, producer, graphic designer, business partner, husband, father and practical powerhouse can not be underestimated.

Thanks to all the skilled and dedicated musicians I've worked with over the years, spending quality time writing, recording, rehearsing and performing. These unique experiences create a deep and special bond. Thanks to the road crews, promoters, producers, technicians, designers, photographers, writers and all the people who have provided ancillary support. There are too many to mention and I don't want to leave anyone out.

Without Russ Bestley and Paul Harvey's approach to Omnibus Press, I would probably never have written this book. Thanks to David Barraclough for taking on the project, all the staff at Omnibus and to Zoë Howe for editing the first draft and guiding me through the process with positivity and enthusiasm. Thanks to Russ for his patience, design and layout expertise and to Paul for his assistance in this process and also for being a loyal friend and long term musical collaborator.

Thanks to all the photographers, artists and collectors who've contributed to the book.

Thanks to my family and friends and to all the people I have met along the way (you know who you are) and to everyone who has supported my activities. Thoughts go out to friends who have left us during the making of this book. R.I.P. Jordan Mooney (Pamela Rooke), Dave Griffiths, Jane Suck, Kev Anderson, Phil Jones and Kris Guidio.

I'm grateful to have been given the opportunity to document my life so far and proud of myself for completing what seemed like a mammoth task at the beginning.

Well, that's me done, for now...

And relax. Photograph by Kit Haigh.